THE C
HO
WEEK
MISSAL

PEOPLE'S EDITION

WITH PRAYERS AND DEVOTIONS

Texts approved for use
in England and Wales, Scotland, and Ireland.

Catholic Truth Society
40-46 Harleyford Road, London, SE11 5AY

First Published 2019

ISBN

Holy Week Missal (RM31): 978 1 78469 606 1

Cover design, compilation and typographical design and layout
© 2019 Catholic Truth Society

Concordat cum originali: Paul Moynihan
Imprimatur: ✠ Peter Smith, Archbishop of Southwark, 10 December 2018.

Acknowledgements:

This volume has been compiled from material previously published under the following titles:

Daily Missal, first published 2011. Cover design, compilation and typographical design and layout © 2011 Catholic Truth Society.

The CTS is grateful for the help of the Association for Latin in the Liturgy in the preparation of this volume.

Extracts from scripture (excepting Psalm texts) from the *Jerusalem Bible* © 1966 Darton, Longman and Todd and Doubleday & Company Inc.

The English translation of the Gospel Readings for the Palm Sunday Procession from the Catholic edition of the Revised Standard Version of the Bible © 1965, 1966 by the Division of Christian Education of the National Council of the Churches of Christ in the United States of America. Used by permission. All rights reserved.

Psalm texts from the *Grail Psalms* © 1963 The Grail (England).

New English Translation 2010, granted recognitio by the Congregation for Divine Worship and the Discipline of the Sacraments, for the dioceses of the Bishops' Conferences of England and Wales (Prot. N. 915/06/L, 28 March 2010), and Scotland, (Prot. N. 1021/07/L, 23 June 2010), and Ireland (Prot. N. 516/05/L, 18 June 2010).

The English translation and chants of *The Roman Missal* © 2010, International Commission on English in the Liturgy Corporation. All rights reserved.

Latin text of *Missale Romanum*, Libreria Editrice Vaticana omnia sibi vindicat iura. Sine eiusdem licentia scripto data nemini liceat hunc Missale denuo imprimere aut in aliam linguam vertere.

Papal Magisterium used for introductions to feasts and seasons © Libreria Editrice Vaticana, Vatican City State.

40 Days and 40 Ways: Year A © 2017 The Incorporated Catholic Truth Society.

40 Days and 40 Ways: Year B © 2018 The Incorporated Catholic Truth Society.

Book of Eucharistic Devotions, compilation and typographical design and layout © 2018 The Incorporated Catholic Truth Society. Scripture readings are taken from the *Jerusalem Bible*, © 1966 Darton, Longman & Todd and Doubleday & Company Inc.

Companion to the Sunday Gospels: Year A © 2016 The Incorporated Catholic Truth Society.

Companion to the Sunday Gospels: Year B © 2017 The Incorporated Catholic Truth Society.

Companion to the Sunday Gospels: Year C © 2015 The Incorporated Catholic Truth Society.

Simple Prayer Book, first compiled and published in 1886, revised and reprinted, © The Incorporated Catholic Truth Society.

Stations of the Cross: The Way of Divine Mercy, first published 1959 by The Incorporated Catholic Truth Society; revised edition © 2015 The Incorporated Catholic Truth Society.

Morning prayer for Holy Saturday text is a part of the The Divine Office, The Liturgy of the Hours According to the Roman Rite compiled by the hierarchies of Australia, England and Wales and Ireland. Compilation © 1974 the hierarchies of Australia, England and Wales, Ireland.

Canticle from the Catholic edition of the Revised Standard Version of the Bible © 1965, 1966; Scripture Reading from the *Jerusalem Bible* © 1966.

The original antiphons, concluding prayers, short responses, responsories and rubrics © 1974 the hierarchies of Australia, England and Wales, Ireland.

Psalms are translated from the Hebrew by the Grail © The Grail England.

Images: From *Missale Romanum* by unknown artist © Renata Sedmakova/Shutterstock.com

This Missal is designed to accompany you through Holy Week. As well as the texts for Mass for the week, it also includes brief reflections on the Mass readings by Dom Henry Wansbrough, and an appendix of prayers containing devotions that will help you to enter into this great feast.

TABLE OF CONTENTS

THE ORDER OF MASS

THE INTRODUCTORY RITES

Before Mass begins, the people gather in a spirit of recollection, preparing for their participation in the Mass.

All stand during the entrance procession.

SIGN OF THE CROSS

After the Entrance Chant, the Priest and the faithful sign themselves with the Sign of the Cross:

Priest: In nómine Patris, et Fílii, et Spíritus Sancti.

A-men.

Response: Amen.

GREETING

The Priest greets the people, with one of the following:

1. Pr. Grátia Dómini nostri Iesu Christi,
et cáritas Dei,
et communicátio Sancti Spíritus
sit cum ómnibus vobis.

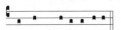

Et cum spí-ri-tu tu-o.

R. Et cum spíritu tuo.

2. Pr. Grátia vobis et pax a Deo Patre nostro
et Dómino Iesu Christo.

R. Et cum spíritu tuo.

3. Pr. Dóminus vobíscum.

R. Et cum spíritu tuo.

The Priest, or a Deacon, or another minister, may very briefly introduce the faithful to the Mass of the day.

THE INTRODUCTORY RITES

Before Mass begins, the people gather in a spirit of recollection, preparing for their participation in the Mass.

All stand during the entrance procession.

SIGN OF THE CROSS

After the Entrance Chant, the Priest and the faithful sign themselves with the Sign of the Cross:

Priest: In the name of the Father, and of the Son, and of the Holy Spirit.

A-men.

Response: Amen.

GREETING

The Priest greets the people, with one of the following:

1. **Pr.** The grace of our Lord Jesus Christ,
      and the love of God,
      and the communion of the Holy Spirit
      be with you all.

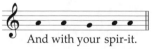

And with your spir-it.

   R. And with your spirit.

2. **Pr.** Grace to you and peace from God our Father
      and the Lord Jesus Christ.
   R. And with your spirit.

3. **Pr.** The Lord be with you.
   R. And with your spirit.

The Priest, or a Deacon, or another minister, may very briefly introduce the faithful to the Mass of the day.

PENITENTIAL ACT

There are three forms of the Penitential Act which may be chosen from as appropriate. Each Penitential Act begins with the invitation to the faithful by the Priest:

Pr. Fratres, agnoscámus peccáta nostra,
ut apti simus ad sacra mystéria celebránda.

A brief pause for silence follows.

Then one of the following forms is used:

**1. Confíteor Deo omnipoténti et vobis, fratres,
quia peccávi nimis
cogitatióne, verbo, ópere et omissióne:**

(and, striking their breast, they say:)
**mea culpa, mea culpa, mea máxima culpa.
Ideo precor beátam Mariám semper Vírginem,
omnes Angelos et Sanctos,
et vos, fratres, oráre pro me
ad Dóminum Deum nostrum.**

---

2. Pr. Miserére nostri, Dómine.

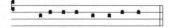

Qui- a peccá- vi- mus ti- bi.

R. **Quia peccávimus tibi.**

Pr. Osténde nobis, Dómine, misericórdiam tuam.

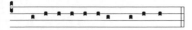

Et sa- lu- tá- re tu- um da no- bis.

R. **Et salutáre tuum da nobis.**

PENITENTIAL ACT

There are three forms of the Penitential Act which may be chosen from as appropriate. Each Penitential Act begins with the invitation to the faithful by the Priest:

Pr. Brethren (brothers and sisters),
let us acknowledge our sins,
and so prepare ourselves to celebrate the sacred mysteries.

A brief pause for silence follows.

Then one of the following forms is used:

**1. I confess to almighty God
and to you, my brothers and sisters,
that I have greatly sinned,
in my thoughts and in my words,
in what I have done and in what I have failed to do,**

(and, striking their breast, they say:)

**through my fault, through my fault,
through my most grievous fault;
therefore I ask blessed Mary ever-Virgin,
all the Angels and Saints,
and you, my brothers and sisters,
to pray for me to the Lord our God.**

---

2. Pr. Have mercy on us, O Lord.

For we have sinned a-gainst you.

R. **For we have sinned against you.**

Pr. Show us, O Lord, your mercy.

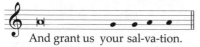

And grant us your sal-va-tion.

R. **And grant us your salvation.**

Invocations naming the gracious works of the Lord may be made, as in the example below:

3. Pr. Qui missus es sanáre contrítos corde:
   Kýrie, eléison.

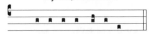

Ký- ri- e,   e- lé- i- son.

   R. Kýrie, eléison.

   Pr. Qui peccatóres vocáre venísti:
   Christe, eléison.

Chri- ste,   e- lé- i- son.

   R. Christe, eléison.

   Pr. Qui ad déxteram Patris sedes, ad interpellándum pro nobis:
   Kýrie, eléison.

Ký- ri- e,   e- lé- i- son.

   R. Kýrie, eléison.

The absolution by the Priest follows:

Pr. Misereátur nostri omnípotens Deus
   et, dimíssis peccátis nostris,
   perdúcat nos ad vitam ætérnam.

   A-men.
R. Amen.

The Kýrie, eléison (Lord, have mercy) invocations follow, unless they have just occurred.

   Pr. Kýrie, eléison.

y-ri-e,   e-lé- i-son.

Invocations naming the gracious works of the Lord may be made, as in the example below:

3. **Pr.** You were sent to heal the contrite of heart:
Lord, have mercy. Or: Kýrie, eléison.

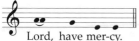
Or: repeat music/words from Latin.

Lord, have mer-cy.

R. **Lord, have mercy.**

Pr. You came to call sinners:
Christ, have mercy. Or: Christe, eléison.

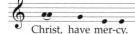
Or: repeat music/words from Latin.

Christ, have mer-cy.

R. **Christ, have mercy.**

Pr. You are seated at the right hand of the Father to intercede for us:
Lord, have mercy. Or: Kýrie, eléison.

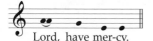
Or: repeat music/words from Latin.

Lord, have mer-cy.

R. **Lord, have mercy.**

The absolution by the Priest follows:

Pr. May almighty God have mercy on us,
forgive us our sins,
and bring us to everlasting life.

A-men.

R. **Amen.**

The Kýrie, eléison (Lord, have mercy) invocations follow, unless they have just occurred.

Pr. Lord, have mercy.

R. Lord, have mer-cy.

Pr. Christe, eléison.

R.   Chris-te, e-lé-i-son.

Pr. Kýrie eléison.

R.   Ky-ri-e, e-lé-i-son. Vel: R.   Ky-ri-e, e-lé-i-son.

THE GLORIA

At the Chrism Mass, the Evening Mass of the Lord's Supper, the Easter Vigil and on Easter Sunday this hymn is either sung or said:

Gló-ri-a in ex-cél-sis De-o.   Et in ter-ra pax ho-mí-ni-bus   bo-næ

vol-un-tá-tis.   Lau-dá-mus te.   Be-ne-dí-ci-mus te   Ado-rá-

mus te.   Glo-ri-fi-cámus te.   Grá-ti-as á-gi-mus ti-bi   prop-ter

mag-nam gló-ri-am tu-am.   Dó-mi-ne De-us, Rex cæ-léstis,   De-us

Pa-ter om-ní-po-tens. Dómi-ne Fi-li uni-gé-ni-te,   Ie-su Christe.

Dómi-ne De-us, Agnus De-i,   Fí-li-us Pa-tris, Qui tollis peccáta

Pr. Christ, have mercy.

R. Christ, have mer-cy.

Pr. Lord, have mercy.

R. Lord, have mer-cy.

THE GLORIA

At the Chrism Mass, the Evening Mass of the Lord's Supper, the Easter Vigil and on Easter Sunday this hymn is either sung or said:

Glo-ry to God in the high-est,

and on earth peace to peo-ple of good will.

We praise you, we bless you, we a-dore you, we glo-ri-fy you,

we give you thanks for your great glo-ry,

Lord God, heav-en-ly King, O God, al-might-y Fa-ther.

Lord Je-sus Christ, On-ly Be-got-ten Son,

Lord God, Lamb of God, Son of the Fa-ther,

you take a-way the sins of the world, have mer-cy on us;

mun- di, mi-se-ré- re nobis. Qui tollis peccáta mundi, súscipe de-

pre-ca-ti-ó-nem no- stram. Qui sedes ad déxteram Patris, mi-seré-

re nobis. Quóni-am tu solus Sanctus. Tu solus Dó-mi-nus Tu so-

lus Al-tíssimus, Ie-su Christe. Cum Sancto Spí-ri-tu, in gló-ri-a

De- i Pa- tris. A- men.

Glória in excélsis Deo
et in terra pax homínibus bonæ voluntátis.

Laudámus te,
benedícimus te,
adorámus te,
glorificámus te,
grátias ágimus tibi propter magnam glóriam tuam,
Dómine Deus, Rex cæléstis,
Deus Pater omnípotens.

Dómine Fili Unigénite, Iesu Christe,
Dómine Deus, Agnus Dei, Fílius Patris,
qui tollis peccáta mundi, miserére nobis;
qui tollis peccáta mundi, súscipe deprecatiónem nostram.
Qui sedes ad déxteram Patris, miserére nobis.
Quóniam tu solus Sanctus, tu solus Dóminus, tu solus Altíssimus,
Iesu Christe, cum Sancto Spíritu: in glória Dei Patris.
Amen.

When this hymn is concluded, the Priest, says: **Pr.** Orémus.
And all pray in silence. Then the Priest says the Collect prayer, which ends:
R. Amen.

you take a-way the sins of the world,   re-ceive our prayer;

you are seat-ed at the right hand of the Fa-ther,   have mer-cy on us.

For you a-lone are the Ho-ly One,   you a-lone are the Lord,

you a-lone are the Most High, Je-sus Christ,   with the Ho-ly Spir-it,

in the glo-ry of God the Fa - ther.   A - men.

Glory to God in the highest,
and on earth peace to people of good will.
We praise you,
we bless you,
we adore you,
we glorify you,
we give you thanks for your great glory,
Lord God, heavenly King,
O God, almighty Father.

Lord Jesus Christ, Only Begotten Son,
Lord God, Lamb of God, Son of the Father,
you take away the sins of the world, have mercy on us;
you take away the sins of the world, receive our prayer;
you are seated at the right hand of the Father,
have mercy on us.

For you alone are the Holy One,
you alone are the Lord,
you alone are the Most High,
Jesus Christ,
with the Holy Spirit,
in the glory of God the Father.
Amen.

When this hymn is concluded, the Priest, says: **Pr.** Let us pray.
And all pray in silence. Then the Priest says the Collect prayer, which ends: **R. Amen.**

THE LITURGY OF THE WORD

By hearing the word proclaimed in worship, the faithful again enter into the unending dialogue between God and the covenant people.

FIRST READING

The reader goes to the ambo and proclaims the First Reading, while all sit and listen. The reader ends:

Verbum Dómini.

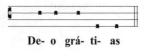

De- o grá- ti- as

R.   **Deo grátias.**

It is appropriate to have a brief time of quiet between readings as those present take the word of God to heart.

PSALM

The psalmist or cantor sings or says the Psalm, with the people making the response.

SECOND READING

On Sundays and certain other days there is a second reading. The reader ends:

Verbum Dómini.

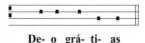

De- o grá- ti- as

R.   **Deo grátias.**

GOSPEL

The assembly stands for the Gospel Acclamation. Except during Lent the Acclamation is:

R.   **Allelúia!**

During Lent the following forms may be used or another similar phrase:

R.   **Laus tibi, Christe, Rex ætérnæ glóriæ!** Or:

R.   **Laus et honor tibi, Dómine Iesu!** Or:

R.   **Glória et laus tibi, Christe!** Or:

R.   **Glória tibi, Christe, Verbo Dei!**

THE LITURGY OF THE WORD

By hearing the word proclaimed in worship, the faithful again enter into the unending dialogue between God and the covenant people.

FIRST READING

The reader goes to the ambo and proclaims the First Reading, while all sit and listen. The reader ends:

The word of the Lord.

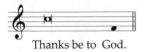

Thanks be to God.

R. **Thanks be to God.**

It is appropriate to have a brief time of quiet between readings as those present take the word of God to heart.

PSALM

The psalmist or cantor sings or says the Psalm, with the people making the response.

SECOND READING

On Sundays and certain other days there is a second reading. The reader ends:

The word of the Lord.

Thanks be to God.

R. **Thanks be to God.**

GOSPEL

The assembly stands for the Gospel Acclamation. Except during Lent the Acclamation is:

R. **Alleluia!**

During Lent the following forms may be used or another similar phrase:

R. **Praise to you, O Christ, king of eternal glory!** Or:

R. **Praise and honour to you, Lord Jesus!** Or:

R. **Glory and praise to you, O Christ!** Or:

R. **Glory to you, O Christ, you are the Word of God!**

At the ambo the Deacon, or the Priest says:

Pr. Dóminus vobíscum.

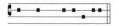

Et cum spíritu tuo.

R. **Et cum spíritu tuo.**

Pr. Léctio sancti Evangélii secúndum **N.**

He makes the Sign of the Cross on the book and, together with the people, on his forehead, lips, and breast.

Glória tibi Dómine.

R. **Glória tibi, Dómine.**

At the end of the Gospel:

Pr. Verbum Dómini.

Laus ti-bi, Christe.

R. **Laus tibi, Christe.**

THE HOMILY

Then follows the Homily, which is preached by a Priest or Deacon. After a brief silence all stand.

THE CREED

On Sundays the Profession of Faith will follow. Especially during Lent and Easter Time, the Apostles' Creed may be used.

THE NICENO-CONSTANTINOPOLITAN CREED

Credo in unum De- um,   Patrem omni-poténtem factó-rem cæli et terræ, vi-sibili-um óm-nium et invi-si-bí- lium.   Et in unum Dó-

At the ambo the Deacon, or the Priest says:

Pr. The Lord be with you.

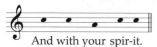

And with your spir-it.

R. **And with your spirit.**

Pr. A reading from the holy Gospel according to **N.**

He makes the Sign of the Cross on the book and, together with the people, on his forehead, lips, and breast.

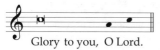

Glory to you, O Lord.

R. **Glory to you, O Lord.**

At the end of the Gospel:

Pr. The Gospel of the Lord.

Praise to you, Lord Je-sus Christ.

R. **Praise to you, Lord Jesus Christ.**

THE HOMILY

Then follows the Homily, which is preached by a Priest or Deacon. After a brief silence all stand.

THE CREED

On Sundays the Profession of Faith will follow. Especially during Lent and Easter Time, the Apostles' Creed may be used.

THE NICENO-CONSTANTINOPOLITAN CREED

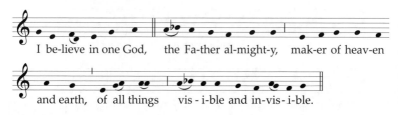

I be-lieve in one God, the Fa-ther al-might-y, mak-er of heav-en and earth, of all things vis-i-ble and in-vis-i-ble.

minum Iesum Christum, Fí-lium De-i uni-gé-ni-tum. Et ex Pa-

tre na- tum ante ómni-a sæ- cu-la. De-um de De-o, lumen de

lumine, De-um verum de De-o vero. Géni-tum, non fac-tum, con-

substanti-á-lem Patri: per quem ómni-a facta sunt. Qui propter nos

At the words

homines et propter nostram sa-lútem descéndit de cæ-lis. Et in-

that follow, up to and including **et homo factus est**, all bow.

carná-tus est de Spí-ri-tu Sancto ex Ma-rí-a Vírgi-ne, et homo

factus est. Cru-ci-fí- xus é-ti-am pro nobis sub Pónti-o Pi-lá-to,

passus et sepúl- tus est. Et resurré-xit térti-a di-e, secúndum Scrip-

turas, Et ascéndit in cæ- lum, sedet ad déxteram Patris. Et í-terum

I be-lieve in one Lord Je-sus Christ, the Only Be-got-ten Son

of God, born of the Father be-fore all a-ges. God from God,

Light from Light, true God from true God, be-got-ten, not made,

con-sub-stan-tial with the Fa-ther; through him all things were

made. For us men and for our sal-va-tion he came down from

At the words that follow, up to and including **and became man**, all bow.

heav-en, and by the Ho-ly Spir-it was in-car-nate of the Vir-gin

Mar-y, and be-came man.

For our sake he was cru-ci-fied un-der Pon-tius Pi-late, he

suffered death and was bur-ied, and rose a-gain on the third day

in accordance with the Scrip-tures. He as-cend-ed in-to heav-en

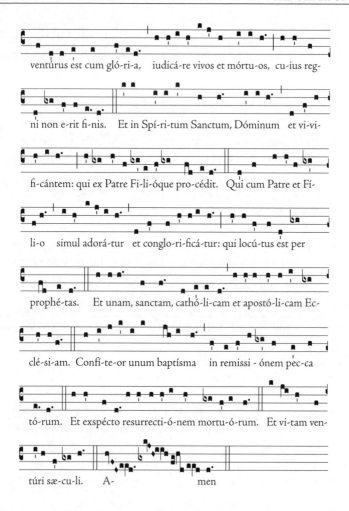

ventúrus est cum gló-ri-a, iudicá-re vivos et mórtu-os, cu-ius reg-

ni non e-rit fi-nis. Et in Spí-ri-tum Sanctum, Dóminum et vi-vi-

fi-cántem: qui ex Patre Fi-li-óque pro-cédit. Qui cum Patre et Fí-

li-o simul adorá-tur et conglo-ri-ficá-tur: qui locú-tus est per

prophé-tas. Et unam, sanctam, cathó-li-cam et apostó-li-cam Ec-

clé-si-am. Confí-te-or unum baptísma in remissi - ónem pec-ca

tó-rum. Et exspécto resurrecti-ó-nem mortu-ó-rum. Et vi-tam ven-

túri sæ-cu-li. A-   men

and is seated at the right hand of the Fa-ther.   He will come a-gain

in glo-ry   to judge the living and the dead   and his kingdom will

have no end.

I be-lieve in the Ho-ly Spir-it,   the Lord, the giv-er of life,   who

pro-ceeds from the Father and the Son,   who with the Fa-ther and

the Son   is   adored and glo-ri-fied,   who has spoken through the

proph-ets.   I be-lieve in one, ho-ly, ca-tho-lic   and a-pos-tol-ic

Church.   I con-fess one Bap-tism   for the for - give-ness of sins

and I look for-ward to the res-ur-rec-tion of the dead   and the life

of the world to come.   A -   men.

Credo in unum Deum,
Patrem omnipoténtem,
factórem cæli et terræ,
visibílium ómnium et invisibílium.

Et in unum Dóminum Iesum Christum,
Fílium Dei Unigénitum,
et ex Patre natum ante ómnia sǽcula.
Deum de Deo, lumen de lúmine,
Deum verum de Deo vero,
génitum, non factum, consubstantiálem Patri:
per quem ómnia facta sunt.
Qui propter nos hómines et propter nostram salútem
descéndit de cælis.

(all bow)

Et incarnátus est de Spíritu Sancto
ex María Vírgine, et homo factus est.

Crucifíxus étiam pro nobis sub Póntio Piláto;
passus et sepúltus est,
et resurréxit tértia die, secúndum Scriptúras,
et ascéndit in cælum, sedet ad déxteram Patris.

Et íterum ventúrus est cum glória,
    iudicáre vivos et mórtuos,
cuius regni non erit finis.
Et in Spíritum Sanctum, Dóminum et vivificántem:
qui ex Patre Filióque procédit.
Qui cum Patre et Fílio simul adorátur et conglorificátur:
qui locútus est per prophétas.

Et unam, sanctam, cathólicam et apostólicam Ecclésiam.
Confíteor unum baptísma in remissiónem peccatórum.
Et exspécto resurrectiónem mortuórum,
et vitam ventúri sǽculi. Amen.

I believe in one God,
the Father almighty,
maker of heaven and earth,
of all things visible and invisible.

I believe in one Lord Jesus Christ,
the Only Begotten Son of God,
born of the Father before all ages.
God from God, Light from Light,
true God from true God,
begotten, not made, consubstantial with the Father;
through him all things were made.
For us men and for our salvation
he came down from heaven,

(all bow)

and by the Holy Spirit was incarnate of the Virgin Mary,
and became man.

For our sake he was crucified under Pontius Pilate,
he suffered death and was buried,
and rose again on the third day
in accordance with the Scriptures.
He ascended into heaven
and is seated at the right hand of the Father.
He will come again in glory
to judge the living and the dead
and his kingdom will have no end.

I believe in the Holy Spirit, the Lord, the giver of life,
who proceeds from the Father and the Son,
who with the Father and the Son is adored and glorified,
who has spoken through the prophets.

I believe in one, holy, catholic and apostolic Church.
I confess one Baptism for the forgiveness of sins
and I look forward to the resurrection of the dead
and the life of the world to come. Amen.

THE APOSTLES' CREED

Credo in Deum, Patrem omnipoténtem,
Creatórem cæli et terræ,
et in Iesum Christum, Fílium eius únicum,
Dóminum nostrum,

at the words that follow up to and including Maria Virgine, *all bow.*

qui concéptus est de Spíritu Sancto,
natus ex María Vírgine,
passus sub Póntio Piláto,
crucifíxus, mórtuus, et sepúltus,
descéndit ad ínferos,
tértia die resurréxit a mórtuis,
ascéndit ad cælos,
sedet ad déxteram Dei Patris omnipoténtis,
inde ventúrus est iudicáre vivos et mórtuos.

Credo in Spíritum Sanctum,
sanctam Ecclésiam cathólicam,
sanctórum communiónem,
remissiónem peccatórum,
carnis resurrectiónem,
vitam ætérnam. Amen.

THE PRAYER OF THE FAITHFUL (BIDDING PRAYERS)

Intentions will normally be for the Church; for the world; for those in particular need; and for the local community. After each there is time for silent prayer, followed by the next intention, or concluded with a sung phrase such as **Christe audi nos**, or **Christe exaudi nos**, or by a responsory such as:

R.   **Præsta, ætérne omnípotens Deus.** Or:
R.   **Te rogámus audi nos.** Or:
R.   **Kýrie, eléison.**

The Priest concludes the Prayer with a collect.

THE APOSTLES' CREED

I believe in God,
the Father almighty
Creator of heaven and earth,
and in Jesus Christ, his only Son, our Lord,

at the words that follow up to and including the Virgin Mary, all bow.

who was conceived by the Holy Spirit,
born of the Virgin Mary,
suffered under Pontius Pilate,
was crucified, died and was buried;
he descended into hell;
on the third day he rose again from the dead;
he ascended into heaven,
and is seated at the right hand of God
the Father almighty;
from there he will come to judge the living and the dead.

I believe in the Holy Spirit,
the holy catholic Church,
the communion of saints,
the forgiveness of sins,
the resurrection of the body,
and life everlasting. Amen.

THE PRAYER OF THE FAITHFUL (BIDDING PRAYERS)

Intentions will normally be for the Church; for the world; for those in particular need; and for the local community. After each there is time for silent prayer, followed by the next intention, or concluded with a sung phrase such as **Christ, hear us,** or **Christ graciously hear us,** or by a responsory such as:

Let us pray to the Lord.
R. Grant this, almighty God. Or:
R. Lord, have mercy. Or:
R. Kýrie, eléison.

The Priest concludes the Prayer with a collect.

THE LITURGY OF THE EUCHARIST

For Catholics, the Eucharist is the source and summit of the whole Christian life.

After the Liturgy of the Word, the people sit and the Offertory Chant begins. The faithful express their participation by making an offering, bringing forward bread and wine for the celebration of the Eucharist and perhaps other gifts to relieve the needs of the Church and of the poor.

PREPARATORY PRAYERS

Standing at the altar, the Priest takes the paten with the bread and holds it slightly raised above the altar with both hands, saying:

Pr. Benedíctus es, Dómine, Deus univérsi,
quia de tua largitáte accépimus panem,
quem tibi offérimus,
fructum terræ et óperis mánuum hóminum:
ex quo nobis fiet panis vitæ.

R. **Benedíctus Deus in sǽcula.**

The Deacon, or the Priest, pours wine and a little water into the chalice, saying quietly:

Pr. Per huius aquæ et vini mysterium
eius efficiamur divinitatis consortes,
qui humanitatis nostræ fieri dignatus est particeps.

The Priest then takes the chalice and holds it slightly raised above the altar with both hands, saying:

Pr. Benedíctus es, Dómine, Deus univérsi,
quia de tua largitáte accépimus vinum,
quod tibi offérimus,
fructum vitis et óperis mánuum hóminum,
ex quo nobis fiet potus spiritális.

R. **Benedíctus Deus in sǽcula.**

After this, the Priest, bowing profoundly, says quietly:

Pr. In spiritu humilitatis et in animo contrito
suscipiamur a te, Domine;
et sic fiat sacrificium nostrum in conspectu tuo hodie,
ut placeat tibi, Domine Deus.

Then the Priest, standing at the side of the altar, washes his hands, saying quietly:

Pr. Lava me, Domine, ab iniquitate mea,
et a peccato meo munda me.

THE LITURGY OF THE EUCHARIST

For Catholics, the Eucharist is the source and summit of the whole Christian life.

After the Liturgy of the Word, the people sit and the Offertory Chant begins. The faithful express their participation by making an offering, bringing forward bread and wine for the celebration of the Eucharist and perhaps other gifts to relieve the needs of the Church and of the poor.

PREPARATORY PRAYERS

Standing at the altar, the Priest takes the paten with the bread and holds it slightly raised above the altar with both hands, saying:

Pr. Blessed are you, Lord God of all creation,
for through your goodness we have received
the bread we offer you:
fruit of the earth and work of human hands,
it will become for us the bread of life.

R. **Blessed be God for ever.**

The Deacon, or the Priest, pours wine and a little water into the chalice, saying quietly:

Pr. By the mystery of this water and wine
may we come to share in the divinity of Christ
who humbled himself to share in our humanity.

The Priest then takes the chalice and holds it slightly raised above the altar with both hands, saying:

Pr. Blessed are you, Lord God of all creation,
for through your goodness we have received
the wine we offer you:
fruit of the vine and work of human hands,
it will become our spiritual drink.

R. **Blessed be God for ever.**

After this, the Priest, bowing profoundly, says quietly:

Pr. With humble spirit and contrite heart
may we be accepted by you, O Lord,
and may our sacrifice in your sight this day
be pleasing to you, Lord God.

Then the Priest, standing at the side of the altar, washes his hands, saying quietly:

Pr. Wash me, O Lord, from my iniquity
and cleanse me from my sin.

The people rise as the Priest says:

Pr. Oráte, fratres:
ut meum ac vestrum sacrifícium
acceptábile fiat apud Deum Patrem omnipoténtem.

R. **Suscípiat Dóminus sacrifícium de mánibus tuis**
ad laudem et glóriam nóminis sui,
ad utilitátem quoque nostram
totiúsque Ecclésiæ suæ sanctæ.

PRAYER OVER THE OFFERINGS

The Priest says the Prayer over the Offerings, at the end of which the people acclaim:

R. **Amen.**

THE EUCHARISTIC PRAYER

Extending his hands, the Priest says:

Pr. Dóminus vobíscum.

Et cum spí-ri-tu tu-o.

R. **Et cum spíritu tuo.**

Pr. Sursum corda.

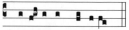

Habémus ad Dóminum.

R. **Habémus ad Dóminum.**

Pr. Grátias agámus Dómino Deo nostro.

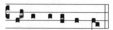

Dignum et iustum est.

R. **Dignum et iustum est.**

The people rise as the Priest says:

Pr. Pray, brethren (brothers and sisters),
　　that my sacrifice and yours
　　may be acceptable to God,
　　the almighty Father.

R. **May the Lord accept the sacrifice at your hands**
　　for the praise and glory of his name,
　　for our good
　　and the good of all his holy Church.

PRAYER OVER THE OFFERINGS

The Priest says the Prayer over the Offerings, at the end of which the people acclaim:

R. **Amen.**

THE EUCHARISTIC PRAYER

Extending his hands, the Priest says:

Pr. The Lord be with you.

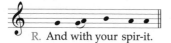

R. And with your spir-it.

R. **And with your spirit.**

Pr. Lift up your hearts.

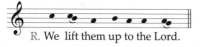

R. We lift them up to the Lord.

R. **We lift them up to the Lord.**

Pr. Let us give thanks to the Lord our God.

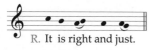

R. It is right and just.

R. **It is right and just.**

The Priest continues with the Preface at the end of which all sing or say:

anc-tus, * Sanc-tus, Sanc-tus Dó-mi-nus De-us Sá-ba-oth. Ple-ni

sunt cæ-li et ter-ra gló-ri-a tu-a.   Ho-sán-na in ex-cél-sis.   Be-ne-díc-

tus qui ve-nit in nómine Dómini.   Ho-sán-na in excél-sis.

Sanctus, Sanctus, Sanctus Dóminus Deus Sábaoth.
Pleni sunt cæli et terra glória tua.
Hosánna in excélsis.
Benedíctus qui venit in nómine Dómini.
Hosánna in excélsis.

After the Sanctus the congregation kneels for the remainder of the Eucharistic Prayer.

The Priest continues with the Preface at the end of which all sing or say:

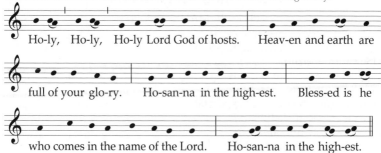

Ho-ly, Ho-ly, Ho-ly Lord God of hosts. Heav-en and earth are full of your glo-ry. Ho-san-na in the high-est. Bless-ed is he who comes in the name of the Lord. Ho-san-na in the high-est.

Holy, Holy, Holy Lord God of hosts.
Heaven and earth are full of your glory.
Hosanna in the highest.
Blessed is he who comes in the name of the Lord.
Hosanna in the highest.

After the Sanctus the congregation kneels for the remainder of the Eucharistic Prayer.

EUCHARISTIC PRAYER I

(THE ROMAN CANON)

Pr. Te ígitur, clementíssime Pater,
per Iesum Christum, Fílium tuum,
Dóminum nostrum,
súpplices rogámus ac pétimus,
uti accépta hábeas
et benedícas ✠ hæc dona, hæc múnera,
hæc sancta sacrifícia illibáta,
in primis, quæ tibi offérimus
pro Ecclésia tua sancta cathólica:
quam pacificáre, custodíre, adunáre
et régere dignéris toto orbe terrárum:
una cum fámulo tuo Papa nostro N.
et Antístite nostro N.
et ómnibus orthodóxis atque cathólicæ
et apostólicæ fídei cultóribus.

Commemoration of the Living.

Meménto, Dómine,
famulórum famularúmque tuárum N. et N.
et ómnium circumstántium,
quorum tibi fides cógnita est et nota devótio,
pro quibus tibi offérimus:
vel qui tibi ófferunt hoc sacrifícium laudis,
pro se suísque ómnibus:
pro redemptióne animarúm suárum,
pro spe salútis et incolumitátis suæ:
tibíque reddunt vota sua
ætérno Deo, vivo et vero.

Within the Action

Communicántes,
et memóriam venerántes,
in primis gloriósæ semper Vírginis Maríæ,
Genetrícis Dei et Dómini nostri Iesu Christi:
† sed et béati Ioseph, eiúsdem Vírginis Sponsi,
et beatórum Apostolórum ac Mártyrum tuórum,
Petri et Pauli, Andréæ,
(Iacóbi, Ioánnis,
Thomæ, Iacóbi, Philíppi,

EUCHARISTIC PRAYER I
(THE ROMAN CANON)

Pr. To you, therefore, most merciful Father,
we make humble prayer and petition
through Jesus Christ, your Son, our Lord:
that you accept
and bless ✠ these gifts, these offerings,
these holy and unblemished sacrifices,
which we offer you firstly
for your holy catholic Church.
Be pleased to grant her peace,
to guard, unite and govern her
throughout the whole world,
together with your servant N. our Pope
and N. our Bishop,
and all those who, holding to the truth,
hand on the catholic and apostolic faith.

Commemoration of the Living.

Remember, Lord, your servants N. and N.
and all gathered here,
whose faith and devotion are known to you.
For them, we offer you this sacrifice of praise
or they offer it for themselves
and all who are dear to them:
for the redemption of their souls,
in hope of health and well-being,
and paying their homage to you,
the eternal God, living and true.

Within the Action

In communion with those whose memory we venerate,
especially the glorious ever-Virgin Mary,
Mother of our God and Lord, Jesus Christ,
† and blessed Joseph, her Spouse,
your blessed Apostles and Martyrs,
Peter and Paul, Andrew,
(James, John,
Thomas, James, Philip,

Bartholomǽi, Matthǽi,
Simónis et Thaddǽi:
Lini, Cleti, Cleméntis, Xysti,
Cornélii, Cypriáni,
Lauréntii, Chrysógoni,
Ioánnis et Pauli,
Cosmæ et Damiáni)
et ómnium Sanctórum tuórum;
quorum méritis precibúsque concédas,
ut in ómnibus protectiónis tuæ muniámur auxílio.
(Per Christum Dóminum nostrum. Amen.)

PROPER FORMS OF THE COMMUNICANTES

From the Mass of the Easter Vigil until the Second Sunday of Easter

Communicántes,
et (noctem sacratíssimam) diem sacratíssimum celebrántes
Resurrectiónis Dómini nostri Iesu Christi secúndum carnem:
sed et memóriam venerántes,
in primis gloriósæ semper Vírginis Maríæ,
Genetrícis eiúsdem Dei et Dómini nostri Iesu Christi: †

Hanc ígitur oblatiónem servitútis nostræ,
sed et cunctæ famíliæ tuæ,
quǽsumus, Dómine, ut placátus accípias:
diésque nostros in tua pace dispónas,
atque ab ætérna damnatióne nos éripi
et in electórum tuórum iúbeas grege numerári.
(Per Christum Dóminum nostrum. Amen.)

From the Mass of the Easter Vigil until the Second Sunday of Easter

Hanc ígitur oblatiónem servitútis nostræ,
sed et cunctæ famíliæ tuæ,
quam tibi offérimus
pro his quoque, quos regeneráre dignátus es ex aqua et Spíritu Sancto,
tríbuens eis remissiónem ómnium peccatórum,
quǽsumus, Dómine, ut placátus accípias:

Bartholomew, Matthew,
Simon and Jude;
Linus, Cletus, Clement, Sixtus,
Cornelius, Cyprian,
Lawrence, Chrysogonus,
John and Paul,
Cosmas and Damian)
and all your Saints;
we ask that through their merits and prayers,
in all things we may be defended
by your protecting help.
(Through Christ our Lord. Amen.)

PROPER FORMS OF THE COMMUNICANTES

From the Mass of the Easter Vigil until the Second Sunday of Easter

Celebrating the most sacred night (day)
of the Resurrection of our Lord Jesus Christ in the flesh,
and in communion with those whose memory we venerate,
especially the glorious ever-Virgin Mary,
Mother of our God and Lord, Jesus Christ, †

Therefore, Lord, we pray:
graciously accept this oblation of our service,
that of your whole family;
order our days in your peace,
and command that we be delivered from eternal damnation
and counted among the flock of those you have chosen.
(Through Christ Our Lord. Amen.)

From the Mass of the Easter Vigil until the Second Sunday of Easter

Therefore, Lord, we pray:
graciously accept this oblation of our service,
that of your whole family,
which we make to you
also for those to whom you have been pleased to give
the new birth of water and the Holy Spirit,
granting them forgiveness of all their sins;

diésque nostros in tua pace dispónas,
atque ab ætérna damnatióne nos éripi
et in electórum tuórum iúbeas grege numerári.
(Per Christum Dóminum nostrum. Amen.)

Quam oblatiónem tu, Deus, in ómnibus, quǽsumus,
benedíctam, adscríptam, ratam,
rationábilem, acceptabilémque fácere dignéris:
ut nobis Corpus et Sanguis fiat dilectíssimi Fílii tui,
Dómini nostri Iesu Christi.

Qui, prídie quam paterétur,
accépit panem in sanctas ac venerábiles manus suas,
et elevátis óculis in cælum
ad te Deum Patrem suum omnipoténtem,
tibi grátias agens benedíxit,
fregit,
dedítque discípulis suis, dicens:

ACCÍPITE ET MANDUCÁTE EX HOC OMNES:
HOC EST ENIM CORPUS MEUM,
QUOD PRO VOBIS TRADÉTUR.

Símili modo, postquam cenátum est,
accípiens et hunc præclárum cálicem
in sanctas ac venerábiles manus suas,
item tibi grátias agens benedíxit,
dedítque discípulis suis dicens:

ACCÍPITE ET BÍBITE EX EO OMNES:
HIC EST ENIM CALIX SÁNGUINIS MEI
NOVI ET ÆTÉRNI TESTAMÉNTI,
QUI PRO VOBIS ET PRO MULTIS EFFUNDÉTUR
IN REMISSIÓNEM PECCATÓRUM.
HOC FÁCITE IN MEAM COMMEMORATIÓNEM.

order our days in your peace,
and command that we be delivered from eternal damnation
and counted among the flock of those you have chosen.
(Through Christ our Lord. Amen.)

Be pleased, O God, we pray,
to bless, acknowledge,
and approve this offering in every respect;
make it spiritual and acceptable,
so that it may become for us
the Body and Blood of your most beloved Son,
our Lord Jesus Christ.

On the day before he was to suffer,
he took bread in his holy and venerable hands,
and with eyes raised to heaven
to you, O God, his almighty Father,
giving you thanks, he said the blessing,
broke the bread
and gave it to his disciples, saying:

TAKE THIS, ALL OF YOU, AND EAT OF IT,
FOR THIS IS MY BODY,
WHICH WILL BE GIVEN UP FOR YOU.

In a similar way, when supper was ended,
he took this precious chalice
in his holy and venerable hands,
and once more giving you thanks, he said the blessing
and gave the chalice to his disciples, saying:

TAKE THIS, ALL OF YOU, AND DRINK FROM IT,
FOR THIS IS THE CHALICE OF MY BLOOD,
THE BLOOD OF THE NEW AND ETERNAL COVENANT,
WHICH WILL BE POURED OUT FOR YOU AND FOR MANY
FOR THE FORGIVENESS OF SINS.
DO THIS IN MEMORY OF ME.

Pr. Mystérium fídei.

The people continue, acclaiming one of the following:

Mortem tu-am annunti-ámus, Dómi-ne,   et tu-am resurrecti-ó-

nem confi-témur, do-nec vé-ni-as.

1. **Mortem tuam annuntiámus, Dómine,**
et tuam resurrectiónem confitémur, donec vénias.

Quoti-escúmque manducámus panem hunc   et cálicem bíbimus,

mortem tu-am annunti-ámus, Dómine, donec vé- ni-as.

2. **Quotiescúmque manducámus panem hunc**
et cálicem bíbimus,
mortem tuam annuntiámus, Dómine, donec vénias.

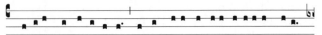

Salvátor mundi, salva nos, qui per crucem et resurrecti-ónem tu-am

li-be-rá- sti nos.

3. **Salvátor mundi, salva nos,**
qui per crucem et resurrectiónem tuam liberásti nos.

Pr. The mystery of faith.

The people continue, acclaiming one of the following:

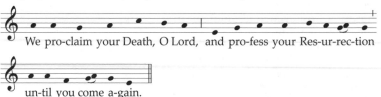

We pro-claim your Death, O Lord, and pro-fess your Res-ur-rec-tion
un-til you come a-gain.

1. **We proclaim your Death, O Lord,**
and profess your Resurrection
until you come again.

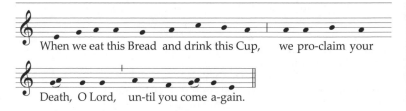

When we eat this Bread and drink this Cup, we pro-claim your
Death, O Lord, un-til you come a-gain.

2. **When we eat this Bread and drink this Cup,**
we proclaim your Death, O Lord,
until you come again.

Save us, Sav-iour of the world, for by your Cross and Res-ur-rec-tion
you have set us free.

3. **Save us, Saviour of the world,**
for by your Cross and Resurrection
you have set us free.

Only in Ireland: **4.** **My Lord and my God.**

Pr. Unde et mémores, Dómine,
nos servi tui,
sed et plebs tua sancta,
eiúsdem Christi, Fílii tui, Dómini nostri,
tam beátæ passiónis,
necnon et ab ínferis resurrectiónis,
sed et in cælos gloriósæ ascensiónis:
offérimus præcláræ maiestáti tuæ
de tuis donis ac datis
hóstiam puram,
hóstiam sanctam,
hóstiam immaculátam,
Panem sanctum vitæ ætérnæ
et Cálicem salútis perpétuæ.

Supra quæ propítio ac seréno vultu
respícere dignéris:
et accépta habére,
sícuti accépta habére dignátus es
múnera púeri tui iusti Abel,
et sacrifícium Patriárchæ nostri Abrahæ,
et quod tibi óbtulit summus sacérdos tuus Melchísedech,
sanctum sacrifícium, immaculátam hóstiam.

Súpplices te rogámus, omnípotens Deus:
iube hæc perférri per manus sancti Angeli tui
in sublíme altáre tuum,
in conspéctu divínæ maiestátis tuæ;
ut, quotquot ex hac altáris participatióne
sacrosánctum Fílii tui Corpus et Sánguinem sumpsérimus,
omni benedictióne cælésti et grátia repleámur
(Per Christum Dóminum nostrum. Amen.)

Commemoration of the Dead.

Meménto étiam, Dómine, famulórum famularúmque tuárum N. et N.,
qui nos præcessérunt cum signo fídei,
et dórmiunt in somno pacis.
Ipsis, Dómine, et ómnibus in Christo quiescéntibus,
locum refrigérii, lucis et pacis,
ut indúlgeas, deprecámur.
(Per Christum Dóminum nostrum. Amen.)

Nobis quoque peccatóribus fámulis tuis,
de multitúdine miseratiónum tuárum sperántibus,

Pr. Therefore, O Lord,
as we celebrate the memorial of the blessed Passion,
the Resurrection from the dead,
and the glorious Ascension into heaven
of Christ, your Son, our Lord,
we, your servants and your holy people,
offer to your glorious majesty
from the gifts that you have given us,
this pure victim,
this holy victim,
this spotless victim,
the holy Bread of eternal life
and the Chalice of everlasting salvation.

Be pleased to look upon these offerings
with a serene and kindly countenance,
and to accept them,
as once you were pleased to accept
the gifts of your servant Abel the just,
the sacrifice of Abraham, our father in faith,
and the offering of your high priest Melchizedek,
a holy sacrifice, a spotless victim.

In humble prayer we ask you, almighty God:
command that these gifts be borne
by the hands of your holy Angel
to your altar on high
in the sight of your divine majesty,
so that all of us, who through this participation at the altar
receive the most holy Body and Blood of your Son,
may be filled with every grace and heavenly blessing.
(Through Christ our Lord. Amen.)

Commemoration of the Dead.

Remember also, Lord, your servants N. and N.,
who have gone before us with the sign of faith
and rest in the sleep of peace.
Grant them, O Lord, we pray,
and all who sleep in Christ,
a place of refreshment, light and peace.
(Through Christ our Lord. Amen.)

To us, also, your servants, who, though sinners,
hope in your abundant mercies,

partem áliquam et societátem donáre dignéris
cum tuis sanctis Apóstolis et Martýribus:
cum Ioánne, Stéphano,
Matthía, Bárnaba,
(Ignátio, Alexándro,
Marcellíno, Petro,
Felicitáte, Perpétua,
Agatha, Lúcia,
Agnéte, Cæcília, Anastásia)
et ómnibus Sanctis tuis:
intra quorum nos consórtium,
non æstimátor mériti,
sed véniæ, quæsumus, largítor admítte.
Per Christum Dóminum nostrum.

Per quem hæc ómnia, Dómine,
semper bona creas, sanctíficas, vivíficas, benedícis,
et præstas nobis.

Per ipsum, et cum ipso, et in ipso,
est tibi Deo Patri omnipoténti,
in unitáte Spíritus Sancti,
omnis honor et glória
per ómnia sǽcula sæculórum.

A-men.
R. **Amen.**

Then follows the Communion Rite, p.62.

graciously grant some share
and fellowship with your holy Apostles and M.
with John the Baptist, Stephen,
Matthias, Barnabas,
(Ignatius, Alexander,
Marcellinus, Peter,
Felicity, Perpetua,
Agatha, Lucy,
Agnes, Cecilia, Anastasia)
and all your Saints;
admit us, we beseech you,
into their company,
not weighing our merits,
but granting us your pardon,
through Christ our Lord.

Through whom
you continue to make all these good things, O Lord;
you sanctify them, fill them with life,
bless them, and bestow them upon us.

Through him, and with him, and in him,
O God, almighty Father,
in the unity of the Holy Spirit,
all glory and honour is yours,
for ever and ever.

A-men.

R. **Amen.**

Then follows the Communion Rite, p.63.

EUCHARISTIC PRAYER II

Pr. ...biscum.

R. ...píritu tuo.

R. ...m corda.

Pr. ...abémus ad Dóminum.

Pr. Grátias agámus Dómino Deo nostro.

R. **Dignum et iustum est.**

Pr. Vere dignum et iustum est, æquum et salutáre, nos tibi, sancte Pater,
semper et ubíque grátias ágere
per Fílium dilectiónis tuæ Iesum Christum,
Verbum tuum per quod cuncta fecísti:
quem misísti nobis Salvatórem et Redemptórem,
incarnátum de Spíritu Sancto et ex Vírgine natum.

Qui voluntátem tuam adímplens
et pópulum tibi sanctum acquírens
exténdit manus cum paterétur,
ut mortem sólveret et resurrectiónem manifestáret.

Et ídeo cum Angelis et ómnibus Sanctis
glóriam tuam prædicámus, una voce dicéntes:

The people sing or say aloud the Sanctus.

S anc-tus, * Sanc-tus, Sanc-tus Dó-mi-nus De-us Sá-ba-oth. Ple-ni
sunt cæ-li et ter-ra gló-ri-a tu-a. Ho-sán-na in ex-cél-sis. Be-ne-díc-
tus qui ve-nit in nómine Dómini. Ho-sán-na in excél-sis.

Sanctus, Sanctus, Sanctus Dóminus Deus Sábaoth.
Pleni sunt cæli et terra glória tua.
Hosánna in excélsis.
Benedíctus qui venit in nómine Dómini.
Hosánna in excélsis.

EUCHARISTIC PRAYER II

Pr. The Lord be with you.
R. And with your spirit.
Pr. Lift up your hearts.
R. We lift them up to the Lord.
Pr. Let us give thanks to the Lord our God.
R. It is right and just.

Pr. It is truly right and just, our duty and our salvation,
always and everywhere to give you thanks, Father most holy,
through your beloved Son, Jesus Christ,
your Word through whom you made all things,
whom you sent as our Saviour and Redeemer,
incarnate by the Holy Spirit and born of the Virgin.

Fulfilling your will and gaining for you a holy people,
he stretched out his hands as he endured his Passion,
so as to break the bonds of death and manifest the resurrection.

And so, with the Angels and all the Saints
we declare your glory,
as with one voice we acclaim:

The people sing or say aloud the Sanctus.

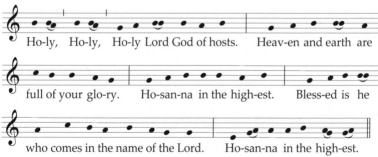

Ho-ly, Ho-ly, Ho-ly Lord God of hosts. Heav-en and earth are
full of your glo-ry. Ho-san-na in the high-est. Bless-ed is he
who comes in the name of the Lord. Ho-san-na in the high-est.

Holy, Holy, Holy Lord God of hosts.
Heaven and earth are full of your glory.
Hosanna in the highest.
Blessed is he who comes in the name of the Lord.
Hosanna in the highest.

Pr. Vere Sanctus es, Dómine, fons omnis sanctitátis.
Hæc ergo dona, quǽsumus,
Spíritus tui rore sanctífica,
ut nobis Corpus et ✠ Sanguis fiant
Dómini nostri Iesu Christi.

Qui cum Passióni voluntárie traderétur,
accépit panem et grátias agens fregit,
dedítque discípulis suis, dicens:

ACCÍPITE ET MANDUCÁTE EX HOC OMNES:
HOC EST ENIM CORPUS MEUM,
QUOD PRO VOBIS TRADÉTUR.

Símili modo, postquam cenátum est,
accípiens et cálicem,
íterum grátias agens dedit discípulis suis, dicens:

ACCÍPITE ET BÍBITE EX EO OMNES:
HIC EST ENIM CALIX SÁNGUINIS MEI
NOVI ET ÆTÉRNI TESTAMÉNTI,
QUI PRO VOBIS ET PRO MULTIS EFFUNDÉTUR
IN REMISSIÓNEM PECCATÓRUM.

HOC FÁCITE IN MEAM COMMEMORATIÓNEM.

Pr. Mystérium fídei.

The people continue, acclaiming one of the following:

Mortem tu-am annunti-ámus, Dómi-ne,   et tu-am resurrecti-ó-

nem confi-témur, do-nec vé-ni-as.

1. **Mortem tuam annuntiámus, Dómine,**
et tuam resurrectiónem confitémur, donec vénias.

Pr. You are indeed Holy, O Lord,
the fount of all holiness.

Make holy, therefore, these gifts, we pray,
by sending down your Spirit upon them like the dewfall,
so that they may become for us
the Body and ✠ Blood of our Lord Jesus Christ.

At the time he was betrayed
and entered willingly into his Passion,
he took bread and, giving thanks, broke it,
and gave it to his disciples, saying:

Take this, all of you, and eat of it,
for this is my Body,
which will be given up for you.

In a similar way, when supper was ended,
he took the chalice
and, once more giving thanks,
he gave it to his disciples, saying:

Take this, all of you, and drink from it,
for this is the chalice of my Blood,
the Blood of the new and eternal covenant,
which will be poured out for you and for many
for the forgiveness of sins.

Do this in memory of me.

Pr. The mystery of faith.

The people continue, acclaiming one of the following:

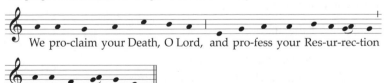

We pro-claim your Death, O Lord, and pro-fess your Res-ur-rec-tion un-til you come a-gain.

**1. We proclaim your Death, O Lord,
and profess your Resurrection
until you come again.**

Quoti-escúmque manducámus panem hunc   et cálicem bíbimus,

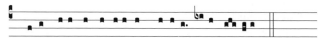

mortem tu-am annunti-ámus, Dómine, donec vé- ni-as.

**2. Quotiescúmque manducámus panem hunc
et cálicem bíbimus,
mortem tuam annuntiámus, Dómine, donec vénias.**

Salvátor mundi, salva nos, qui per crucem et resurrecti-ónem tu-am

li-be-rá- sti nos.

**3. Salvátor mundi, salva nos,
qui per crucem et resurrectiónem tuam liberásti nos.**

Pr. Mémores ígitur mortis et resurrectiónis eius,
tibi, Dómine, panem vitæ
et cálicem salútis offérimus,
grátias agéntes quia nos dignos habuísti
astáre coram te et tibi ministráre.

Et súpplices deprecámur
ut Córporis et Sánguinis Christi partícipes
a Spíritu Sancto congregémur in unum.

Recordáre, Dómine, Ecclésiæ tuæ toto orbe diffúsæ,
ut eam in caritáte perfícias
una cum Papa nostro N. et Epíscopo nostro N.
et univérso clero.

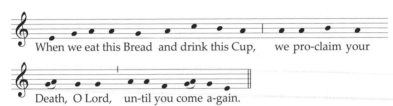

When we eat this Bread and drink this Cup, we pro-claim your

Death, O Lord, un-til you come a-gain.

**2. When we eat this Bread and drink this Cup,
we proclaim your Death, O Lord,
until you come again.**

Save us, Sav-iour of the world, for by your Cross and Res-ur-rec-tion

you have set us free.

**3. Save us, Saviour of the world,
for by your Cross and Resurrection
you have set us free.**

Only in Ireland: **4. My Lord and my God.**

Pr. Therefore, as we celebrate
the memorial of his Death and Resurrection,
we offer you, Lord,
the Bread of life and the Chalice of salvation,
giving thanks that you have held us worthy
to be in your presence and minister to you.

Humbly we pray
that, partaking of the Body and Blood of Christ,
we may be gathered into one by the Holy Spirit.

Remember, Lord, your Church,
spread throughout the world,
and bring her to the fullness of charity,
together with N. our Pope and N. our Bishop
and all the clergy.

Meménto étiam fratrum nostrórum,
qui in spe resurrectiónis dormiérunt,
omniúmque in tua miseratióne defunctórum,
et eos in lumen vultus tui admítte.
Omnium nostrum, quǽsumus, miserére,
ut cum beáta Dei Genetríce Vírgine María,
beáto Ioseph, eius Sponso,
beátis Apostólis et ómnibus Sanctis,
qui tibi a sǽculo placuérunt,
ætérnæ vitæ mereámur esse consórtes,
et te laudémus et glorificémus
per Fílium tuum Iesum Christum.

Per ipsum, et cum ipso, et in ipso,
est tibi Deo Patri omnipoténti,
in unitáte Spíritus Sancti,
omnis honor et glória
per ómnia sǽcula sæculórum.

A-men.

R.   **Amen.**

Then follows the Communion Rite, p.62.

Remember also our brothers and sisters
who have fallen asleep in the hope of the resurrection,
and all who have died in your mercy:
welcome them into the light of your face.
Have mercy on us all, we pray,
that with the Blessed Virgin Mary, Mother of God,
with blessed Joseph, her Spouse,
with the blessed Apostles,
and all the Saints who have pleased you throughout the ages,
we may merit to be coheirs to eternal life,
and may praise and glorify you
through your Son, Jesus Christ.

Through him, and with him, and in him,
O God, almighty Father,
in the unity of the Holy Spirit,
all glory and honour is yours,
for ever and ever.

A-men.

R. **Amen.**

Then follows the Communion Rite, p.63.

EUCHARISTIC PRAYER III

Pr. Vere Sanctus es, Dómine,
et mérito te laudat omnis a te cóndita creatúra,
quia per Fílium tuum,
Dóminum nostrum Iesum Christum,
Spíritus Sancti operánte virtúte,
vivíficas et sanctíficas univérsa,
et pópulum tibi congregáre non désinis,
ut a solis ortu usque ad occásum
oblátio munda offerátur nómini tuo.

Súpplices ergo te, Dómine, deprecámur,
ut hæc múnera, quæ tibi sacránda detúlimus,
eódem Spíritu sanctificáre dignéris,
ut Corpus et ✠ Sanguis fiant
Fílii tui Dómini nostri Iesu Christi,
cuius mandáto hæc mystéria celebrámus.

Ipse enim in qua nocte tradebátur
accépit panem
et tibi grátias agens benedíxit,
fregit, dedítque discípulis suis, dicens:

Accípite et manducáte ex hoc omnes:
hoc est enim Corpus meum,
quod pro vobis tradétur.

Símili modo, postquam cenátum est,
accípiens cálicem,
et tibi grátias agens benedíxit,
dedítque discípulis suis, dicens:

Accípite et bíbite ex eo omnes:
hic est enim calix Sánguinis mei
novi et ætérni testaménti,
qui pro vobis et pro multis effundétur
in remissiónem peccatórum.
Hoc fácite in meam commemoratiónem.

EUCHARISTIC PRAYER III

Pr. You are indeed Holy, O Lord,
and all you have created
rightly gives you praise,
for through your Son our Lord Jesus Christ,
by the power and working of the Holy Spirit,
you give life to all things and make them holy,
and you never cease to gather a people to yourself,
so that from the rising of the sun to its setting
a pure sacrifice may be offered to your name.

Therefore, O Lord, we humbly implore you:
by the same Spirit graciously make holy
these gifts we have brought to you for consecration,
that they may become the Body and ✠ Blood
of your Son our Lord Jesus Christ,
at whose command we celebrate these mysteries.

For on the night he was betrayed
he himself took bread,
and, giving you thanks, he said the blessing,
broke the bread and gave it to his disciples, saying:

TAKE THIS, ALL OF YOU, AND EAT OF IT,
FOR THIS IS MY BODY,
WHICH WILL BE GIVEN UP FOR YOU.

In a similar way, when supper was ended,
he took the chalice,
and, giving you thanks, he said the blessing,
and gave the chalice to his disciples, saying:

TAKE THIS, ALL OF YOU, AND DRINK FROM IT,
FOR THIS IS THE CHALICE OF MY BLOOD,
THE BLOOD OF THE NEW AND ETERNAL COVENANT,
WHICH WILL BE POURED OUT FOR YOU AND FOR MANY
FOR THE FORGIVENESS OF SINS.
DO THIS IN MEMORY OF ME.

Pr. Mystérium fídei.

The people continue, acclaiming one of the following:

Mortem tu-am annunti-ámus, Dómi-ne,　et tu-am resurrecti-ó-

nem confi-témur, do-nec vé-ni-as.

**1. Mortem tuam annuntiámus, Dómine,
et tuam resurrectiónem confitémur, donec vénias.**

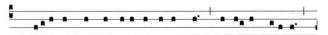

Quoti-escúmque manducámus panem hunc　et cálicem bíbimus,

mortem tu-am annunti-ámus, Dómine,　donec vé-　ni-as.

**2. Quotiescúmque manducámus panem hunc
et cálicem bíbimus,
mortem tuam annuntiámus, Dómine, donec vénias.**

Salvátor mundi, salva nos, qui per crucem et resurrecti-ónem tu-am

li-be-rá- sti nos.

**3. Salvátor mundi, salva nos,
qui per crucem et resurrectiónem tuam liberásti nos.**

Pr. The mystery of faith.

The people continue, acclaiming one of the following:

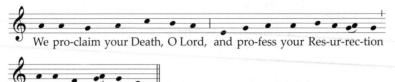

We pro-claim your Death, O Lord, and pro-fess your Res-ur-rec-tion un-til you come a-gain.

1. **We proclaim your Death, O Lord,**
and profess your Resurrection
until you come again.

When we eat this Bread and drink this Cup, we pro-claim your Death, O Lord, un-til you come a-gain.

2. **When we eat this Bread and drink this Cup,**
we proclaim your Death, O Lord,
until you come again.

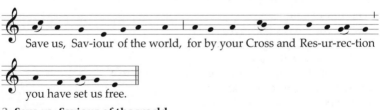

Save us, Sav-iour of the world, for by your Cross and Res-ur-rec-tion you have set us free.

3. **Save us, Saviour of the world,**
for by your Cross and Resurrection
you have set us free.

Only in Ireland: **4.** **My Lord and my God.**

Pr. Mémores ígitur, Dómine,
eiúsdem Fílii tui salutíferæ passiónis
necnon mirábilis resurrectiónis
et ascensiónis in cælum,
sed et præstolántes álterum eius advéntum,
offérimus tibi, grátias referéntes,
hoc sacrifícium vivum et sanctum.

Réspice, quæsumus, in oblatiónem Ecclésiæ tuæ
et, agnóscens Hóstiam,
cuius volúisti immolatióne placári,
concéde, ut qui Córpore et Sánguine Fílii tui refícimur,
Spíritu eius Sancto repléti,
unum corpus et unus spíritus inveniámur in Christo.

Ipse nos tibi perfíciat munus ætérnum,
ut cum eléctis tuis hereditátem cónsequi valeámus,
in primis cum beátissima Vírgine, Dei Genetríce, María,
cum beáto Ioseph, eius Sponso,
cum beátis Apóstolis tuis et gloriósis Martýribus
(cum Sancto N.: the saint of the day or Patron Saint)
et ómnibus Sanctis,
quorum intercessióne
perpétuo apud te confídimus adiuvári.

Hæc Hóstia nostræ reconciliatiónis profíciat,
quæsumus, Dómine,
ad totíus mundi pacem atque salútem.
Ecclésiam tuam, peregrinántem in terra,
in fide et caritáte firmáre dignéris
cum fámulo tuo Papa nostro N. et Epíscopo nostro N.,
cum episcopáli órdine et univérso clero
et omni pópulo acquisitiónis tuæ.

Votis huius famíliæ, quam tibi astáre voluísti,
adésto propítius.
Omnes fílios tuos ubíque dispérsos
tibi, clemens Pater, miserátus coniúnge.

Pr. Therefore, O Lord, as we celebrate the memorial
of the saving Passion of your Son,
his wondrous Resurrection
and Ascension into heaven,
and as we look forward to his second coming,
we offer you in thanksgiving
this holy and living sacrifice.

Look, we pray, upon the oblation of your Church
and, recognising the sacrificial Victim by whose death
you willed to reconcile us to yourself,
grant that we, who are nourished
by the Body and Blood of your Son
and filled with his Holy Spirit,
may become one body, one spirit in Christ.

May he make of us
an eternal offering to you,
so that we may obtain an inheritance with your elect,
especially with the most Blessed Virgin Mary, Mother of God,
with blessed Joseph, her Spouse,
with your blessed Apostles and glorious Martyrs
(with Saint N.: the Saint of the day or Patron Saint)
and with all the Saints,
on whose constant intercession in your presence
we rely for unfailing help.

May this Sacrifice of our reconciliation,
we pray, O Lord,
advance the peace and salvation of all the world.
Be pleased to confirm in faith and charity
your pilgrim Church on earth,
with your servant N. our Pope and N. our Bishop,
the Order of Bishops, all the clergy,
and the entire people you have gained for your own.

Listen graciously to the prayers of this family,
whom you have summoned before you:
in your compassion, O merciful Father,
gather to yourself all your children
scattered throughout the world.

Fratres nostros defúnctos
et omnes qui, tibi placéntes, ex hoc sǽculo transiérunt,
in regnum tuum benígnus admítte,
ubi fore sperámus,
ut simul glória tua perénniter satiémur,
per Christum Dóminum nostrum,
per quem mundo bona cuncta largíris.

Per ipsum, et cum ipso, et in ipso,
est tibi Deo Patri omnipoténti,
in unitáte Spíritus Sancti,
omnis honor et glória
per ómnia sǽcula sæculórum.

A-men.

R.   **Amen.**

Then follows the Communion Rite, p.62.

To our departed brothers and sisters
and to all who were pleasing to you
at their passing from this life,
give kind admittance to your kingdom.
There we hope to enjoy for ever the fullness of your glory
through Christ our Lord,
through whom you bestow on the world all that is good.

Through him, and with him, and in him,
O God, almighty Father,
in the unity of the Holy Spirit,
all glory and honour is yours,
for ever and ever.

A-men.

R. **Amen.**

Then follows the Communion Rite, p.63.

THE COMMUNION RITE

The eating and drinking together of the Lord's Body and Blood in a Paschal meal is the culmination of the Eucharist

THE LORD'S PRAYER

After the chalice and paten have been set down, the congregation stands and the Priest says:

Pr. Præcéptis salutáribus móniti,
et divína institutióne formáti,
audémus dícere:

Together with the people, he continues:

P a-ter noster, qui es in cæ-lis: sancti-fi-cé-tur nomen tu-um; advéni-at

regnum tu-um; fi-at volúntas tu-a, sic-ut in cæ-lo, et in terra. Pa-

nem nostrum coti-di-ánum da nobis hódi-e; et dimítte nobis débi-

ta nostra, sicut et nos dimíttimus de-bi-tó-ribus nostris; et ne nos

indúcas in tenta-ti-ó-nem; sed líbera nos a ma-lo.

THE COMMUNION RITE

The eating and drinking together of the Lord's Body and Blood in a Paschal meal is the culmination of the Eucharist

THE LORD'S PRAYER

After the chalice and paten have been set down, the congregation stands and the Priest says:

Pr. At the Saviour's command
and formed by divine teaching,
we dare to say:

Together with the people, he continues:

Our Fa-ther, who art in heav-en, hal-lowed be thy name; thy king-dom come, thy will be done on earth as it is in heav-en. Give us this day our dai-ly bread, and for-give us our tres-pass-es, as we for-give those who tres-pass a-gainst us; and lead us not in-to temp-ta-tion, but de-liv-er us from e-vil.

R. **Pater noster, qui es in cælis:**
sanctificétur nomen tuum;
advéniat regnum tuum;
fiat volúntas tua, sicut in cælo, et in terra.
Panem nostrum cotidiánum da nobis hódie;
et dimítte nobis debíta nostra,
sicut et nos dimíttimus debitóribus nostris;
et ne nos indúcas in tentatiónem;
sed líbera nos a malo.

Pr. Líbera nos, quǽsumus, Dómine, ab ómnibus malis,
da propítius pacem in diébus nostris,
ut, ope misericórdiæ tuæ adiúti,
et a peccáto simus semper líberi
et ab omni perturbatióne secúri:
exspectántes beátam spem
et advéntum Salvatóris nostri Iesu Christi.

Qui-a tu-um est regnum, et po-téstas,

et gló- ri- a in saecu-la.

R. **Quia tuum est regnum,**
et potéstas, et glória
in sǽcula.

THE PEACE

Pr. Dómine Iesu Christe, qui dixísti Apostólis tuis:
Pacem relínquo vobis, pacem meam do vobis:
ne respícias peccáta nostra,
sed fidem Ecclésiæ tuæ;
eámque secúndum voluntátem tuam
pacificáre et coadunáre dignéris.
Qui vivis et regnas in sǽcula sæculórum.

R. **Amen.**

R. **Our Father, who art in heaven,**
hallowed be thy name;
thy kingdom come,
thy will be done
on earth as it is in heaven.
Give us this day our daily bread,
and forgive us our trespasses,
as we forgive those who trespass against us;
and lead us not into temptation,
but deliver us from evil.

Pr. Deliver us, Lord, we pray, from every evil,
graciously grant peace in our days,
that, by the help of your mercy,
we may be always free from sin
and safe from all distress,
as we await the blessed hope
and the coming of our Saviour, Jesus Christ.

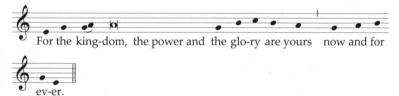

For the king-dom, the power and the glo-ry are yours now and for
ev-er.

R. **For the kingdom,**
the power and the glory are yours
now and for ever.

THE PEACE

Pr. Lord Jesus Christ,
who said to your Apostles:
Peace I leave you, my peace I give you;
look not on our sins,
but on the faith of your Church,
and graciously grant her peace and unity
in accordance with your will.
Who live and reign for ever and ever.
R. **Amen.**

Pr. Pax Dómini sit semper vobíscum.

Et cum spí-ri- tu tu- o.

R. **Et cum spíritu tuo.**

Then, if appropriate, the Deacon, or the Priest, adds:

Pr. Offérte vobis pacem.

And all offer one another the customary sign of peace.

BREAKING OF THE BREAD

Then he takes the host, breaks it over the paten, and places a small piece in the chalice, saying quietly:

Hæc commixtio Corporis et Sanguinis

Domini nostri Iesu Christi

fiat accipientibus nobis in vitam æternam.

Then the Priest takes the host, breaks it over the paten, and places a small piece in the chalice. Meanwhile the following is sung or said:

A g-nus De-i, * qui tol-lis pec-cá-ta mundi:

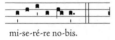

mi-se-ré-re no-bis.

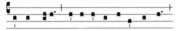

Ag-nus De-i, * qui tol-lis pec-cá-ta mundi:

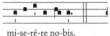

mi-se-ré-re no-bis.

Ag-nus De-i, * qui tol-lis pec-cá-ta mun-di:

do-na no-bis pa-cem.

Pr. The peace of the Lord be with you always.

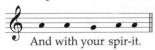

And with your spir-it.

R. And with your spirit.

Then, if appropriate, the Deacon, or the Priest, adds:

Pr. Let us offer each other the sign of peace.

And all offer one another the customary sign of peace.

BREAKING OF THE BREAD

Then he takes the host, breaks it over the paten, and places a small piece in the chalice, saying quietly:

May this mingling of the Body and Blood
of our Lord Jesus Christ
bring eternal life to us who receive it.

Then the Priest takes the host, breaks it over the paten, and places a small piece in the chalice. Meanwhile the following is sung or said:

Lamb of God, * you take a-way the sins of the world,

have mer-cy on us.

Lamb of God, * you take a-way the sins of the world,

have mer-cy on us.

Lamb of God, * you take a-way the sins of the world,

grant us peace.

The invocation may even be repeated several times if the fraction is prolonged. Only the final time, however, is grant us peace said.

Agnus Dei, qui tollis peccáta mundi: miserére nobis.
Agnus Dei, qui tollis peccáta mundi: miserére nobis.
Agnus Dei, qui tollis peccáta mundi: dona nobis pacem.

Then the Priest, with hands joined, says quietly:

Domine Iesu Christe, Fili Dei vivi,
qui ex voluntate Patris,
cooperante Spiritu Sancto,
per mortem tuam mundum vivificasti:
libera me per hoc sacrosanctum Corpus et Sanguinem tuum
ab omnibus iniquitatibus meis et universis malis:
et fac me tuis semper inhærere mandatis,
et a te numquam separari permittas.

Or:

Perceptio Corporis et Sanguinis tui, Domine Iesu Christe,
non mihi proveniat in iudicium et condemnationem:
sed pro tua pietate prosit mihi
ad tutamentum mentis et corporis,
et ad medelam percipiendam.

INVITATION TO COMMUNION

All kneel. The Priest genuflects, takes the host and, holding it slightly raised above the paten or above the chalice says aloud:

Pr. Ecce Agnus Dei, ecce qui tollit peccáta mundi.
     Beáti qui ad cenam Agni vocáti sunt.
R. **Dómine, non sum dignus, ut intres sub tectum meum,**
     sed tantum dic verbo, et sanábitur ánima mea.

The Priest, facing the altar, says quietly:

Corpus Christi custodiat me in vitam æternam.

And he reverently consumes the Body of Christ.
Then he takes the chalice and says quietly:

Sanguis Christi custodiat me in vitam æternam.

And he reverently consumes the Blood of Christ.
While the Priest is receiving the Body of Christ, the Communion Chant begins.

Lamb of God, you take away the sins of the world, have mercy on us.
Lamb of God, you take away the sins of the world, have mercy on us.
Lamb of God, you take away the sins of the world, grant us peace.

Then the Priest, with hands joined, says quietly:

Lord Jesus Christ, Son of the living God,
who, by the will of the Father
and the work of the Holy Spirit,
through your Death gave life to the world,
free me by this, your most holy Body and Blood,
from all my sins and from every evil;
keep me always faithful to your commandments,
and never let me be parted from you.

Or:

May the receiving of your Body and Blood,
Lord Jesus Christ,
not bring me to judgement and condemnation,
but through your loving mercy
be for me protection in mind and body
and a healing remedy.

INVITATION TO COMMUNION

All kneel. The Priest genuflects, takes the host and, holding it slightly raised above
the paten or above the chalice says aloud:

Pr. Behold the Lamb of God,
    behold him who takes away the sins of the world.
    Blessed are those called to the supper of the Lamb.

R. **Lord, I am not worthy**
   that you should enter under my roof,
   but only say the word
   and my soul shall be healed.

The Priest, facing the altar, says quietly:

May the Body of Christ
keep me safe for eternal life.

And he reverently consumes the Body of Christ.
Then he takes the chalice and says quietly:

May the Blood of Christ
keep me safe for eternal life.

And he reverently consumes the Blood of Christ.
While the Priest is receiving the Body of Christ, the Communion Chant begins.

COMMUNION PROCESSION

After the priest has reverently consumed the Body and Blood of Christ he takes the paten or ciborium and approaches the communicants.

The Priest raises the host slightly and shows it to each of the communicants, saying:

Pr. Corpus Christi.

R. **Amen.**

When Communion is ministered from the chalice:

Pr. Sanguis Christi.

R. **Amen.**

When the distribution of Communion is over, the Priest or a Deacon or an acolyte purifies the paten over the chalice and also the chalice itself.

While he carries out the purification, the Priest says quietly:

Quod ore sumpsimus, Domine, pura mente capiamus,
et de munere temporali fiat nobis remedium sempiternum.

After the distribution of Communion, if appropriate, a sacred silence may be observed for a while, or a psalm or other canticle of praise or a hymn may be sung.

PRAYER AFTER COMMUNION

Then, the Priest says:

Pr. Orémus.

All stand and pray in silence for a while, unless silence has just been observed. Then the Priest says the Prayer after Communion, at the end of which the people acclaim:

R. **Amen.**

THE CONCLUDING RITES

The Mass closes, sending the people forth to put what they have celebrated into effect in their daily lives.

Any brief announcements follow here. Then the dismissal takes place.

Pr. Dóminus vóbiscum.

Et cum spí-ri-tu tu-o.

R. **Et cum spíritu tuo.**

COMMUNION PROCESSION

After the priest has reverently consumed the Body and Blood of Christ he takes the paten or ciborium and approaches the communicants.

The Priest raises the host slightly and shows it to each of the communicants, saying:

Pr. The Body of Christ.

R. **Amen.**

When Communion is ministered from the chalice:

Pr. The Blood of Christ.

R. **Amen.**

When the distribution of Communion is over, the Priest or a Deacon or an acolyte purifies the paten over the chalice and also the chalice itself.

While he carries out the purification, the Priest says quietly:

What has passed our lips as food, O Lord,

may we possess in purity of heart,

that what has been given to us in time

may be our healing for eternity.

After the distribution of Communion, if appropriate, a sacred silence may be observed for a while, or a psalm or other canticle of praise or a hymn may be sung.

PRAYER AFTER COMMUNION

Then, the Priest says:

Pr. Let us pray.

All stand and pray in silence for a while, unless silence has just been observed. Then the Priest says the Prayer after Communion, at the end of which the people acclaim:

R. **Amen.**

THE CONCLUDING RITES

The Mass closes, sending the people forth to put what they have celebrated into effect in their daily lives.

Any brief announcements follow here. Then the dismissal takes place.

Pr. The Lord be with you.

And with your spir-it.

R. **And with your spirit.**

The Priest blesses the people, saying:

Pr. Benedícat vos omnípotens Deus,
    Pater, et Fílius, ✠ et Spíritus Sanctus.

  A-men.

R. **Amen.**

Then the Deacon, or the Priest himself says the Dismissal:

Pr. Ite, missa est.

    Or:

Pr. Ite, ad Evangélium Dómini annuntiándum.

    Or:

Pr. Ite in pace, glorificándo vita vestra Dóminum.

De-   o grá- ti-as.

R. **Deo grátias.**

    Or:

Pr. Ite in pace.

    De- o grá- ti- as.

R. **Deo grátias.**

Then the Priest venerates the altar as at the beginning. After making a profound bow with the ministers, he withdraws.

The Priest blesses the people, saying:

Pr. May almighty God bless you,
the Father, and the Son, ✠ and the Holy Spirit.

A-men.

R. **Amen.**

Then the Deacon, or the Priest himself says the Dismissal:

Pr. Go forth, the Mass is ended.

Or:

Pr. Go and announce the Gospel of the Lord.

Or:

Pr. Go in peace, glorifying the Lord by your life.

R. Thanks be to God.

R. **Thanks be to God.**

Or:

Pr. Go in peace.

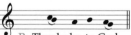
R. Thanks be to God.

R. **Thanks be to God.**

Then the Priest venerates the altar as at the beginning. After making a profound bow with the ministers, he withdraws.

HOLY WEEK

PALM SUNDAY OF THE PASSION OF THE LORD

(YEAR A,B,C)

It is a moving experience each year on Palm Sunday as we go up the mountain with Jesus, towards the Temple, accompanying him on his ascent. But what are we really doing when we join this procession as part of the throng which went up with Jesus to Jerusalem and hailed him as King of Israel? Does it have anything to do with the reality of our life and our world? To answer this, we must first be clear about what Jesus himself wished to do and actually did. He was journeying towards the Temple in the Holy City, towards that place which for Israel ensured in a particular way God's closeness to his people. The ultimate goal of his pilgrimage was the heights of God himself; to those heights he wanted to lift every human being. Our procession today is meant, then, to be an image of something deeper, to reflect the fact that, together with Jesus, we are setting out on pilgrimage along the high road that leads to the living God.

(Pope Benedict XVI)

On this day the Church recalls the entrance of Christ the Lord into Jerusalem to accomplish his Paschal Mystery. Accordingly, the memorial of this entrance of the Lord takes place at all Masses, by means of the Procession or the Solemn Entrance before the principal Mass or the Simple Entrance before other Masses. The Solemn Entrance, but not the Procession, may be repeated before other Masses that are usually celebrated with a large gathering of people.

It is desirable that, where neither the Procession nor the Solemn Entrance can take place, there be a sacred celebration of the Word of God on the messianic entrance and on the Passion of the Lord, either on Saturday evening or on Sunday at a convenient time.

The Commemoration of the Lord's Entrance into Jerusalem

First Form: The Procession

At an appropriate hour, a gathering takes place at a smaller church or other suitable place other than inside the church to which the procession will go. The faithful hold branches in their hands.

Wearing the red sacred vestments as for Mass, the Priest and the Deacon, accompanied by other ministers, approach the place where the people are gathered. Instead of the chasuble, the Priest may wear a cope, which he leaves aside when the procession is over, and puts on a chasuble.

Meanwhile, the following antiphon or another appropriate chant is sung.

Ant. Mt 21:9	Ant.
Hosanna to the Son of David;	Hosanna filio David:
blessed is he who comes	benedictus qui venit
in the name of the Lord,	in nomine Domini.
the King of Israel.	Rex Israel:
Hosanna in the highest.	Hosanna in excelsis.

After this, the Priest and people sign themselves, while the Priest says: **In the name of the Father, and of the Son, and of the Holy Spirit**. Then he greets the people in the usual way. A brief address is given, in which the faithful are invited to participate actively and consciously in the celebration of this day, in these or similar words:

Dear brethren (brothers and sisters),	Fratres carissimi,
since the beginning of Lent until now	postquam iam ab initio
we have prepared our hearts	Quadragesimæ corda nostra
by penance and charitable works.	pænitentia et operibus
Today we gather together to herald	caritatis præparavimus,
with the whole Church	hodierna die congregamur,
the beginning of the celebration	ut cum tota Ecclesia præludamus
of our Lord's Paschal Mystery,	paschale Domini nostri mysterium,
that is to say, of his Passion	eius nempe passionem
and Resurrection.	atque resurrectionem,
For it was to accomplish this mystery	ad quod implendum
that he entered his own city	ipse ingressus est civitatem
of Jerusalem.	suam Ierusalem.
Therefore, with all faith	Quare cum omni fide et devotione
and devotion,	memoriam agentes
let us commemorate	huius salutiferi ingressus,
the Lord's entry into the city	sequamur Dominum,
for our salvation,	ut, per gratiam consortes
following in his footsteps,	effecti crucis,
so that, being made by his grace	partem habeamus resurrectionis
partakers of the Cross,	et vitæ.
we may have a share also in his	
Resurrection and in his life.	

After the address, the Priest says one of the following prayers with hands extended.

Let us pray.

Almighty ever-living God,
sanctify ✠ these branches
    with your blessing,
that we, who follow Christ the King
    in exultation,
may reach the eternal Jerusalem
    through him.
Who lives and reigns
    for ever and ever.
R. Amen.

Or:

Increase the faith of those who
    place their hope in you, O God,
and graciously hear the prayers
    of those who call on you,
that we, who today hold high
    these branches
to hail Christ in his triumph,
may bear fruit for you by good
    works accomplished in him.
Who lives and reigns
    for ever and ever.
R. Amen.

Oremus.

Omnipotens sempiterne Deus,
hos palmites tua
    benedictione ✠ sanctifica,
ut nos, qui Christum Regem
    exsultando prosequimur,
per ipsum valeamus ad æternam
    Ierusalem pervenire.
Qui vivit et regnat
    in sæcula sæculorum.
R. Amen.

Vel:

Auge fidem in te sperantium, Deus,
et supplicum preces
    clementer exaudi,
ut, qui hodie Christo triumphanti
    palmites exhibemus,
in ipso fructus tibi bonorum
    operum afferamus.
Qui vivit et regnat
    in sæcula sæculorum.
R. Amen.

He sprinkles the branches with holy water without saying anything.

Then a Deacon or, if there is no Deacon, a Priest, proclaims in the usual way the Gospel concerning the Lord's entrance according to one of the four Gospels. If appropriate, incense may be used.

YEAR A

A reading from the holy Gospel according to Matthew   21:1-11

'Blessed is he who comes in the name of the Lord.'

When they drew near to Jerusalem
and came to Bethphage, to the Mount of Olives,
Jesus sent two disciples, saying to them,
'Go into the village opposite you,
and immediately you will find an ass tied,
and a colt with her; untie them and bring them to me.

If any one says anything to you, you shall say,
"The Lord has need of them,"
and he will send them immediately.'
This took place to fulfil
what was spoken by the prophet, saying,

> 'Tell the daughter of Sion,
> Behold, your king is coming to you,
> humble, and mounted on an ass,
> and on a colt, the foal of an ass.'

The disciples went and did as Jesus had directed them;
they brought the ass and the colt,
and put their garments on them, and he sat thereon.
Most of the crowd spread their garments on the road,
and others cut branches from the trees
and spread them on the road.
And the crowds that went before him
and that followed him shouted,
'Hosanna to the Son of David!
Blessed is he who comes in the name of the Lord!
Hosanna in the highest!'
And when he entered Jerusalem,
all the city was stirred, saying, 'Who is this?'
And the crowds said,
'This is the prophet Jesus from Nazareth of Galilee.'

The Gospel of the Lord.

YEAR B

A reading from the holy Gospel according to Mark   11:1-10

Blessings on him who comes in the name of the Lord.

When they drew near to Jerusalem,
to Bethphage and Bethany, at the Mount of Olives,
Jesus sent two of his disciples, and said to them,
'Go into the village opposite you,
and immediately as you enter it
you will find a colt tied, on which no one has ever sat;
untie it and bring it.
If any one says to you,
"Why are you doing this?" say,

"The Lord has need of it
and will send it back here immediately.'"
And they went away,
and found a colt tied at the door out in the open street;
and they untied it.
And those who stood there said to them,
'What are you doing, untying the colt?'
And they told them what Jesus had said;
and they let them go.
And they brought the colt to Jesus,
and threw their garments on it;
and he sat upon it.
And many spread their garments on the road,
and others spread leafy branches
which they had cut from the fields.
And those who went before
and those who followed cried out,
'Hosanna!
Blessed is he who comes in the name of the Lord!
Blessed is the kingdom of our father David that is coming!
Hosanna in the highest!'

    The Gospel of the Lord.

ALTERNATIVE GOSPEL FOR YEAR B

A reading from the holy Gospel according to John   12:12-16

Blessings on him who comes in the name of the Lord.

A great crowd who had come to the feast
heard that Jesus was coming to Jerusalem.
So they took branches of palm trees
and went out to meet him, crying,
'Hosanna!
Blessed is he who comes in the name of the Lord,
even the king of Israel!'
And Jesus found a young ass and sat upon it; as is written,
    'Fear not, daughter of Sion;
    behold, your king is coming,
    sitting on an ass's colt!'

His disciples did not understand this at first;
but when Jesus was glorified,
then they remembered that this had been written of him
and had been done to him.

The Gospel of the Lord.

YEAR C

A reading from the holy Gospel according to Luke   19:28-40

Blessings on him who comes in the name of the Lord.

Jesus went on ahead, going up to Jerusalem.
When he drew near to Bethphage and Bethany,
at the mount that is called Olivet,
he sent two disciples,
saying, 'Go into the village opposite,
where on entering you will find a colt tied,
on which no one has ever yet sat;
untie it and bring it here.
If any one asks you,
"Why are you untying it?"
you shall say this,
"The Lord has need of it."'
So those who were sent
went away and found it as he had told them.
And as they were untying the colt,
its owners said to them,
'Why are you untying the colt?'
And they said,
'The Lord has need of it.'
And they brought it to Jesus,
and throwing their garments on the colt
they set Jesus upon it.
And as he rode along,
they spread their garments on the road.
As he was drawing near,
at the descent of the Mount of Olives,
the whole multitude of the disciples
began to rejoice and praise God with a loud voice

for all the mighty works that they had seen,
saying,
'Blessed is the King who comes in the name of the Lord!
Peace in heaven and glory in the highest!'
And some of the Pharisees in the multitude said to him,
'Teacher, rebuke your disciples.'
He answered,
'I tell you, if these were silent,
the very stones would cry out.'

The Gospel of the Lord.

After the Gospel, a brief homily may be given. Then, to begin the Procession, an invitation may be given by a Priest or a Deacon or a lay minister, in these or similar words:

Dear brethren (brothers and sisters), like the crowds who acclaimed　Jesus in Jerusalem, let us go forth in peace.	Imitemur, fratres carissimi,　turbas acclamantes Iesum, et procedamus in pace.

Or:	Vel:
Let us go forth in peace.	Procedamus in pace.

In this latter case, all respond:

In the name of Christ. Amen.	In nomine Christi. Amen.

The Procession to the church where Mass will be celebrated then sets off in the usual way. If incense is used, the thurifer goes first, carrying a thurible with burning incense, then an acolyte or another minister, carrying a cross decorated with palm branches according to local custom, between two ministers with lighted candles. Then follow the Deacon carrying the Book of the Gospels, the Priest with the ministers, and, after them, all the faithful carrying branches.

As the Procession moves forward, the following or other suitable chants in honour of Christ the King are sung by the choir and people.

Antiphon 1	Antiphona 1
The children of the Hebrews,　carrying olive branches, went to meet the Lord,　crying out and saying: Hosanna in the highest.	Pueri Hebræorum,　portantes ramos olivarum, obviaverunt Domino,　clamantes et dicentes: Hosanna in excelsis.

If appropriate, this antiphon is repeated between the strophes of the following Psalm.

PSALM 23

The Lord's is the earth
   and its fullness,*
the world, and those who dwell in it.
It is he who set it on the seas;*
on the rivers he made it firm. Ant.

Who shall climb the mountain
   of the Lord?*
The clean of hands and pure of heart,
whose soul is not set on vain things,†
who has not sworn
   deceitful words.* Ant.

Blessings from the Lord
   shall he receive,*
and right reward from the God
   who saves him.
Such are the people who seek him,*
who seek the face of the God
   of Jacob. Ant.

O gates, lift high your heads,†
grow higher, ancient doors.*
Let him enter, the king of glory!
Who is this king of glory?*
The Lord, the mighty, the valiant;
the Lord, the valiant in war. Ant.

O gates, lift high your heads;†
grow higher, ancient doors.*
Let him enter, the king of glory!
Who is this king of glory?*
He, the Lord of hosts,
he is the king of glory. Ant.

Domini est terra et plenitudo eius,*
orbis terrarum et qui habitant in eo.
Quia ipse super maria fundavit eum*
et super flumina firmavit eum. Ant.

Quis ascendet in montem Domini,*
aut quis stabit in loco sancto eius?
Innocens manibus et mundo corde,†
qui non levavit ad vana
   animam suam,*
nec iuravit in dolum. Ant.

Hic accipiet benedictionem
   a Domino*
et iustificationem a Deo salutari suo.
Hæc est generatio
   quærentium eum,*
quærentium faciem Dei Iacob. Ant.

Attollite, portæ, capita vestra,†
et elevamini, portæ æternales,*
et introibit rex gloriæ.
Quis est iste rex gloriæ?*
Dominus fortis et potens,
Dominus potens in prœlio. Ant.

Attollite, portæ, capita vestra, †
et elevamini, portæ æternales,*
et introibit rex gloriæ.
Quis est iste rex gloriæ?*
Dominus virtutum ipse est rex
   gloriæ. Ant.

Antiphon 2

The children of the Hebrews spread
   their garments on the road,
crying out and saying:
   Hosanna to the Son of David;
blessed is he who comes
   in the name of the Lord.

Antiphona 2

Pueri Hebræorum vestimenta
   prosternebant in via,
et clamabant dicentes:
   Hosanna filio David;
benedictus, qui venit
   in nomine Domini.

If appropriate, this antiphon is repeated between the strophes of the following Psalm.

PSALM 46

All peoples, clap your hands.*
Cry to God with shouts of joy!
For the Lord, the Most high,
　　is awesome,*
the great king over all the earth. Ant.

He humbles peoples under us*
and nations under our feet.
Our heritage he chose for us,*
the pride of Jacob whom he loves.
God goes up with shouts of joy.*
The Lord goes up
　　with trumpet blast. Ant.

Sing praise for God; sing praise!*
Sing praise to our king; sing praise!
God is king of all earth.*
Sing praise with all your skill. Ant.

God reigns over the nations.*
God sits upon his holy throne.
The princes of the peoples
　　are assembled
with the people of the God
　　of Abraham.†
The rulers of the earth belong
　　to God,*
who is greatly exalted. Ant.

Omnes gentes, plaudite manibus,*
iubilate Deo in voce exsultationis,
quoniam Dominus Altissimus,
　　terribilis,*
rex magnus super omnem terram.
　　Ant.

Subiecit populos nobis,*
et gentes sub pedibus nostris.
Elegit nobis hereditatem nostram,*
gloriam Iacob, quem dilexit.
Ascendit Deus in iubilo,*
et Dominus in voce tubæ. Ant.

Psallite Deo, psallite;*
psallite regi nostro, psallite.
Quoniam rex omnis terræ Deus,*
psallite sapienter. Ant.

Regnavit Deus super gentes,*
Deus sedet super sedem
　　sanctam suam.
Principes populorum congregati sunt
cum populo Dei Abraham,†
quoniam Dei sunt scuta terræ:*
vehementer elevatus est. Ant.

Hymn to Christ the King

Chorus:

Glory and honour and praise be to
　　you, Christ, King and Redeemer,
to whom young children cried out
　　loving Hosannas with joy.
All repeat: Glory and honour...

Chorus:

Israel's King are you, King David's
　　magnificent offspring;
you are the ruler who come blest
　　in the name of the Lord.
All repeat: Glory and honour...

Hymnus ad Christum Regem

Gloria, laus et honor tibi sit,
　　rex Christe redemptor,
cui puerile decus prompsit
　　Hosanna pium.
Omnes repetunt: Gloria, laus...

Israel es tu rex, Davidis
　　et inclita proles,
nomine qui in Domini,
　　rex benedicte, venis.
Omnes repetunt: Gloria, laus...

Chorus:
Heavenly hosts on high unite
   in singing your praises;
men and women on earth
   and all creation join in.
All repeat: Glory and honour...

Chorus:
Bearing branches of palm, Hebrews
   came crowding to greet you;
see how with prayers and hymns
   we come to pay you our vows.
All repeat: Glory and honour...

Chorus:
They offered gifts of praise to you,
   so near to your Passion;
see how we sing this song now
   to you reigning on high.
All repeat: Glory and honour...

Chorus:
Those you were pleased to accept;
   now accept our gifts of devotion,
good and merciful King,
   lover of all that is good.
All repeat: Glory and honour...

Cœtus in excelsis te laudat
   cælicus omnis,
et mortalis homo,
   et cuncta creata simul.
Omnes repetunt: Gloria, laus...

Plebs Hebræa tibi cum palmis
   obvia venit;
cum prece, voto,
   hymnis adsumus ecce tibi.
Omnes repetunt: Gloria, laus...

Hi tibi passuro solvebant
   munia laudis;
nos tibi regnanti
   pangimus ecce melos.
Omnes repetunt: Gloria, laus...

Hi placuere tibi,
   placeat devotio nostra:
rex bone, rex clemens,
   cui bona cuncta placent.
Omnes repetunt: Gloria, laus...

As the procession enters the church, there is sung the following responsory or another chant, which should speak of the Lord's entrance.

R. As the Lord entered the holy city,
the children of the Hebrews
proclaimed the resurrection of life.
*Waving their branches of palm,
   they cried:
Hosanna in the Highest.

V. When the people heard that
   Jesus was coming to Jerusalem,
   they went out to meet him.

*Waving their branches...

R. Ingrediente Domino
   in sanctam civitatem,
Hebræorum pueri, resurrectionem
   vitæ pronuntiantes,
*Cum ramis palmarum:
Hosanna, clamabant, in excelsis.

V. Cum audisset populus, quod
   Iesus veniret Hierosolymam,
   exierunt obviam ei.

*Cum ramis...

When the Priest arrives at the altar, he venerates it and, if appropriate, incenses it. Then he goes to the chair, where he puts aside the cope, if he has worn one, and puts on the chasuble. Omitting the other Introductory Rites of the Mass and, if appropriate, the Kyrie (Lord, have mercy), he says the Collect of the Mass, and then continues the Mass in the usual way.

Second Form: The Solemn Entrance

When a procession outside the church cannot take place, the entrance of the Lord is celebrated inside the church by means of a Solemn Entrance before the principal Mass.

Holding branches in their hands, the faithful gather either outside, in front of the church door, or inside the church itself. The Priest and ministers and a representative group of the faithful go to a suitable place in the church outside the sanctuary, where at least the greater part of the faithful can see the rite.

While the Priest approaches the appointed place, the antiphon Hosanna or another appropriate chant is sung. Then the blessing of branches and the proclamation of the Gospel of the Lord's entrance into Jerusalem take place. After the Gospel, the Priest processes solemnly with the ministers and the representative group of the faithful through the church to the sanctuary, while the responsory As the Lord entered or another appropriate chant is sung.

Arriving at the altar, the Priest venerates it. He then goes to the chair and, omitting the Introductory Rites of the Mass and, if appropriate, the Kyrie (Lord, have mercy), he says the Collect of the Mass, and then continues the Mass in the usual way.

Third Form: The Simple Entrance

At all other Masses of this Sunday at which the Solemn Entrance is not held, the memorial of the Lord's entrance into Jerusalem takes place by means of a Simple Entrance.

While the Priest proceeds to the altar, the Entrance Antiphon with its Psalm or another chant on the same theme is sung. Arriving at the altar, the Priest venerates it and goes to the chair. After the Sign of the Cross, he greets the people and continues the Mass in the usual way.

At other Masses, in which singing at the entrance cannot take place, the Priest, as soon as he has arrived at the altar and venerated it, greets the people, reads the Entrance Antiphon, and continues the Mass in the usual way.

Entrance Antiphon Cf. Jn 12:1,12-13; Ps 23:9-10

S IX days before the Passover,
  when the Lord came into
    the city of Jerusalem,
the children ran to meet him;
in their hands they carried
    palm branches
and with a loud voice cried out:

*Hosanna in the highest!
Blessed are you, who have come
    in your abundant mercy!

O gates, lift high your heads;
grow higher, ancient doors.
Let him enter, the king of glory!
Who is this king of glory?
He, the Lord of hosts,
    he is the king of glory.

*Hosanna in the highest!
Blessed are you, who have come
    in your abundant mercy!

Ant. ad introitum

A NTE sex dies sollemnis Paschæ,
  quando venit Dominus
    in civitatem Ierusalem,
occurrerunt ei pueri:
et in manibus portabant
    ramos palmarum
et clamabant voce magna, dicentes:

*Hosanna in excelsis:
Benedictus, qui venisti
    in multitudine misericordiæ tuæ.
Attollite, portæ, capita vestra,
et elevamini, portæ æternales,
et introibit rex gloriæ.
Quis est iste rex gloriæ?
Dominus virtutum ipse est
    rex gloriæ.

*Hosanna in excelsis:
Benedictus, qui venisti
    in multitudine misericordiæ tuæ.

At the Mass

After the Procession or Solemn Entrance the Priest begins the Mass with the Collect.

Collect

Almighty ever-living God,
who as an example of humility
    for the human race to follow
caused our Saviour to take flesh
    and submit to the Cross,
graciously grant that we may heed
    his lesson of patient suffering
and so merit a share
    in his Resurrection.
Who lives and reigns with you
    in the unity of the Holy Spirit,
one God, for ever and ever.

Collecta

Omnipotens sempiterne Deus,
qui humano generi, ad imitandum
    humilitatis exemplum,
Salvatorem nostrum carnem sumere,
et crucem subire fecisti,
concede propitius,
ut et patientiæ ipsius
    habere documenta
et resurrectionis consortia mereamur.
Qui tecum vivit et regnat
    in unitate Spiritus Sancti,
Deus, per omnia sæcula sæculorum.

FIRST READING

A reading from the prophet Isaiah   50:4-7

I did not cover my face against insult – I know I shall not be shamed.

The Lord has given me
a disciple's tongue.
So that I may know how to reply to the wearied
he provides me with speech.
Each morning he wakes me to hear,
to listen like a disciple.
The Lord has opened my ear.
For my part, I made no resistance,
neither did I turn away.
I offered my back to those who struck me,
my cheeks to those who tore at my beard;
I did not cover my face
against insult and spittle.
The Lord comes to my help,
so that I am untouched by the insults.
So, too, I set my face like flint,
I know I shall not be shamed.

The word of the Lord.

Responsorial Psalm   Ps 21:8-9,17-20,23-24. R. v.2

R. **My God, my God, why have you forsaken me?**

All who see me deride me.
They curl their lips, they toss their heads.
'He trusted in the Lord, let him save him;
let him release him if this is his friend.' R.

Many dogs have surrounded me,
a band of the wicked beset me.
They tear holes in my hands and my feet.
I can count every one of my bones. R.

They divide my clothing among them.
They cast lots for my robe.
O Lord, do not leave me alone,
my strength, make haste to help me! R.

I will tell of your name to my brethren
and praise you where they are assembled.
'You who fear the Lord give him praise;
all sons of Jacob, give him glory.
Revere him, Israel's sons.' R.

R. **My God, my God, why have you forsaken me?**

SECOND READING

A reading from the letter of St Paul to the Philippians   2:6-11
He humbled himself, but God raised him high.

His state was divine,
yet Christ Jesus did not cling
to his equality with God
but emptied himself
to assume the condition of a slave,
and became as men are;
and being as all men are,
he was humbler yet,
even to accepting death,
death on a cross.
But God raised him high
and gave him the name
which is above all other names
so that all beings
in the heavens, on earth and in the underworld,
should bend the knee at the name of Jesus
and that every tongue should acclaim
Jesus Christ as Lord,
to the glory of God the Father.

   The word of the Lord.

Gospel Acclamation   Ph 2:8-9

R. **Praise to you, O Christ, king of eternal glory.**
Christ was humbler yet,
even to accepting death, death on a cross.
But God raised him high
and gave him the name which is above all names.
R. **Praise to you, O Christ, king of eternal glory.**

The narrative of the Lord's Passion is read without candles and without incense, with no greeting or signing of the book. It is read by a Deacon or, if there is no Deacon, by a Priest. It may also be read by readers, with the part of Christ, if possible, reserved to a Priest.

Deacons, but not others, ask for the blessing of the Priest before singing the Passion, as at other times before the Gospel.

GOSPEL

YEAR A

The passion of our Lord Jesus Christ according to Matthew   26:14-27:66

The symbols in the following passion narrative represent:

N Narrator   J Jesus   O Other single speaker
C Crowd, or more than one speaker

N One of the Twelve, the man called Judas Iscariot, went to the chief priests and said:

O What are you prepared to give me if I hand him over to you?

N They paid him thirty silver pieces, and from that moment he looked for an opportunity to betray him.

Now on the first day of Unleavened Bread the disciples came to Jesus to say,

C Where do you want us to make the preparations for you to eat the Passover?

N He replied:

J Go to so-and-so in the city and say to him, 'The Master says: My time is near. It is at your house that I am keeping Passover with my disciples.'

N The disciples did what Jesus told them and prepared the Passover. When the evening came he was at table with the twelve disciples. And while they were eating he said:

J I tell you solemnly, one of you is about to betray me.

N They were greatly distressed and started asking him in turn,

C Not I, Lord, surely?

N He answered:

J Someone who has dipped his hand into the dish with me, will betray me. The Son of Man is going to his fate, as the scriptures say he will, but alas for that man by whom the Son of Man is betrayed! Better for that man if he had never been born!

N Judas, who was to betray him, asked in his turn,

O Not I, Rabbi, surely?

N Jesus answered:

J   They are your own words.

N   Now as they were eating, Jesus took some bread, and when he had said the blessing he broke it and gave it to the disciples and said:

J   Take it and eat; this is my body.

N   Then he took a cup, and when he had returned thanks he gave it to them saying:

J   Drink all of you from this, for this is my blood, the blood of the covenant, which is to be poured out for many for the forgiveness of sins. From now on, I tell you, I shall not drink wine until the day I drink the new wine with you in the kingdom of my Father.

N   After psalms had been sung they left for the Mount of Olives. Then Jesus said to them,

J   You will all lose faith in me this night, for the scripture says: I shall strike the shepherd and the sheep of the flock will be scattered. But after my resurrection I shall go before you to Galilee.

N   At this, Peter said:

O   Though all lose faith in you, I will never lose faith.

N   Jesus answered him,

J   I tell you solemnly, this very night, before the cock crows, you will have disowned me three times.

N   Peter said to him,

O   Even if I have to die with you, I will never disown you.

N   And all the disciples said the same.

     Then Jesus came with them to a small estate called Gethsemane; and he said to his disciples,

J   Stay here while I go over there to pray.

N   He took Peter and the two sons of Zebedee with him. And sadness came over him, and great distress. Then he said to them:

J   My soul is sorrowful to the point of death. Wait here and keep awake with me.

N   And going on a little further he fell on his face and prayed:

J   My Father, if it is possible let this cup pass me by. Nevertheless, let it be as you, not I, would have it.

N   He came back to the disciples and found them sleeping, and he said to Peter:

J   So you had not the strength to keep awake with me one hour? You should be awake, and praying not to be put to the test. The spirit is willing, but the flesh is weak.

N Again, a second time, he went away and prayed:

J My Father, if this cup cannot pass by without my drinking it, your will be done!

N And he came again back and found them sleeping, their eyes were so heavy. Leaving them there, he went away again and prayed for the third time, repeating the same words. Then he came back to the disciples and said to them,

J You can sleep on now and take your rest. Now the hour has come when the Son of Man is to be betrayed into the hands of sinners. Get up! Let us go! My betrayer is already close at hand.

N He was still speaking when Judas, one of the Twelve, appeared, and with him a large number of men armed with swords and clubs, sent by the chief priests and elders of the people Now the traitor had arranged a sign with them. He had said:

O 'The one I kiss, he is the man. Take him in charge.'

N So he went straight up to Jesus and said:

O Greetings, Rabbi,

N and kissed him. Jesus said to him,

J My friend, do what you are here for.

N Then they came forward, seized Jesus and took him in charge. At that, one of the followers of Jesus grasped his sword and drew it; he struck out at the high priest's servant and cut off his ear. Jesus then said:

J Put your sword back, for all who draw the sword will die by the sword. Or do you think that I cannot appeal to my Father who would promptly send more than twelve legions of angels to my defence? But then, how would the scriptures be fulfilled that say this is the way it must be?

N It was at this time that Jesus said to the crowds:

J Am I a brigand, that you had to set out to capture me with swords and clubs? I sat teaching in the Temple day after day and you never laid hands on me.

N Now all this happened to fulfil the prophecies in scripture. Then all the disciples deserted him and ran away.

  The men who had arrested Jesus led him off to Caiaphas the high priest, where the scribes and the elders were assembled. Peter followed him at a distance, and when he reached the high priest's palace, he went in and sat down with the attendants to see what the end would be.

  The chief priests and the whole Sanhedrin were looking for evidence against Jesus, however false, on which they might pass the death-sentence. But they could not find any, though several lying witnesses came forward. Eventually two stepped forward and made a statement,

O   This man said: 'I have power to destroy the Temple of God and in three days build it up.'

N   The high priest then stood up and said to him:

O   Have you no answer to that? What is this evidence these men are bringing against you?

N   But Jesus was silent. And the high priest said to him:

O   I put you on oath by the living God to tell us if you are the Christ, the Son of God.

N   Jesus answered:

J   The words are your own. Moreover, I tell you that from this time onward you will see the Son of Man seated at the right hand of the Power and coming on the clouds of heaven.

N   At this, the high priest tore his clothes and said:

O   He has blasphemed. What need of witnesses have we now? There! You have just heard the blasphemy. What is your opinion?

N   They answered:

C   He deserves to die

N   Then they spat in his face and hit him with their fists; others said as they struck him:

C   Play the prophet, Christ! Who hit you then?

N   Meanwhile Peter was sitting outside in the courtyard, and a servant-girl came up to him and said:

O   You too were with Jesus the Galilean.

N   But he denied it in front of them all, saying:

O   I do not know what you are talking about.

N   When he went out to the gateway another servant-girl saw him and said to the people there:

O   This man was with Jesus the Nazarene.

N   And again, with an oath, he denied it,

O   I do not know the man.

N   A little later the bystanders came up and said to Peter:

C   You are one of them for sure! Why, your accent gives you away.

N   Then he started calling down curses on himself and swearing:

O   I do not know the man.

N   At that moment the cock crew, and Peter remembered what Jesus had said, 'Before the cock crows you will have disowned me three times.'

And he went outside and wept bitterly.

When morning came, all the chief priests and the elders of the people met in council to bring about the death of Jesus. They had him bound, and led him away to hand him over to Pilate, the governor. When he found that Jesus had been condemned, Judas his betrayer was filled with remorse and took the thirty pieces of silver back to the chief priests and elders, saying:

O I have sinned. I have betrayed innocent blood.

N They replied:

C What is that to us? That is your concern.

N And flinging down the silver pieces in the sanctuary he made off, and went and hanged himself. The chief priests picked up the silver pieces and said:

C It is against the Law to put this into the treasury; it is blood money.

N So they discussed the matter and bought the potter's field with it as a graveyard for foreigners, and this is why the field is called the Field of Blood today. The words of the prophet Jeremiah were then fulfilled: And they took the thirty silver pieces, the sum at which the precious One was priced by children of Israel, and they gave them for the potter's field, just as the Lord directed me.

[Jesus, then, was brought before the governor, and the governor put to him this question:

O Are you the king of the Jews?

N Jesus replied:

J It is you who say it.

N But when he was accused by the chief priests and the elders he refused to answer at all. Pilate then said to him:

O Do you not hear how many charges they have brought against you?

N But to the governor's complete amazement, he offered no reply to any of the charges.

At festival time it was the governor's practice to release a prisoner for the people, anyone they chose. Now there was at that time a notorious prisoner whose name was Barabbas. So when the crowd gathered, Pilate said to them,

O Which do you want me to release for you: Barabbas or Jesus who is called Christ?

N For Pilate knew it was out of jealousy that they had handed him over. Now as he was seated in the chair of judgement, his wife sent him a message,

O   Have nothing to do with that man; I have been upset all day by a dream I had about him.

N   The chief priests and the elders, however, had persuaded the crowd to demand the release of Barabbas and the execution of Jesus. So when the governor spoke and asked them:

O   Which of the two do you want me to release for you?

N   They said:

C   Barabbas.

N   Pilate said to them:

O   What am I to do with Jesus who is called Christ?

N   They all said:

C   Let him be crucified!

N   Pilate asked:

O   Why? What harm has he done?

N   But they shouted all the louder,

C   Let him be crucified!

N   Then Pilate saw that he was making no impression, that in fact a riot was imminent. So he took some water, washed his hands in front of the crowd and said:

O   I am innocent of this man's blood. It is your concern.

N   And the people, to a man, shouted back:

C   His blood be on us and on our children!

N   Then he released Barabbas for them. He ordered Jesus to be first scourged and then handed over to be crucified.

     The governor's soldiers took Jesus with them into the Praetorium and collected the whole cohort round him. Then they stripped him and made him wear a scarlet cloak, and having twisted some thorns into a crown they put this on his head and placed a reed in his right hand. To make fun of him they knelt to him saying:

C   Hail, king of the Jews!

N   And they spat on him and took the reed and struck him on the head with it. And when they had finished making fun of him, they took off the cloak and dressed him in his own clothes and led him away to crucify him.

     On their way out, they came across a man from Cyrene, Simon by name, and enlisted him to carry his cross. When they had reach a place called Golgotha, that is, the place of the skull, they gave him wine to drink. When they had finished crucifying him they shared out his clothing by casting lots, and then sat down and stayed there keeping guard over him. Above his head was placed the charge against him; it read: 'This is Jesus, the King of the Jews.' At the same time two robbers were crucified with him, one on the right and one on the left.

The passers-by jeered at him; they shook their heads and said:

C So you would destroy the Temple and rebuild it in three days! Then save yourself! If you are God's son, come down from the cross!

N The chief priests with the scribes and elders mocked him in the same way, saying:

C He saved others; he cannot save himself. He is the King of Israel; let him come down from the cross now, and we will believe in him. He put his trust in God; now let God rescue him if he wants him. For he did say, 'I am the son of God.'

N Even the robbers who were crucified with him taunted him in the same way.

From the sixth hour there was darkness over all the land until the ninth hour. And about the ninth hour, Jesus cried out in a loud voice:

J Eli, Eli, lama sabachthani?

N That is: 'My God, my God, why have you deserted me?' When some of those who stood there heard this, they said:

C The man is calling on Elijah,

N and one of them quickly ran to get a sponge which he dipped in vinegar and, putting it on a reed, gave it him to drink. The rest of them said:

C Wait! See if Elijah will come to save him.

N But Jesus, again crying out in a loud voice, yielded up his spirit.

All kneel and pause a moment.

N At that, the veil of the Temple was torn in two from top to bottom; the earth quaked; the rocks were split; the tombs opened and the bodies of many holy men rose from the dead, and these, after his resurrection, came out of the tombs, entered the Holy City and appeared to a number of people.

Meanwhile the centurion, together with the others guarding Jesus, had seen the earthquake and all that was taking place, and they were terrified and said:

C In truth this was a son of God.]

N And many women were there, watching from a distance, the same women who had followed Jesus from Galilee and looked after him. Among them were Mary of Magdala, Mary the mother of James and

Joseph, and the mother of Zebedee's sons.

When it was evening, there came a rich man of Arimathaea called Joseph, who had himself become a disciple of Jesus. This man went to Pilate and asked for the body of Jesus. Pilate thereupon ordered it to be handed over. So Joseph took the body, wrapped it in a clean shroud and put it in his own new tomb which he had hewn out of the rock. He then rolled a large stone across the entrance of the tomb and went away. Now Mary of Magdala and the other Mary were there, sitting opposite the sepulchre.

Next day, that is, when Preparation Day was over, the chief priests and the Pharisees went in a body to Pilate and said to him,

C Your Excellency, we recall that this impostor said, while he was still alive, 'After three days I shall rise again.' Therefore give the order to have the sepulchre kept secure until the third day, for fear his disciples come and steal him away and tell the people, 'He has risen from the dead.' This last piece of fraud would be worse than what went before.

N Pilate said to them:

O You may have your guards. Go and make all as secure as you know how.

N So they went and made the sepulchre secure, putting seals on the stone and mounting a guard.

| [The Gospel of the Lord.]

Shorter Form, verses 27:11-54. Read between [ ]

YEAR B

The symbols in the following passion narrative represent:

N Narrator   J Jesus   O Other single speaker
C Crowd, or more than one speaker

The passion of our Lord Jesus Christ according to Mark   14:1-15:47

N It was two days before the Passover and the feast of Unleavened Bread, and the chief priests and scribes were looking for a way to arrest Jesus by some trick and have him put to death. For they said,

C It must not be during the festivities, or there will be a disturbance among the people.

N Jesus was at Bethany in the house of Simon the leper; he was at dinner when a woman came in with an alabaster jar of very costly ointment, pure nard. She broke the jar and poured the ointment on his head. Some who were there said to one another indignantly,

C Why this waste of ointment? Ointment like this could have been sold for over three hundred denarii and the money given to the poor;

N   and they were angry with her. But Jesus said,

J   Leave her alone. Why are you upsetting her? What she has done for me is one of the good works. You have the poor with you always and you can be kind to them whenever you wish but you will not always have me. She has done what was in her power to do; she has anointed my body beforehand for its burial. I tell you solemnly, wherever throughout all the world the Good News is proclaimed, what she has done will be told also, in remembrance of her.

N   Judas Iscariot, one of the Twelve, approached the chief priests with an offer to hand Jesus over to them. They were delighted to hear it, and promised to give him money; and he looked for a way of betraying him when the opportunity should occur.

On the first day of Unleavened Bread, when the Passover lamb was sacrificed, his disciples said to him,

C   Where do you want us to go and make the preparations for you to eat the Passover?

N   So he sent two of his disciples, saying to them,

J   Go into the city and you will meet a man carrying a pitcher of water. Follow him, and say to the owner of the house which he enters, 'The Master says: Where is my dining room in which I can eat the Passover with my disciples?' He will show you a large upper room furnished with couches, all prepared. Make the preparations for us there.

N   The disciples set out and went to the city and found everything as he had told them, and prepared the Passover.

When evening came he arrived with the Twelve. And while they were at table eating, Jesus said,

J   I tell you solemnly, one of you is about to betray me, one of you eating with me.

N   They were distressed and asked him, one after another,

O   Not I, surely?

N   He said to them,

J   It is one of the Twelve, one who is dipping into the same dish with me. Yes, the Son of Man is going to his fate, as the scriptures say he will, but alas for that man by whom the Son of Man is betrayed! Better for that man if he had never been born!

N   And as they were eating he took some bread, and when he had said the blessing he broke it and gave it to them, saying,

J   Take it; this is my body.

N   Then he took a cup, and when he had returned thanks he gave it to them, and all drank from it, and he said to them,

J   This is my blood, the blood of the covenant, which is to be poured out for many. I tell you solemnly, I shall not drink any more wine until the day I drink the new wine in the kingdom of God.

N   After psalms had been sung they left for the Mount of Olives. And Jesus said to them,

J   You will all lose faith, for the scripture says, 'I shall strike the shepherd and the sheep will be scattered.' However after my resurrection I shall go before you to Galilee.

N   Peter said,

O   Even if all lose faith, I will not.

N   And Jesus said to him,

J   I tell you solemnly, this day, this very night, before the cock crows twice, you will have disowned me three times.

N   But he repeated still more earnestly,

O   If I have to die with you, I will never disown you.

N   And they all said the same.

       They came to a small estate called Gethsemane, and Jesus said to his disciples,

J   Stay here while I pray.

N   Then he took Peter and James and John with him. And a sudden fear came over him, and great distress. And he said to them,

J   My soul is sorrowful to the point of death. Wait here, and keep awake.

N   And going on a little further he threw himself on the ground and prayed that, if it were possible, this hour might pass him by. He said,

J   Abba (Father)! Everything is possible for you. Take this cup away from me. But let it be as you, not I, would have it.

N   He came back and found them sleeping, and he said to Peter,

J   Simon, are you asleep? Had you not the strength to keep awake one hour? You should be awake, and praying not to be put to the test. The spirit is willing but the flesh is weak.

N   Again he went away and prayed, saying the same words. And once more he came back and found them sleeping, their eyes were so heavy; and they could find no answer for him. He came back a third time and said to them,

J   You can sleep on now and take your rest. It is all over. The hour has come. Now the Son of Man is to be betrayed into the hands of sinners. Get up! Let us go! My betrayer is close at hand already.

N   Even while he was still speaking, Judas, one of the Twelve, came up with a number of men armed with swords and clubs, sent by the chief priests and the scribes and the elders. Now the traitor had arranged a signal with them. He had said,

O The one I kiss, he is the man. Take him in charge, and see he is well guarded when you lead him away.'

N So when the traitor came, he went straight up to Jesus and said,

O Rabbi!

N and kissed him. The others seized him and took him in charge. Then one of the bystanders drew his sword and struck out at the high priest's servant, and cut off his ear.

Then Jesus spoke,

J Am I a brigand that you had to set out to capture me with swords and clubs? I was among you teaching in the Temple day after day and you never laid hands on me. But this is to fulfil the scriptures.

N And they all deserted him and ran away. A young man who followed him had nothing on but a linen cloth. They caught hold of him, but he left the cloth in their hands and ran away naked.

They led Jesus off to the high priest; and all the chief priests and the elders and the scribes assembled there. Peter had followed him at a distance, right into the high priest's palace, and was sitting with the attendants warming himself at the fire.

The chief priests and the whole Sanhedrin were looking for evidence against Jesus on which they might pass the death-sentence. But they could not find any. Several, indeed, brought false evidence against him, but their evidence was conflicting. Some stood up and submitted this false evidence against him,

C We heard him say, 'I am going to destroy this Temple made by human hands, and in three days build another, not made by human hands.'

N But even on this point their evidence was conflicting. The high priest then stood up before the whole assembly and put this question to Jesus,

O Have you no answer to that? What is this evidence these men are bringing against you?

N But he was silent and made no answer at all. The high priest put a second question to him,

O Are you the Christ the Son of the Blessed One?

N Jesus said,

J I am, and you will see the Son of Man seated at the right hand of the Power and coming with the clouds of heaven.

N The high priest tore his robes, and said,

O   What need of witnesses have we now? You heard the blasphemy. What is your finding?

N   And they all gave their verdict: he deserved to die.
Some of them started spitting at him and, blindfolding him, began hitting him with their fists and shouting,

C   Play the prophet!

N   And the attendants rained blows on him.

While Peter was down below in the courtyard, one of the high-priest's servant-girls came up. She saw Peter warming himself there, stared at him and said,

O   You too were with Jesus, the man from Nazareth.

N   But he denied it, saying,

O   I do not know, I do not understand what you are talking about.

N   And he went out into the forecourt. The servant-girl saw him and again started telling the bystanders,

O   This fellow is one of them.

N   But he again denied it. A little later the bystanders themselves said to Peter,

C   You are one of them for sure! Why, you are a Galilean.

N   But he started calling down curses on himself and swearing,

O   I do not know the man you speak of.

N   At that moment the cock crew for the second time, and Peter recalled how Jesus had said to him, 'Before the cock crows twice, you will have disowned me three times.' And he burst into tears.

[First thing in the morning, the chief priest together with the elders and scribes, in short the whole Sanhedrin, had their plan ready. They had Jesus bound and took him away and handed him over to Pilate.
Pilate questioned him,

O   Are you the king of the Jews?

N   He answered,

J   It is you who say it.

N   And the chief priests brought many accusations against him. Pilate questioned him again,

O   Have you no reply at all? See how many accusations they are bringing against you!

N   But to Pilate's amazement, Jesus made no further reply.

At festival time Pilate used to release a prisoner for them, anyone they asked for. Now a man called Barabbas was then in prison with the rioters who had committed murder during the uprising. When the

N crowd went up and began to ask Pilate the customary favour, Pilate answered them,

O Do you want me to release for you the king of the Jews?

N For he realised it was out of jealousy that the chief priests had handed Jesus over. The chief priests, however, had incited the crowd to demand that he should release Barabbas for them instead. Then Pilate spoke again.

O But in that case, what am I to do with the man you call king of the Jews?

N They shouted back.

C Crucify him!

N Pilate asked them,

O Why? What harm has he done?

N But they shouted all the louder,

C Crucify him!

N So Pilate, anxious to placate the crowd, released Barabbas for them and, having ordered Jesus to be scourged, handed him over to be crucified.

  The soldiers led him away to the inner part of the palace, that is, the Praetorium, and called the whole cohort together. They dressed him up in purple, twisted some thorns into a crown and put it on him. And they began saluting him,

C Hail, king of the Jews!

N They struck his head with a reed and spat on him; and they went down on their knees to do him homage. And when they had finished making fun of him, they took off the purple and dressed him in his own clothes.

  They led him out to crucify him. They enlisted a passer-by, Simon of Cyrene, father of Alexander and Rufus, who was coming in from the country, to carry his cross. They brought Jesus to the place called Golgotha, which means the place of the skull.

  They offered him wine mixed with myrrh, but he refused it. Then they crucified him, and shared out his clothing, casting lots to decide what each should get. It was the third hour when they crucified him. The inscription giving the charge against him read: 'The King of the Jews.' And they crucified two robbers with him, one on his right and one on his left.

  The passers-by jeered at him; they shook their heads and said,

C Aha! So you would destroy the Temple and rebuild it in three days! Then save yourself: come down from the cross!

N   The chief priests and the scribes mocked him among themselves in the same way. They said,

C   He saved others, he cannot save himself. Let the Christ, the king of Israel, come down from the cross now, for us to see it and believe.

N   Even those who were crucified with him taunted him.

When the sixth hour came there was darkness over the whole land until the ninth hour. And at the ninth hour Jesus cried out in a loud voice,

J   Eloi, Eloi, lama sabachthani?

N   This means 'My God, my God, why have you deserted me?' When some of those who stood by heard this, they said,

C   Listen, he is calling on Elijah.

N   Someone ran and soaked a sponge in vinegar and, putting it on a reed, gave it him to drink, saying,

O   Wait and see if Elijah will come to take him down.

N   But Jesus gave a loud cry and breathed his last.

All kneel and pause a moment.

N   And the veil of the Temple was torn in two from top to bottom. The centurion, who was standing in front of him, had seen how he had died, and he said,

O   In truth this man was a son of God.]

N   There were some women watching from a distance. Among them were Mary of Magdala, Mary who was the mother of James the younger, and Joset, and Salome. These used to follow him and look after him when he was in Galilee. And there were many other women there who had come up to Jerusalem with him.

It was now evening, and since it was Preparation Day (that is the vigil of the sabbath), there came Joseph of Arimathaea, a prominent member of the Council, who himself lived in the hope of seeing the kingdom of God, and he boldly went to Pilate and asked for the body of Jesus. Pilate, astonished that he should have died so soon, summoned the centurion and enquired if he was already dead. Having been assured of this by the centurion, he granted the corpse to Joseph who brought a shroud, took Jesus down from the cross, wrapped him in the shroud and laid him in a tomb which had been hewn out of the rock. He then rolled a stone against the entrance to the tomb. Mary of Magdala and Mary the mother of Joset were watching and took note of where he was laid.

[The Gospel of the Lord.]

Shorter Form, verses 15:1-39. Read between [ ]

YEAR C

The passion of our Lord Jesus Christ according to Luke   22:14-23:56

N   When the hour came Jesus took his place at table, and the apostles with him. And he said to them,

J   I have longed to eat this Passover with you before I suffer; because, I tell you, I shall not eat it again until it is fulfilled in the kingdom of God.

N   Then, taking a cup, he gave thanks and said,

J   Take this and share it among you, because from now on, I tell you, I shall not drink wine until the kingdom of God comes.

N   Then he took some bread, and when he had given thanks, broke it and gave it to them, saying,

J   This is my body which will be given for you; do this as a memorial of me.

N   He did the same with the cup after supper, and said,

J   This cup is the new covenant in my blood which will be poured out for you.

   And yet, here with me on the table is the hand of the man who betrays me. The Son of Man does indeed go to his fate even as it has been decreed, but alas for that man by whom he is betrayed!

N   And they began to ask one another which of them it could be who was to do this thing.

   A dispute arose also between them about which should be reckoned the greatest, but he said to them,

J   Among pagans it is the kings who lord it over them, and those who have authority over them are given the title Benefactor. This must not happen with you. No; the greatest among you must behave as if he were the youngest, the leader as if he were the one who serves. For who is the greater: the one at table or the one who serves? The one at table, surely? Yet here I am among you as one who serves!

   You are the men who have stood by me faithfully in my trials; and now I confer a kingdom on you, just as my Father conferred one on me: you will eat and drink at my table in my kingdom, and you will sit on thrones to judge the twelve tribes of Israel.

   Simon, Simon! Satan, you must know, has got his wish to sift you all like wheat; but I have prayed for you, Simon, that your faith may not fail, and once you have recovered, you in your turn must strengthen your brothers.

N   He answered,

O   Lord, I would be ready to go to prison with you, and to death.

N   Jesus replied,

J   I tell you, Peter, by the time the cock crows today you will have denied three times that you know me.

N   He said to them,

J   When I sent you out without purse or haversack or sandals, were you short of anything?

N   They answered,

C   No.

N   He said to them,

J   But now if you have a purse, take it: if you have a haversack, do the same; if you have no sword, sell your cloak and buy one, because I tell you these words of scripture have to be fulfilled in me: He let himself be taken for a criminal. Yes, what scripture says about me is even now reaching its fulfilment.

N   They said,

C   Lord, there are two swords here now.

N   He said to them,

J   That is enough!

N   He then left the upper room to make his way as usual to the Mount of Olives, with the disciples following. When they reached the place he said to them,

J   Pray not to be put to the test.

N   Then he withdrew from them, about a stone's throw away, and knelt down and prayed, saying,

J   Father, if you are willing, take this cup away from me. Nevertheless, let your will be done, not mine.

N   Then an angel appeared to him coming from heaven to give him strength. In his anguish he prayed even more earnestly and his sweat fell to the ground like great drops of blood.

     When he rose from prayer he went to the disciples and found them sleeping for sheer grief. He said to them,

J   Why are you asleep? Get up and pray not to be put to the test.

N   He was still speaking when a number of men appeared, and at the head of them the man called Judas, one of the Twelve, who went up to Jesus to kiss him. Jesus said,

J   Judas, are you betraying the Son of Man with a kiss?

N   His followers, seeing what was happening, said,

C   Lord, shall we use our swords?

N   And one of them struck out at the high priest's servant, and cut off his right ear. But at this Jesus spoke,

J   Leave off! That will do!

N   And touching the man's ear he healed him.

Then Jesus spoke to the chief priests and captains of the Temple guard and elders who had come for him. He said,

J   Am I a brigand that you had to set out with swords and clubs? When I was among you in the Temple day after day you never moved to lay hands on me. But this is your hour; this is the reign of darkness.

N   They seized him then and led him away, and they took him to the high priest's house. Peter followed at a distance. They had lit a fire in the middle of the courtyard and Peter sat down among them, and as he was sitting there by the blaze a servant-girl saw him, peered at him and said,

O   This person was with him too.

N   But he denied it, saying,

O   Woman, I do not know him.

N   Shortly afterwards, someone else saw him and said,

O   You are another of them.

N   But Peter replied,

O   I am not, my friend.

N   About an hour later, another man insisted, saying,

O   This fellow was certainly with him. Why, he is a Galilean.

N   Peter said,

O   My friend, I do not know what you are talking about.

N   At that instant, while he was still speaking, the cock crew, and the Lord turned and looked straight at Peter, and Peter remembered what the Lord had said to him, 'Before the cock crows today, you will have disowned me three times.' And he went outside and wept bitterly.

Meanwhile the men who guarded Jesus were mocking and beating him. They blindfolded him and questioned him, saying,

C   Play the prophet. Who hit you then?

N   And they continued heaping insults on him.

When day broke there was a meeting of the elders of the people, attended by the chief priests and scribes. He was brought before their council, and they said to him,

C   If you are the Christ, tell us.

N   He replied,

J   If I tell you, you will not believe me, and if I question you, you will not answer. But from now on, the Son of Man will be seated at the right hand of the Power of God.

N   Then they all said,

C   So you are the Son of God then?

N He answered,

J It is you who say I am.

N They said,

C What need of witnesses have we now? We have heard it for ourselves from his own lips.

N [The whole assembly then rose, and they brought him before Pilate. They began their accusation by saying,

C We found this man inciting our people to revolt, opposing payment of the tribute to Caesar, and claiming to be Christ, a king.

N Pilate put to him this question,

O Are you the king of the Jews?

N He replied,

J It is you who say it.

N Pilate then said to the chief priests and the crowd,

O I find no case against this man.

N But they persisted,

C He is inflaming the people with his teaching all over Judaea; it has come all the way from Galilee, where he started, down to here.

N When Pilate heard this, he asked if the man were a Galilean; and finding that he came under Herod's jurisdiction he passed him over to Herod who was also in Jerusalem at that time.

Herod was delighted to see Jesus; he had heard about him and had been wanting for a long time to set eyes on him; moreover, he was hoping to see some miracle worked by him. So he questioned him at some length; but without getting any reply. Meanwhile the chief priests and the scribes were there, violently pressing their accusations. Then Herod, together with his guards, treated him with contempt and made fun of him; he put a rich cloak on him and sent him back to Pilate. And though Herod and Pilate had been enemies before, they were reconciled that same day.

Pilate then summoned the chief priests and the leading men and the people. He said,

O You brought this man before me as a political agitator. Now I have gone into the matter myself in your presence and found no case against the man in respect of all the charges you bring against him. Nor has Herod either, since he has sent him back to us. As you can see, the man has done nothing that deserves death, so I shall have him flogged and then let him go.

N But as one man they howled,

C Away with him! Give us Barabbas!

N This man had been thrown into prison for causing a riot in the city and for murder.

Pilate was anxious to set Jesus free and addressed them again, but they shouted back,

C Crucify him! Crucify him!

N And for the third time he spoke to them,

O Why? What harm has this man done? I have found no case against him that deserves death, so I shall have him punished and let him go.

N But they kept on shouting at the top of their voices, demanding that he should be crucified, and their shouts were growing louder.

Pilate then gave his verdict: their demand was to be granted. He released the man they asked for, who had been imprisoned for rioting and murder, and handed Jesus over to them to deal with as they pleased.

As they were leading him away they seized on a man, Simon from Cyrene, who was coming in from the country, and made him shoulder the cross and carry it behind Jesus. Large numbers of people followed him, and of women too who mourned and lamented for him. But Jesus turned to them and said,

J Daughters of Jerusalem, do not weep for me; weep rather for yourselves and for your children. For the days will surely come when people will say, 'Happy are those who are barren, the wombs that have never borne, the breasts that have never suckled!' Then they will begin to say to the mountains, 'Fall on us!'; to the hills, 'Cover us!' For if men use the green wood like this, what will happen when it is dry?

N Now with him they were also leading out two other criminals to be executed.

When they reached the place called The Skull, they crucified him there and the criminals also, one on the right, the other on the left. Jesus said,

J Father, forgive them; they do not know what they are doing.

N Then they cast lots to share out his clothing. The people stayed there watching him. As for the leaders, they jeered at him, saying,

C He saved others; let him save himself if he is the Christ of God, the Chosen One.

N The soldiers mocked him too, and when they approached to offer him vinegar they said,

C If you are the king of the Jews, save yourself.

N Above him there was an inscription: 'This is the King of the Jews.'
One of the criminals hanging there abused him, saying,

O Are you not the Christ? Save yourself and us as well.

N But the other spoke up and rebuked him,

O Have you no fear of God at all? You got the same sentence as he did, but in our case we deserved it: we are paying for what we did. But this man has done nothing wrong. Jesus, remember me when you come into your kingdom.

N He replied,

J Indeed, I promise you, today you will be with me in paradise.

N It was now about the sixth hour and, with the sun eclipsed, a darkness came over the whole land until the ninth hour. The veil of the Temple was torn right down the middle; and when Jesus had cried out in a loud voice, he said,

J Father, into your hands I commit my spirit.

N With these words he breathed his last.

All kneel and pause a moment.

When the centurion saw what had taken place, he gave praise to God and said,

O This was a great and good man.

N And when all the people who had gathered for the spectacle saw what had happened, they went home beating their breasts.

All his friends stood at a distance; so also did the women who had accompanied him from Galilee, and they saw all this happen.]

Then a member of the council arrived, an upright and virtuous man named Joseph. He had not consented to what the others had planned and carried out. He came from Arimathaea, a Jewish town, and he lived in the hope of seeing the kingdom of God. This man went to Pilate and asked for the body of Jesus. He then took it down, wrapped it in a shroud and put him in a tomb which was hewn in stone in which no one had yet been laid. It was Preparation Day and the sabbath was imminent.

Meanwhile the women who had come from Galilee with Jesus were following behind. They took note of the tomb and of the position of the body.

Then they returned and prepared spices and ointments. And on the sabbath day they rested, as the law required.

[The Gospel of the Lord.]

Shorter Form, verses 23:1-49. Read between [ ]

After the narrative of the Passion, a brief homily should take place, if appropriate. A period of silence may also be observed.

The Creed is said, and the Universal Prayer takes place.

Prayer over the Offerings

Through the Passion of your Only
    Begotten Son, O Lord,
may our reconciliation with you
    be near at hand,
so that, though we do not merit it
    by our own deeds,
yet by this sacrifice made once
    for all,
we may feel already the effects
    of your mercy.
Through Christ our Lord.

Super oblata

Per Unigeniti tui passionem
placatio tua nobis, Domine,
    sit propinqua,
quam, etsi nostris operibus
    non meremur,
interveniente sacrificio singulari,
tua percipiamus
    miseratione præventi.
Per Christum Dominum nostrum.

Preface: The Passion of the Lord.

It is truly right and just,
    our duty and our salvation,
always and everywhere to give
    you thanks,
Lord, holy Father, almighty
    and eternal God,
through Christ our Lord.

For, though innocent, he suffered
    willingly for sinners
and accepted unjust condemnation
    to save the guilty.
His Death has washed away our sins,
and his Resurrection has purchased
    our justification.

And so, with all the Angels,
we praise you, as in joyful
    celebration we acclaim:
Holy, Holy, Holy
    Lord God of hosts...

Præfatio: De dominica Passione.

Vere dignum et iustum est,
    æquum et salutare,
nos tibi semper et ubique
    gratias agere:
Domine, sancte Pater, omnipotens
    æterne Deus:
per Christum Dominum nostrum.

Qui pati pro impiis dignatus
    est innocens,
et pro sceleratis
    indebite condemnari.
Cuius mors delicta nostra detersit,
et iustificationem nobis
    resurrectio comparavit.

Unde et nos cum omnibus Angelis
    te laudamus,
iucunda celebratione clamantes:
Sanctus, Sanctus, Sanctus
    Dominus Deus Sabaoth...

Communion Antiphon   Mt 26:42

Father, if this chalice cannot pass
    without my drinking it,
your will be done.

Prayer after Communion

Nourished with these sacred gifts,
we humbly beseech you, O Lord,
that, just as through the death
    of your Son
you have brought us to hope
    for what we believe,
so by his Resurrection
you may lead us to where you call.
Through Christ our Lord.

Prayer over the People

Look, we pray, O Lord,
    on this your family,
for whom our Lord Jesus Christ
did not hesitate to be delivered
    into the hands of the wicked
and submit to the agony
    of the Cross.
Who lives and reigns
    for ever and ever.

Ant. ad communionem

Pater, si non potest
    hic calix transire,
nisi bibam illum, fiat voluntas tua.

Post communionem

Sacro munere satiati,
supplices te, Domine, deprecamur,
ut, qui fecisti nos
morte Filii tui sperare
    quod credimus,
facias nos, eodem resurgente,
pervenire quo tendimus.
Per Christum Dominum nostrum.

Oratio super populum

Respice, quæsumus, Domine,
    super hanc familiam tuam,
pro qua Dominus noster
    Iesus Christus
non dubitavit manibus
    tradi nocentium,
et crucis subire tormentum.
Qui vivit et regnat
    in sæcula sæculorum.

REFLECTION

The Passion According to Matthew (Year A)

✠

The accounts of the Passion given by the four evangelists are not identical. The basic outline of these dreadful events was clear enough. It is confirmed by the contemporary Jewish historian Josephus, who tells us that Jesus was crucified by Pontius Pilate at the instigation of the Jewish leaders. The task of the Gospel writers is not to relay to us the raw facts, but to help us understand their significance. Each stresses a particular aspect. For instance, John underlines that this was the triumph of Jesus: he shows his divinity already at the arrest scene. He himself yielded up his Spirit only when he had completed his task. Matthew's pre-occupation with Judaism dictates that he show in detail how the events accord with God's plan revealed in the scriptures. Almost every incident is told in such a way that hearers familiar with the scriptures would catch allusions to the biblical writings: nowhere is this more obvious than in the account of the death of Judas. Though Pilate the governor must bear the final responsibility, Matthew also stresses the pressure put on him by the crowd manipulated by the politically adept Jewish authorities, culminating in the horrific cry: "His blood be on us and on our children" – an allusion to the sufferings undergone by the next generation during the siege of Jerusalem by the Romans. The significance of the events is further underlined by the apocalyptic earthquake at Jesus's death, and by the immediate release of the blessed dead, who come at last into the Holy City.

The Passion According to Mark (Year B)

✠

The Gospel of Mark is concerned to show Jesus as a real, human person. So the story of the Passion begins with the very real fear and horror of Jesus in the garden. Mark represents Jesus as almost beside himself with apprehension at the torture which he knew he would suffer. Again and again he returns to seek companionship from his disciples, to find them callously asleep. The Passion-story ends, too, with a loud cry of agony as Jesus breathes his last.

The core of the Passion-story is the trial scene. Before the high priest, Jesus acknowledges that he is the Messiah of Judaism, and the Son of the Blessed One. To these titles he joins "Son of Man". In the Book of Daniel the Son of Man is a glorious figure who triumphs over persecution to receive from God all power on earth. So now Jesus claims to share God's throne as that Son of Man. It is for these divine claims that he is rejected as a blasphemer and handed over to the Romans.

When Jesus cries out on the cross "My God, my God, why have you deserted me?", he is not in despair, but is beginning Psalm 22. The Psalm begins in persecution, but ends in the triumph of God and the vindication of the sufferer. This gives the meaning of his Passion: by it Jesus brings the triumph of God and his own vindication by God. The Cross is the moment, not of abandonment by God, but of the most complete union of Jesus to the Father. Jesus here establishes the Sovereignty of his Father by his total, loving obedience. This is why the centurion proclaims, "In truth, this man was a son of God." It is also significant that here for the first time in the gospels a human being recognises Jesus as Son of God. It is not a Jew but a gentile – the beginning of the spread of the gospel to all nations of the world.

The Passion According to Luke (Year C)

✠

Each of the Gospel writers has a slightly different account of the Passion and Death of Jesus, for it was their task not so much to record history as to explain how these dreadful events could be the central focus of the Good News of Jesus Christ. Each has a different emphasis, and that of Luke is precisely repentance and forgiveness by the mercy of God.

The account of the Last Supper is not so much an account of the final Passover meal as an account of two incidents. First comes the identification of the traitor, not by name, but stressing the enormity of his betrayal: to betray a friend with whom he has shared a meal, and even more the same dish, is an unthinkable act of treachery. In all the synoptic Gospels next comes the account of the institution of the Eucharist: the focus is on the blood of Jesus which seals the new covenant, a personal covenant promised by the prophets, by which each of us is sealed into a new and intimate relationship with the Lord. Blood is the symbol of life, and the new covenant gives new life. Luke adds a third element, in the Hellenistic manner gathering together sayings of the Master which will underpin the continuation of his mission by the disciples in the Church. Already we look towards Peter's failure and his repentance and forgiveness.

The Agony in the Garden has a new angle. Luke's accent is not on Jesus falling to the ground in distraught anticipation of the torture to come. Instead, he kneels nobly in fervent prayer, as an example for his followers, "Pray that you enter not into temptation". At the arrest he continues his saving mission by healing the man whose ear has been cut off.

At Peter's betrayal in the courtyard of the high priest's house the tender glance of Jesus brings Peter to repentance; he bursts into bitter tears and disappears from the scene. The subsequent interrogation (Luke positions it in the morning, not in the night) is more a disorderly kangaroo court. There is no sign of the high priest, and the rabble merely ask Jesus to identify himself as Christ/Messiah and son of God. This Jesus does, adding his own preferred title of "Son of Man", no doubt with allusion to the glorious Son of Man in Daniel's vision who 'from now on' will be coming on the clouds of heaven.

In the trial before Pilate all the accent is on Pilate's desperate attempts to evade responsibility, even sending Jesus over to Herod Antipas, the ruler of Galilee – with the one result that the friendship between Pilate and Herod is restored. Pilate suggests that Jesus should be whipped rather than brutally flogged, but finally rejects all responsibility by handing him over to the Jews to do with him as they wish.

In Luke the mission of Jesus to Jerusalem is bracketed at he enters the city by his weeping over its refusal to repent, and now as he leaves the city by his warning to the mourning women of the horrors of the coming siege and sack of Jerusalem. Then at the Crucifixion itself there follows a scene characterised above all by repentance and forgiveness. Jesus forgives his executioners, then the "good thief" admits his guilt and turns to Jesus for forgiveness. Jesus promises him Paradise, and in full control yields his spirit into the hands of the Father. Finally the centurion gives glory to God and the crowds depart, beating their breasts in repentance.

MONDAY OF HOLY WEEK

Entrance Antiphon Cf. Ps 34:1-2;139:8

Contend, O Lord,
   with my contenders;
fight those who fight me.
Take up your buckler and shield;
arise in my defence, Lord,
   my mighty help.

Collect

Grant, we pray, almighty God,
that, though in our weakness we fail,
we may be revived through
   the Passion of your Only
   Begotten Son.
Who lives and reigns with you
   in the unity of the Holy Spirit,
one God, for ever and ever.

Ant. ad introitum

Iudica, Domine, nocentes me,
expugna impugnantes me:
apprehende arma et scutum,
et exsurge in adiutorium meum,
Domine, virtus salutis meæ.

Collecta

Da, quæsumus, omnipotens Deus,
ut, qui ex nostra
   infirmitate deficimus,
intercedente Unigeniti Filii tui
   passione, respiremus.
Qui tecum vivit et regnat
   in unitate Spiritus Sancti,
Deus, per omnia sæcula sæculorum.

FIRST READING

A reading from the prophet Isaiah   42:1-7

He does not cry out or shout aloud.

Here is my servant whom I uphold,
my chosen one in whom my soul delights.
I have endowed him with my spirit
that he may bring true justice to the nations.

He does not cry out or shout aloud,
or make his voice heard in the streets.
He does not break the crushed reed,
nor quench the wavering flame.

Faithfully he brings true justice;
he will neither waver, nor be crushed
until true justice is established on earth,
for the islands are awaiting his law.

Thus says God, the Lord,
he who created the heavens and spread them out,

who gave shape to the earth and what comes from it,
who gave breath to its people
and life to the creatures that move in it:

> I, the Lord, have called you to serve the cause of right;
> I have taken you by the hand and formed you;
> I have appointed you as covenant of the people and light of the nations,
> to open the eyes of the blind,
> to free captives from prison,
> and those who live in darkness from the dungeon.

The word of the Lord.

Responsorial Psalm   Ps 26:1-3,13-14. R. v.1

R. **The Lord is my light and my help.**

The Lord is my light and my help;
whom shall I fear?
The Lord is the stronghold of my life;
before whom shall I shrink? R.

When evil-doers draw near
to devour my flesh,
it is they, my enemies and foes,
who stumble and fall. R.

Though an army encamp against me
my heart would not fear.
Though war break out against me
even then would I trust. R.

I am sure I shall see the Lord's goodness
in the land of the living.
Hope in him, hold firm and take heart.
Hope in the Lord! R.

Gospel Acclamation

R. **Praise and honour to you, Lord Jesus!**
Hail to you, our King!
You alone have had compassion for our sins.
R. **Praise and honour to you, Lord Jesus!**

GOSPEL

A reading from the holy Gospel according to John   12:1-11

Leave her alone; she had to keep this scent for the day of my burial.

Six days before the Passover, Jesus went to Bethany, where Lazarus was, whom he had raised from the dead. They gave a dinner for him there; Martha waited on them and Lazarus was among those at table. Mary brought in a pound of very costly ointment, pure nard, and with it anointed the feet of Jesus, wiping them with her hair; the house was full of the scent of the ointment. Then Judas Iscariot – one of his disciples, the man who was to betray him – said, 'Why wasn't this ointment sold for three hundred denarii, and the money given to the poor?' He said this, not because he cared about the poor, but because he was a thief; he was in charge of the common fund and used to help himself to the contributions. So Jesus said, 'Leave her alone; she had to keep this scent for the day of my burial. You have the poor with you always, you will not always have me.'

Meanwhile a large number of Jews heard that he was there and came not only on account of Jesus but also to see Lazarus whom he had raised from the dead. Then the chief priests decided to kill Lazarus as well, since it was on his account that many of the Jews were leaving them and believing in Jesus.

The Gospel of the Lord.

Prayer over the Offerings	Super oblata
Look graciously, O Lord,	Respice, Domine, propitius sacra
upon the sacred mysteries	mysteria quæ gerimus,
we celebrate here,	et, quod ad nostra
and may what you	evacuanda præiudicia
have mercifully provided	misericors prævidisti,
to cancel the judgement we incurred	vitam nobis tribue
bear for us fruit in eternal life.	fructificare perpetuam.
Through Christ our Lord.	Per Christum Dominum nostrum.

Preface: The victory of the Passion.	Præfatio: De victoria Passionis.
It is truly right and just,	Vere dignum et iustum est,
our duty and our salvation,	æquum et salutare,
always and everywhere to give	nos tibi semper et ubique
you thanks,	gratias agere:

Lord, holy Father, almighty
and eternal God,
through Christ our Lord.
For the days of his saving Passion
and glorious Resurrection are
approaching,
by which the pride of the
ancient foe is vanquished
and the mystery of our redemption
in Christ is celebrated.
Through him the host of Angels
adores your majesty
and rejoices in your presence
for ever.
May our voices, we pray, join with
theirs in one chorus of exultant
praise, as we acclaim:
Holy, Holy, Holy
Lord God of hosts...

Domine, sancte Pater, omnipotens
æterne Deus:
per Christum Dominum nostrum.
Cuius salutiferæ passionis
et gloriosæ resurrectionis dies
appropinquare noscuntur,
quibus et de antiqui hostis
superbia triumphatur,
et nostræ redemptionis recolitur
sacramentum.
Per quem maiestatem tuam adorat
exercitus Angelorum,
ante conspectum tuum in
æternitate lætantium.
Cum quibus et nostras voces ut
admitti iubeas, deprecamur,
socia exsultatione dicentes:
Sanctus, Sanctus, Sanctus
Dominus Deus Sabaoth...

Communion Antiphon Cf. Ps 101:3

Do not hide your face from me
in the day of my distress.
Turn your ear towards me; on the day
when I call, speedily answer me.

Ant. ad communionem

Non avertas faciem tuam a me;
in quacumque die tribulor,
inclina ad me aurem tuam;
in quacumque die invocavero te,
velociter exaudi me.

Prayer after Communion

Visit your people, O Lord, we pray,
and with ever-watchful love
look upon the hearts dedicated
to you by means
of these sacred mysteries,
so that under your protection
we may keep safe this remedy
of eternal salvation,
which by your mercy
we have received.
Through Christ our Lord.

Post communionem

Visita, quæsumus, Domine,
plebem tuam,
et corda sacris dicata mysteriis
pietate tuere pervigili,
ut remedia salutis æternæ,
quæ te miserante percipit,
te protegente custodiat.
Per Christum Dominum nostrum.

Prayer over the People

for optional use

May your protection, O Lord,
    we pray,
defend the humble
and keep ever safe those who trust
    in your mercy,
that they may celebrate
    the paschal festivities
not only with bodily observance
but above all with purity of mind.
Through Christ our Lord.

Oratio super populum

Defensio tua, Domine, quæsumus,
    adsit humilibus,
et iugiter protegat in tua
    misericordia confidentes,
ut, ad festa paschalia celebranda,
non solum
    observantiam corporalem,
sed, quod est potius,
    habeant mentium puritatem.
Per Christum Dominum nostrum.

REFLECTION

✠

In the second part of the Book of Isaiah, dating from the Babylonian Exile, are four Poems of the Task of a Servant of the Lord. It is unclear whether this servant is an individual or a personification of the People of Israel, serving the Lord by witnessing to the values of God's covenant with Israel, and eventually suffering for them. They depict a servant of the Lord, wholly dedicated to the Lord, and pleasing to him, who will bring true justice to Israel and to the nations, and will suffer hideously and die in the Lord's service, and will eventually be justified. Whatever the original meaning, Christian tradition has applied these songs to Jesus and his mission. Three of these "Servant" poems are read on the first three days of Holy Week, and the fourth on Good Friday. It is most likely that Jesus himself had this task of the servant in mind when he speaks so frequently of his own task of service – "the Son of man came not to be served but to serve" (*Mk* 10:45) – or says that the first of his followers must be "last of all and servant of all" (9:35). The Voice from heaven to Jesus at the Baptism echoes the opening of the first song, "Here is my servant whom I uphold, my chosen one in whom my soul delights" (*Is* 42:1); this was the signal that his public mission should begin. So in a way these poems sum up the mission of Jesus.

There seem to have been various stories circulating in the Christian tradition about a woman paying homage to Jesus by anointing him and wiping his feet with her hair. In Mark 14:3-9 at Bethany a woman anoints his head just before the Passion, and Jesus interprets this as preparation for his burial (as he would not later be anointed for his burial). In Luke 7:36-50 a woman sheds tears of repentance on his feet and anoints them with oil at the house of Simon the Pharisee; Jesus praises her for her unbounded love. Stressing repentance contrasted with Simon's lack of courteous hospitality, this is a characteristic Lukan story. There may be some crossover between the different stories, for anointing the feet is unusual (it makes them sticky!), whereas anointing the head is more normal (the warmth then diffuses the perfume). This reaction of Jesus in putting homage to his own person before attention to the poor is unusual. Perhaps it is intended to counter the horror that is so soon to overtake him; it is certainly a useful reminder of the honour due to his person in every circumstance.

TUESDAY OF HOLY WEEK

Entrance Antiphon   Cf. Ps 26:12

Do not leave me to the will
    of my foes, O Lord,
for false witnesses rise up against me
and they breathe out violence.

Ant. ad introitum

Ne tradideris me, Domine,
in animas persequentium me:
quoniam insurrexerunt in me
    testes iniqui,
et mentita est iniquitas sibi.

Collect

Almighty ever-living God,
grant us so to celebrate
the mysteries of the Lord's Passion
that we may merit to receive
    your pardon.
Through our Lord Jesus Christ,
    your Son,
who lives and reigns with you
    in the unity of the Holy Spirit,
one God, for ever and ever.

Collecta

Omnipotens sempiterne Deus,
da nobis ita dominicæ passionis
    sacramenta peragere,
ut indulgentiam percipere mereamur.
Per Dominum nostrum Iesum
    Christum Filium tuum,
qui tecum vivit et regnat
    in unitate Spiritus Sancti,
Deus, per omnia sæcula sæculorum.

FIRST READING

A reading from the prophet Isaiah   49:1-6

I will make you the light of the nations so that my salvation may reach to the ends of the earth.

Islands, listen to me,
pay attention, remotest peoples.
The Lord called me before I was born,
from my mother's womb he pronounced my name.

He made my mouth a sharp sword,
and hid me in the shadow of his hand.
He made me into a sharpened arrow,
and concealed me in his quiver.

He said to me, 'You are my servant Israel,
in whom I shall be glorified';
while I was thinking, 'I have toiled in vain,
I have exhausted myself for nothing';

and all the while my cause was with the Lord,
my reward with my God.

I was honoured in the eyes of the Lord,
my God was my strength.

And now the Lord has spoken,
he who formed me in the womb to be his servant,
to bring Jacob back to him,
to gather Israel to him:

> 'It is not enough for you to be my servant,
> to restore the tribes of Jacob and bring back the survivors of Israel;
> I will make you the light of the nations
> so that my salvation may reach to the ends of the earth.'

The word of the Lord.

Responsorial Psalm   Ps 70:1-6,15,17. R. v.15

R. **My lips will tell of your help.**

In you, O Lord, I take refuge;
let me never be put to shame.
In your justice rescue me, free me:
pay heed to me and save me. R.

Be a rock where I can take refuge,
a mighty stronghold to save me;
for you are my rock, my stronghold.
Free me from the hand of the wicked. R.

It is you, O Lord, who are my hope,
my trust, O Lord, since my youth.
On you I have leaned from my birth,
from my mother's womb you have been my help. R.

My lips will tell of your justice
and day by day of your help
(though I can never tell it all).
O God, you have taught me from my youth
and I proclaim your wonders still. R.

Gospel Acclamation

R. **Glory and praise to you, O Christ!**
Hail to you, our King!
Obedient to the Father, you were led to your crucifixion
as a meek lamb is led to the slaughter.
R. **Glory and praise to you, O Christ!**

GOSPEL

A reading from the holy Gospel according to John   13:21-33,36-38

One of you will betray me; before the cock crows, you will have disowned me three times.

While at supper with his disciples, Jesus was troubled in spirit and declared, 'I tell you most solemnly, one of you will betray me.' The disciples looked at one another, wondering which he meant. The disciple Jesus loved was reclining next to Jesus; Simon Peter signed to him and said, 'Ask who it is he means', so leaning back on Jesus's breast he said, 'Who is it, Lord?' 'It is the one' replied Jesus 'to whom I give the piece of bread that I shall dip in the dish.' He dipped the piece of bread and gave it to Judas son of Simon Iscariot. At that instant, after Judas had taken the bread, Satan entered him. Jesus then said, 'What you are going to do, do quickly.' None of the others at table understood the reason he said this. Since Judas had charge of the common fund, some of them thought Jesus was telling him, 'Buy what we need for the festival', or telling him to give something to the poor. As soon as Judas had taken the piece of bread he went out. Night had fallen.

When he had gone Jesus said:

'Now has the Son of Man been glorified,
and in him God has been glorified.
If God has been glorified in him,
God will in turn glorify him in himself,
and will glorify him very soon.
My little children,
I shall not be with you much longer.
You will look for me,
and, as I told the Jews,
where I am going,
you cannot come.'

Simon Peter said, 'Lord, where are you going?' Jesus replied, 'Where I am going you cannot follow me now; you will follow me later.' Peter said to him, 'Why can't I follow you now? I will lay down my life for you.' 'Lay down your life for me?' answered Jesus. 'I tell you most solemnly, before the cock crows you will have disowned me three times.'

The Gospel of the Lord.

Prayer over the Offerings

Look favourably, O Lord, we pray,
on these offerings of your family,
and to those you make partakers of
    these sacred gifts
grant a share in their fullness.
Through Christ our Lord.

Super oblata

Hostias familiæ tuæ,
    quæsumus, Domine,
placatus intende,
et, quam sacris muneribus facis
    esse participem,
tribuas ad eorum
    plenitudinem pervenire.
Per Christum Dominum nostrum.

Preface II of the Passion of the Lord, pp.118-119

Communion Antiphon   Rm 8:32

God did not spare his own Son,
but handed him over for us all.

Ant. ad communionem

Proprio Filio suo
    non pepercit Deus,
sed pro nobis omnibus tradidit illum.

Prayer after Communion

Nourished by your saving gifts,
we beseech your mercy, Lord,
that by this same Sacrament,
with which you have fed us in
    the present age
you may make us partakers
    of life eternal.
Through Christ our Lord.

Post communionem

Satiati munere salutari,
tuam, Domine,
    misericordiam deprecamur,
ut, hoc eodem sacramento,
quo nos voluisti
    temporaliter vegetari,
perpetuæ vitæ facias esse participes.
Per Christum Dominum nostrum.

Prayer over the People
for optional use

May your mercy, O God,
cleanse the people that are subject
    to you
from all seduction of former ways
and make them capable
    of new holiness.
Through Christ our Lord.

Oratio super populum

Tua misericordia, Deus,
    populum tibi subditum
et ab omni subreptione
    vetustatis expurget,
et capacem sanctæ novitatis efficiat.
Per Christum Dominum nostrum.

REFLECTION

✠

In this second Song of the Servant the stress is upon the mission of the servant for the nations. Here the Servant is named "Israel" (though some think this name is an addition), and his task is not merely to bring back the survivors of Israel, but also to be the light to the nations, a phrase picked up in Simeon's canticle. These Songs find their place in the central section of Isaiah, written during the Exile at Babylon, when Israel was beginning to be aware that the vocation of Israel was to bring salvation to other nations of the world. On the other hand, the two mentions of "born from my mother's womb", "formed in the womb" do suggest that it is the song of an individual. Perhaps it is an individual representing Israel, just as Jesus is the focal point, in whom all the hopes of Israel find their realisation.

The Gospel reading jumps a little ahead, to the Last Supper. Rather than telling us the story of the Last Supper, the Gospels give us only two incidents at the Supper, the marking of the traitor and the Institution of the Eucharist. The latter is absent from John, who reserves the sacraments till after the death of Jesus and the foundation of the Church. John identifies the traitor, but the synoptic Gospels stress not his identity, but his treachery, the one who dips his hand in the dish with Jesus and immediately betrays this gesture of fellowship. In our readings we have the betrayal on Tuesday (John) and Wednesday (Matthew), while the Eucharist is reserved for Thursday.

The Church puts before us the failure of the disciples, or rather the failure of the whole body of disciples, led by Peter. Throughout Jesus' ministry this has been a theme, especially in Mark. Three times the disciples are rebuked for their failure to understand who Jesus is, each time on the Lake of Galilee, before – immediately after the gift of sight to the blind man of Bethsaida – Peter bursts out with his profession of faith, "You are the Christ/Messiah" (*Mk* 8:29). After this turning point of the Gospel, again three times they fail to grasp the teaching on suffering, that as Messiah Jesus can accomplish his mission only by suffering and death, and that his disciples must share this suffering. The theme reaches its climax with Peter's repeated protestation at the Supper that he is ready to die with Jesus, and his panicked denial when he is accosted by the diminutive servant girl outside the High Priest's house. In John at any rate we hear the story of his repentance and response to the Risen Christ's threefold challenge at the Lakeside. The prominence given to this theme is surely a reminder that the Twelve are role models for future disciples even in their failure – and in their repentance. Perfection is not required, only repentance.

WEDNESDAY OF HOLY WEEK

At the name of Jesus,
    every knee should bend,
of those in heaven and on
    the earth and under the earth,
for the Lord became obedient
    to death, death on a cross:
therefore Jesus Christ is Lord,
    to the glory of God the Father.

Ant. ad introitum

In nomine Iesu omne genu
    flectatur,
cælestium, terrestrium
    et infernorum:
quia Dominus factus est obœdiens
    usque ad mortem,
mortem autem crucis:
ideo Dominus Iesus Christus
    in gloria est Dei Patris.

Collect

O God, who willed your Son
    to submit for our sake
to the yoke of the Cross,
so that you might drive from us
    the power of the enemy,
grant us, your servants, to attain
    the grace of the resurrection.
Through our Lord Jesus Christ,
    your Son,
who lives and reigns with you
    in the unity of the Holy Spirit,
one God, for ever and ever.

Collecta

Deus, qui pro nobis Filium tuum
crucis patibulum subire voluisti,
ut inimici a nobis
    expelleres potestatem,
concede nobis famulis tuis,
ut resurrectionis
    gratiam consequamur.
Per Dominum nostrum Iesum
    Christum Filium tuum,
qui tecum vivit et regnat
    in unitate Spiritus Sancti,
Deus, per omnia sæcula sæculorum.

FIRST READING

A reading from the prophet Isaiah   50:4-9
I did not cover my face against insult and spittle.

The Lord has given me
a disciple's tongue.
So that I may know how to reply to the wearied
he provides me with speech.
Each morning he wakes me to hear,
to listen like a disciple.
The Lord has opened my ear.
For my part, I made no resistance,
neither did I turn away.

I offered my back to those who struck me,
my cheeks to those who tore at my beard;
I did not cover my face
against insult and spittle.
The Lord comes to my help
so that I am untouched by the insults.
So, too, I set my face like flint;
I know I shall not be shamed.
My vindicator is here at hand. Does anyone start proceedings against me?
Then let us go to court together.
Who thinks he has a case against me?
Let him approach me.
The Lord is coming to my help, who dare condemn me?

    The word of the Lord.

Responsorial Psalm   Ps 68:8-10,21-22,31,33-34. R. v.14

R. **In your great love, O Lord,
   answer my prayer for your favour.**

    It is for you that I suffer taunts,
    that shame covers my face,
    that I have become a stranger to my brothers,
    an alien to my own mother's sons.
    I burn with zeal for your house
    and taunts against you fall on me. R.

    Taunts have broken my heart;
    I have reached the end of my strength.
    I looked in vain for compassion,
    for consolers; not one could I find.
    For food they gave me poison;
    in my thirst they gave me vinegar to drink. R.

    I will praise God's name with a song;
    I will glorify him with thanksgiving.
    The poor when they see it will be glad
    and God-seeking hearts will revive;
    for the Lord listens to the needy
    and does not spurn his servants in their chains. R.

Gospel Acclamation

R. **Glory to you, O Christ, you are the Word of God!**
Hail to you, our King!
Obedient to the Father, you were led to your crucifixion
as a meek lamb is led to the slaughter.
R. **Glory to you, O Christ, you are the Word of God!**

Or:

R. **Glory to you, O Christ, you are the Word of God!**
Hail to you, our King!
You alone have had compassion on our sins.
R. **Glory to you, O Christ, you are the Word of God!**

GOSPEL

A reading from the holy Gospel according to Matthew   26:14-25

The Son of Man is going to his fate, as the scriptures say he will, but alas for that man by whom he is betrayed

One of the Twelve, the man called Judas Iscariot, went to the chief priests and said, 'What are you prepared to give me if I hand him over to you?' They paid him thirty silver pieces, and from that moment he looked for an opportunity to betray him.

Now on the first day of Unleavened Bread the disciples came to Jesus to say, 'Where do you want us to make the preparations for you to eat the passover?' 'Go to so-and-so in the city' he replied 'and say to him, "The Master says: My time is near. It is at your house that I am keeping Passover with my disciples."' The disciples did what Jesus told them and prepared the Passover.

When evening came he was at table with the twelve disciples. And while they were eating he said, 'I tell you solemnly, one of you is about to betray me.' They were greatly distressed and started asking him in turn, 'Not I, Lord, surely?' He answered, 'Someone who has dipped his hand into the dish with me, will betray me. The Son of Man is going to his fate, as the scriptures say he will, but alas for that man by whom the Son of Man is betrayed! Better for that man if he had never been born!' Judas, who was to betray him, asked in his turn, 'Not I, Rabbi, surely?' 'They are your own words' answered Jesus.

The Gospel of the Lord.

Prayer over the Offerings

Receive, O Lord, we pray,
    the offerings made here,
and graciously grant
that, celebrating your Son's Passion
    in mystery,
we may experience the grace
    of its effects.
Through Christ our Lord.

Super oblata

Suscipe, quæsumus, Domine,
    munus oblatum,
et dignanter operare,
ut, quod gerimus Filii
    tui mysterio passionis,
piis effectibus consequamur.
Per Christum Dominum nostrum.

Preface II of the Passion of the Lord, pp.118-119

Communion Antiphon   Mt 20:28

The Son of Man did not come
    to be served but to serve
and to give his life as a ransom
    for many.

Ant. ad communionem

Filius hominis non venit ministrari,
    sed ministrare,
et dare animam suam
    redemptionem pro multis.

Prayer after Communion

Endow us, almighty God,
    with the firm conviction
that through your Son's Death
    in time,
to which the revered mysteries
    bear witness,
we may be assured of perpetual life.
Through Christ our Lord.

Post communionem

Largire sensibus nostris,
    omnipotens Deus,
ut per temporalem Filii tui mortem,
quam mysteria veneranda testantur,
vitam te nobis dedisse
    perpetuam confidamus.
Per Christum Dominum nostrum.

Prayer over the People
for optional use

Grant your faithful, O Lord, we pray,
to partake unceasingly
    of the paschal mysteries
and to await with longing the gifts
    to come,
that, persevering in the Sacraments
    of their rebirth,
they may be led by Lenten works
    to newness of life.
Through Christ our Lord.

Oratio super populum

Da, quæsumus, Domine,
    fidelibus tuis
et sine cessatione capere
    paschalia sacramenta,
et desideranter exspectare
    dona ventura,
ut, mysteriis quibus renati
    sunt permanentes,
ad novam vitam his
    operibus perducantur.
Per Christum Dominum nostrum.

REFLECTION

✠

The day before Maundy Thursday is often unofficially known as "Spy Wednesday" to give it special status as the day on which we hear the Gospel readings about the treacherous arrangements between Judas and the chief priests. Speculations about Judas and studies of his character have been endless. At one end it has been suggested that the financial motive, and indeed all evil intention, was a later addition, and that he was originally merely "the one who handed Jesus over", not the traitor; he merely arranged a meeting with the authorities so that Jesus and the chief priests could sort things out, and that when this went horribly wrong Judas despaired at the catastrophe and so committed suicide. At the other end Judas is simply the symbol of all evil, lacking any redeeming feature. Between these extremes are such strange theories as that of the recently rediscovered ancient manuscript, *The Gospel of Judas*, according to which Jesus is grateful to Judas for enabling him to fulfil his purpose.

In today's Gospel reading financial greed is paramount, and perhaps also disappointment or contempt, for thirty silver pieces is the price of a slave in Exodus 21:32. In recounting the death of Judas, Matthew 27:5 concentrates on the thought of the betrayal of a friend, for the only suicide in the Hebrew Bible is that of Ahitophel, the counsellor of King David, who betrayed his master, and then committed suicide when his advice to the rebellious Solomon was disregarded; he also hanged himself (*2 S* 17:23). In any case, it is perhaps useful to regard Spy Wednesday as the day of evil, the day when evil temporarily prevails. In sketching his own struggle against evil (or perhaps the struggle of humanity as a whole against evil) Paul writes:

> I do not do what I want to do, but I do the thing that I hate, for while it is open to me to want to do good, the power to do it is not; for the good thing I want to do, I do not do; the evil thing which I do not want – that is what I accomplish. But if I do what I do not want to, then it is not myself acting, but the sin that lives in me. So I find this law for myself, that when I want to do good, evil opens up to me. In my inmost self I delight in God's law, but I find another law in my body battling against the law of my mind and taking me prisoner to the law of sin which lives in my body (*Rm* 7:15-22).

We all know the moment at which we give in to evil: "The baby is crying – let it cry" or "No one will notice that the DVD is missing" or more simply, "I don't care whether it is right or wrong; that is what I am going to do." It might be that Spy Wednesday could function as the symbol of that motivation in ourselves, the very opposite of the love and generosity of Christ which we are to celebrate and commemorate in the three days of Easter.

THURSDAY OF HOLY WEEK

The Chrism Mass

The blessing of the Oil of the Sick and of the Oil of Catechumens and the consecration of the Chrism are carried out by the Bishop, according to the Rite described in the Roman Pontifical, usually on this day, at a proper Mass to be celebrated during the morning.

If, however, it is very difficult for the clergy and the people to gather with the Bishop on this day, the Chrism Mass may be anticipated on another day, but near to Easter.

This Mass, which the Bishop concelebrates with his presbyterate, should be, as it were, a manifestation of the Priests' communion with their Bishop. Accordingly it is desirable that all the Priests participate in it, insofar as is possible, and during it receive Communion even under both kinds. To signify the unity of the presbyterate of the diocese, the Priests who concelebrate with the Bishop should be from different regions of the diocese.

In accord with traditional practice, the blessing of the Oil of the Sick takes place before the end of the Eucharistic Prayer, but the blessing of the Oil of Catechumens and the consecration of the Chrism take place after Communion. Nevertheless, for pastoral reasons, it is permitted for the entire rite of blessing to take place after the Liturgy of the Word.

Entrance Antiphon Rv 1:6	Ant. ad introitum
JESUS Christ has made us into a kingdom, priests for his God and Father. To him be glory and power for ever and ever. Amen.	IESUS Christus fecit nos regnum et sacerdotes Deo et Patri suo: ipsi gloria et imperium in sæcula sæculorum. Amen.

The Gloria in excelsis (Glory to God in the highest) is said.

Collect	Collecta
O God, who anointed your Only Begotten Son with the Holy Spirit and made him Christ and Lord, graciously grant that, being made sharers in his consecration, we may bear witness to your Redemption in the world.	Deus, qui Unigenitum Filium tuum unxisti Spiritu Sancto Christumque Dominum constituisti, concede propitius, ut, eiusdem consecrationis participes effecti, testes Redemptionis inveniamur in mundo.

Through our Lord Jesus Christ, your Son, who lives and reigns with you in the unity of the Holy Spirit, one God, for ever and ever.	Per Dominum nostrum Iesum Christum Filium tuum, qui tecum vivit et regnat in unitate Spiritus Sancti, Deus, per omnia sæcula sæculorum.

FIRST READING

A reading from the prophet Isaiah   61:1-3,6,8-9

The Lord has anointed me and has sent me to bring Good News to the poor, to give them the oil of gladness.

The spirit of the Lord has been given to me,
for the Lord has anointed me.
He has sent me to bring good news to the poor,
to bind up hearts that are broken;

to proclaim liberty to captives,
freedom to those in prison;
to proclaim a year of favour from the Lord,
a day of vengeance for our God;

to comfort all those who mourn and to give them
for ashes a garland;
for mourning robe the oil of gladness,
for despondency, praise.

But you, you will be named 'priests of the Lord',
they will call you 'ministers of our God'.
I reward them faithfully
and make an everlasting covenant with them.

Their race will be famous throughout the nations,
their descendants throughout the peoples.
All who see them will admit
that they are a race whom the Lord has blessed.

    The word of the Lord.

Responsorial Psalm   Ps 88:21-22,25,27. R. v.2

R. **I will sing for ever of your love, O Lord.**

    I have found David my servant
    and with my holy oil anointed him.
    My hand shall always be with him
    and my arm shall make him strong. R.

My truth and my love shall be with him;
> by my name his might shall be exalted.
> He will say to me: 'You are my father,
> my God, the rock who saves me.' R.

SECOND READING

A reading from the book of the Apocalypse   1:5-8

He made us a line of kings, priests to serve his God and Father.

Grace and peace to you from Jesus Christ, the faithful witness, the First-born from the dead, the Ruler of the kings of the earth. He loves us and has washed away our sins with his blood, and made us a line of kings, priests to serve his God and Father; to him, then, be glory and power for ever and ever. Amen. It is he who is coming on the clouds; everyone will see him, even those who pierced him, and all the races of the earth will mourn over him. This is the truth. Amen. 'I am the Alpha and the Omega' says the Lord God, who is, who was, and who is to come, the Almighty.

> The word of the Lord

Gospel Acclamation   Is 61:1 (Lk 4:18)

R. **Praise to you, O Christ, King of eternal glory!**
The spirit of the Lord has been given to me;
he sent me to bring the good news to the poor.
R. **Praise to you, O Christ, King of eternal glory!**

GOSPEL

A reading from the holy Gospel according to Luke   4:16-21

The spirit of the Lord has been given to me, for he has anointed me.

Jesus came to Nazara, where he had been brought up, and went into the synagogue on the sabbath day as he usually did. He stood up to read, and they handed him the scroll of the prophet Isaiah. Unrolling the scroll he found the place where it is written:

> The spirit of the Lord has been given to me,
> for he has anointed me.
> He has sent me to bring the good news to the poor,
> to proclaim liberty to captives
> and to the blind new sight,
> to set the downtrodden free,
> to proclaim the Lord's year of favour.

He then rolled up the scroll, gave it back to the assistant and sat down.

And all eyes in the synagogue were fixed on him. Then he began to speak to them, 'This text is being fulfilled today even as you listen.'

The Gospel of the Lord.

Renewal of Priestly Promises

Beloved sons,
on the anniversary of that day
when Christ our Lord conferred
    his priesthood
on his Apostles and on us,
are you resolved to renew,
in the presence of your Bishop
    and God's holy people, the
    promises you once made?

Priests, all together, respond: **I am.**

Are you resolved to be more united
    with the Lord Jesus
and more closely conformed to him,
denying yourselves and confirming
    those promises
about sacred duties towards
    Christ's Church
which, prompted by love of him,
you willingly and joyfully pledged
on the day of your
    priestly ordination?

Priests: **I am.**

Are you resolved to be faithful
    stewards of the mysteries of God
in the Holy Eucharist and the other
    liturgical rites
and to discharge faithfully

Filii carissimi,
    annua redeunte memoria diei,
qua Christus Dominus sacerdotium
    suum cum Apostolis
    nobisque communicavit,
vultis olim factas promissiones
    coram Episcopo vestro
et populo sancto Dei renovare?

Presbyteri: Volo.

Vultis Domino Iesu arctius
    coniungi et conformari,
vobismetipsis abrenuntiantes atque
    promissa confirmantes sacrorum
    officiorum,
quæ, Christi amore inducti, erga
    eius Ecclesiam,
sacerdotalis vestræ ordinationis die,
    cum gaudio suscepistis?

Presbyteri: Volo.

Vultis fideles esse dispensatores
    mysteriorum Dei
per sanctam Eucharistiam
    ceterasque liturgicas actiones,
    atque sacrum docendi munus,

the sacred office of teaching,
following Christ the Head
and Shepherd,
not seeking any gain,
but moved only by zeal for souls?
Priests: **I am.**

Then the Bishop addresses the people:

As for you, dearest sons
and daughters,
pray for your Priests,
that the Lord may pour out his gifts
abundantly upon them,
and keep them faithful as ministers
of Christ, the High Priest,
so that they may lead you to him,
who is the source of salvation.
People: **Christ, hear us.
Christ, graciously hear us.**

And pray also for me,
that I may be faithful
to the apostolic office
entrusted to me in my lowliness
and that in your midst I may be
made day by day
a living and more perfect image
of Christ,
the Priest, the Good Shepherd,
the Teacher and the Servant of all.
People: **Christ, hear us.
Christ, graciously hear us.**

May the Lord keep us all
in his charity
and lead all of us,
shepherds and flock,
to eternal life.
All: Amen.

Christum Caput atque
Pastorem sectando,
fideliter implere,
non bonorum cupidi,
sed animarum zelo tantum inducti?
Presbyteri: Volo.

Vos autem, filii dilectissimi,
pro presbyteris vestris orate,
ut Dominus super eos bona sua
abundanter effundat,
quatenus fideles ministri Christi,
Summi Sacerdotis,
vos ad eum perducant,
qui fons est salutis.
Populus: **Christe, audi nos.
Christe, exaudi nos.**

Et pro me etiam orate:
ut fidelis sim muneri apostolico
humilitati meæ commisso,
et inter vos efficiar viva
et perfectior in dies imago
Christi Sacerdotis,
Boni Pastoris,
Magistri et omnium Servi.
Populus: **Christe, audi nos.
Christe, exaudi nos.**

Dominus nos omnes
in sua caritate custodiat,
et ipse nos universos,
pastores et oves,
ad vitam perducat æternam.
Omnes: Amen.

The Creed is not said.

Prayer over the Offerings

May the power of this sacrifice,
  O Lord, we pray,
mercifully wipe away what is old in us
and increase in us grace
  of salvation and newness of life.
Through Christ our Lord.

Preface: The Priesthood of Christ
and the Ministry of Priests.

It is truly right and just,
  our duty and our salvation,
always and everywhere
  to give you thanks,
Lord, holy Father,
  almighty and eternal God.

For by the anointing
  of the Holy Spirit
you made your Only Begotten Son
High Priest of the new
  and eternal covenant,
and by your wondrous design
  were pleased to decree
that his one Priesthood should
  continue in the Church.

For Christ not only adorns
  with a royal priesthood
the people he has made his own,
but with a brother's kindness
  he also chooses men
to become sharers
  in his sacred ministry
through the laying on of hands.

They are to renew in his name
the sacrifice of human redemption,
to set before your children
  the paschal banquet,
to lead your holy people in charity,
to nourish them with the word

Super oblata

Huius sacrificii potentia,
Domine, quæsumus,
et vetustatem nostram
  clementer abstergat,
et novitatem nobis augeat et salutem.
Per Christum Dominum nostrum.

Præfatio: De sacerdotio Christi
et de ministerio sacerdotum.

Vere dignum et iustum est,
  æquum et salutare,
nos tibi semper et ubique
  gratias agere:
Domine, sancte Pater,
  omnipotens æterne Deus:

Qui Unigentitum tuum
  Sancti Spiritus unctione
novi et æterni testamenti
  constituisti Pontificem,
et ineffabili dignatus es
  dispositione sancire,
ut unicum eius sacerdotium in
  Ecclesia servaretur.

Ipse enim non solum
  regali sacerdotio
populum acquisitionis exornat,
sed etiam fraterna homines
  eligit bonitate,
ut sacri sui ministerii fiant
  manuum impositione participes.

Qui sacrificium renovent,
  eius nomine,
redemptionis humanæ,
tuis apparantes filiis
  paschale convivium,
et plebem tuam sanctam
  caritate præveniant,
verbo nutriant, reficiant sacramentis.

and strengthen them
   with the Sacraments.

As they give up their lives for you
and for the salvation of their
   brothers and sisters,
they strive to be conformed
   to the image of Christ himself
and offer you a constant witness
   of faith and love.

And so, Lord,
   with all the Angels and Saints,
we, too, give you thanks,
   as in exultation we acclaim:
**Holy, Holy, Holy
   Lord God of hosts...**

Qui, vitam pro te fratrumque
   salute tradentes,
ad ipsius Christi nitantur
   imaginem conformari,
et constantes tibi fidem
   amoremque testentur.

Unde et nos, Domine, cum Angelis
   et Sanctis universis
tibi confitemur,
   in exsultatione dicentes:
**Sanctus, Sanctus, Sanctus
   Dominus Deus Sabaoth...**

Communion Antiphon   Ps 88:2

I will sing for ever of your mercies,
   O Lord;
through all ages my mouth will
   proclaim your fidelity.

Ant. ad communionem

Misericordias Domini
   in æternum cantabo;
in generationem et generationem
annuntiabo veritatem tuam
   in ore meo.

Prayer after Communion

We beseech you, almighty God,
that those you renew by
   your Sacraments
may merit to become the
   pleasing fragrance of Christ.
Who lives and reigns
   for ever and ever.

Post communionem

Supplices te rogamus,
   omnipotens Deus,
ut, quos tuis reficis sacramentis,
Christi bonus odor
   effici mereantur.
Qui vivit et regnat in
   sæcula sæculorum.

The reception of the Holy Oils may take place in individual parishes either before
the celebration of the Evening Mass of the Lord's Supper or at another time that
seems more appropriate.

THE SACRED PASCHAL TRIDUUM

(YEAR A,B,C)

In the Sacred Triduum, the Church solemnly celebrates the greatest mysteries of our redemption, keeping by means of special celebrations the memorial of her Lord, crucified, buried, and risen.

The Paschal Fast should also be kept sacred. It is to be celebrated everywhere on the Friday of the Lord's Passion and, where appropriate, prolonged also through Holy Saturday as a way of coming, with spirit uplifted, to the joys of the Lord's Resurrection.

For a fitting celebration of the Sacred Triduum, a sufficient number of lay ministers is required, who must be carefully instructed as to what they are to do.

The singing of the people, the ministers, and the Priest Celebrant has a special importance in the celebrations of these days, for when texts are sung, they have their proper impact.

Pastors should, therefore, not fail to explain to the Christian faithful, as best they can, the meaning and order of the celebrations and to prepare them for active and fruitful participation.

The celebrations of the Sacred Triduum are to be carried out in cathedral and parochial churches and only in those churches in which they can be performed with dignity, that is, with a good attendance of the faithful, an appropriate number of ministers, and the means to sing at least some of the parts.

Consequently, it is desirable that small communities, associations, and special groups of various kinds join together in these churches to carry out the sacred celebrations in a more noble manner.

THURSDAY OF THE LORD'S SUPPER

(MAUNDY THURSDAY)

If we listen attentively to the Gospel, we can discern two different dimensions in the event of the washing of the feet. The cleansing that Jesus offers his disciples is first and foremost simply his action – the gift of purity, of the "capacity for God" that is offered to them. But the gift then becomes a model, the duty to do the same for one another. The gift and example overall, which we find in the passage on the washing of the feet, is a characteristic of the nature of Christianity in general. Christianity is not a type of moralism, simply a system of ethics. It does not originate in our action, our moral capacity. Christianity is first and foremost a gift: God gives himself to us – he does not give something, but himself. And this does not only happen at the beginning, at the moment of our conversion. He constantly remains the One who gives.

He continually offers us his gifts. He always precedes us. This is why the central act of Christian being is the Eucharist: gratitude for having been gratified, joy for the new life that he gives us.

(Pope Benedict XVI)

In accordance with a most ancient tradition of the Church, on this day all Masses without the people are forbidden.

At the Evening Mass

The Mass of the Lord's Supper is celebrated in the evening, at a convenient time, with the full participation of the whole local community and with all the Priests and ministers exercising their office.

All Priests may concelebrate even if they have already concelebrated the Chrism Mass on this day, or if they have to celebrate another Mass for the good of the Christian faithful.

Where a pastoral reason requires it, the local Ordinary may permit another Mass to be celebrated in churches and oratories in the evening and, in case of genuine necessity, even in the morning, but only for the faithful who are in no way able to participate in the evening Mass. Care should, nevertheless, be taken that celebrations of this sort do not take place for the advantage of private persons or special small groups, and do not prejudice the evening Mass.

Holy Communion may only be distributed to the faithful during Mass; but it may be brought to the sick at any hour of the day.

The altar may be decorated with flowers with a moderation that accords with the character of this day. The tabernacle should be entirely empty; but a sufficient amount of bread should be consecrated in this Mass for the Communion of the clergy and the people on this and the following day.

Entrance Antiphon Cf. Ga 6:14	Ant. ad introitum
WE should glory in the Cross of our Lord Jesus Christ, in whom is our salvation, life and resurrection, through whom we are saved and delivered.	NOS autem gloriari oportet in cruce Domini nostri Iesu Christi, in quo est salus, vita et resurrectio nostra, per quem salvati et liberati sumus.

The **Gloria in excelsis** (Glory to God in the highest) is said. While the hymn is being sung, bells are rung, and when it is finished, they remain silent until the **Gloria in excelsis** of the Easter Vigil, unless, if appropriate, the Diocesan Bishop has decided otherwise. Likewise, during this same period, the organ and other musical instruments may be used only so as to support the singing.

Collect

O God, who have called us
    to participate
in this most sacred Supper,
in which your Only Begotten Son,
when about to hand himself over
    to death,
entrusted to the Church a sacrifice
    new for all eternity,
the banquet of his love,
grant, we pray,
that we may draw from so great
    a mystery,
the fullness of charity and of life.
Through our Lord Jesus Christ,
    your Son,
who lives and reigns with you
    in the unity of the Holy Spirit,
one God, for ever and ever.

Collecta

Sacratissimam, Deus,
    frequentantibus Cenam,
in qua Unigenitus tuus,
    morti se traditurus,
novum in sæcula sacrificium
dilectionisque suæ convivium
    Ecclesiæ commendavit,
da nobis, quæsumus,
    ut ex tanto mysterio
plenitudinem caritatis hauriamus
    et vitæ.
Per Dominum nostrum Iesum
    Christum Filium tuum,
qui tecum vivit et regnat
    in unitate Spiritus Sancti,
Deus, per omnia sæcula sæculorum.

FIRST READING

A reading from the book of Exodus   12:1-8,11-14

Instructions concerning the Passover meal.

The Lord said to Moses and Aaron in the land of Egypt, 'This month is to be
the first of all the others for you, the first month of your year. Speak to the
whole community of Israel and say, "On the tenth day of this month each
man must take an animal from the flock, one for each family: one animal
for each household. If the household is too small to eat the animal, a man
must join with his neighbour, the nearest to his house, as the number of
persons requires. You must take into account what each can eat in deciding
the number for the animal. It must be an animal without blemish, a male
one year old; you may take it from either sheep or goats. You must keep
it till the fourteenth day of the month when the whole assembly of the
community of Israel shall slaughter it between the two evenings. Some of
the blood must then be taken and put on the two doorposts and the lintel
of the houses where it is eaten. That night, the flesh is to be eaten, roasted
over the fire; it must be eaten with unleavened bread and bitter herbs. You
shall eat it like this: with a girdle round your waist, sandals on your feet, a
staff in your hand. You shall eat it hastily; it is a passover in honour of the

Lord. That night, I will go through the land of Egypt and strike down all the first-born in the land of Egypt, man and beast alike, and I shall deal out punishment to all the gods of Egypt, I am the Lord. The blood shall serve to mark the houses that you live in. When I see the blood I will pass over you and you shall escape the destroying plague when I strike the land of Egypt. This day is to be a day of remembrance for you, and you must celebrate it as a feast in the Lord's honour. For all generations you are to declare it a day of festival, for ever."'

The word of the Lord.

Responsorial Psalm   Ps 115:12-13,15-18. R. Cf. 1 Co 10:16

R. **The blessing-cup that we bless**
   is a communion with the blood of Christ.

How can I repay the Lord
for his goodness to me?
The cup of salvation I will raise;
I will call on the Lord's name. R.

O precious in the eyes of the Lord
is the death of his faithful.
Your servant, Lord, your servant am I;
you have loosened my bonds. R.

A thanksgiving sacrifice I make:
I will call on the Lord's name.
My vows to the Lord I will fulfil
before all his people. R.

SECOND READING

A reading from the first letter of St Paul to the Corinthians   11:23-26

Every time you eat this bread and drink this cup, you are proclaiming the death of the Lord.

This is what I received from the Lord, and in turn passed on to you: that on the same night that he was betrayed, the Lord Jesus took some bread, and thanked God for it and broke it, and he said, 'This is my body, which is for you; do this as a memorial of me.' In the same way he took the cup after supper, and said,'This cup is the new covenant in my blood. Whenever you drink it, do this as a memorial of me.' Until the Lord comes, therefore, every time you eat this bread and drink this cup, you are proclaiming his death.

The word of the Lord.

Gospel Acclamation   Jn 13:34

R. **Praise and honour to you, Lord Jesus!**
I give you a new commandment:
love one another just as I have loved you, says the Lord.
R. **Praise and honour to you, Lord Jesus!**

GOSPEL

A reading from the holy Gospel according to John   13:1-15

Now he showed how perfect his love was.

It was before the festival of the Passover, and Jesus knew that the hour had come for him to pass from this world to the Father. He had always loved those who were his in the world, but now he showed how perfect his love was.

They were at supper, and the devil had already put it into the mind of Judas Iscariot son of Simon, to betray him. Jesus knew that the Father had put everything into his hands, and that he had come from God and was returning to God, and he got up from table, removed his outer garment and, taking a towel, wrapped it round his waist; he then poured water into a basin and began to wash the disciples' feet and to wipe them with the towel he was wearing.

He came to Simon Peter, who said to him, 'Lord, are you going to wash my feet?' Jesus answered, 'At the moment you do not know what I am doing, but later you will understand.' 'Never!' said Peter 'You shall never wash my feet.' Jesus replied, 'If I do not wash you, you can have nothing in common with me.' 'Then, Lord,' said Simon Peter 'not only my feet, but my hands and my head as well!' Jesus said, 'No one who has taken a bath needs washing, he is clean all over. You too are clean, though not all of you are.' He knew who was going to betray him, that was why he said, 'though not all of you are.'

When he had washed their feet and put on his clothes again he went back to the table. 'Do you understand' he said 'what I have done to you? You call me Master and Lord, and rightly; so I am. If I, then, the Lord and Master, have washed your feet, you should wash each other's feet. I have given you an example so that you may copy what I have done to you.'

The Gospel of the Lord.

After the proclamation of the Gospel, the Priest gives a homily in which light is shed on the principal mysteries that are commemorated in this Mass, namely, the institution of the Holy Eucharist and of the priestly Order, and the commandment of the Lord concerning fraternal charity.

The Washing of Feet

After the Homily, where a pastoral reason suggests it, the Washing of Feet follows. Those who have been chosen are led by the ministers to seats prepared in a suitable place. Then the Priest (removing his chasuble if necessary) goes to each one, and, with the help of the ministers, pours water over each one's feet and then dries them.

Meanwhile some of the following antiphons or other appropriate chants are sung.

Antiphon 1   Cf. Jn 13:4,5,15

After the Lord had risen from supper,
he poured water into a basin
and began to wash the feet
    of his disciples:
he left them this example.

Antiphona 1

Postquam surrexit Dominus a cena,
misit aquam in pelvim,
et cœpit lavare
    pedes discipulorum:
hoc exemplum reliquit eis.

Antiphon 2   Cf. Jn 13:12,13,15

The Lord Jesus,
    after eating supper
    with his disciples,
washed their feet and said to them:
Do you know what I, your Lord
    and Master, have done for you?
I have given you an example,
    that you should do likewise.

Antiphona 2

Dominus Iesus, postquam cenavit
    cum discipulis suis,
lavit pedes eorum, et ait illis:
'Scitis quid fecerim vobis ego,
    Dominus et Magister?
Exemplum dedi vobis,
    ut et vos ita faciatis.'

Antiphon 3   Jn 13:6,7,8

Lord, are you to wash my feet?
    Jesus said to him in answer:
If I do not wash your feet,
    you will have no share with me.
V. So he came to Simon Peter
    and Peter said to him:
– Lord, are you to wash my feet?...
V. What I am doing,
    you do not know for now,
    but later you will come to know.
– Lord, are you to wash my feet?...

Antiphona 3

Domine, tu mihi lavas pedes?
    Respondit Iesus et dixit ei:
Se non lavero tibi pedes,
    non habebis partem mecum.
V. Venit ergo ad Simonem Petrum,
    et dixit ei Petrus:
– Domine, tu mihi lavas pedes?...
V. Quod ego facio,
    tu nescis modo:
    scies autem postea.
– Domine, tu mihi lavas pedes?...

Antiphon 4 Cf. Jn 13:14	Antiphona 4

If I, your Lord and Master,
   have washed your feet,
how much more should you wash
   each other's feet?
	Si ego, Dominus et Magister vester,
	   lavi vobis pedes:
	quanto magis debetis alter alterius
	   lavare pedes?

Antiphon 5 Jn 13:35	Antiphona 5

This is how all will know that you
   are my disciples:
if you have love for one another.
 	
V. Jesus said to his disciples:
– This is how all will know...
	In hoc cognoscent omnes,
	   quia discipuli mei estis,
	si dilectionem habueritis
	   ad invicem.
	
	V. Dixit Iesus discipulis suis.
	– In hoc cognoscent omnes...

Antiphon 6 Jn 13:34	Antiphona 6

I give you a new commandment, that you love one another as I have loved you, says the Lord.	Mandatum novum do vobis, ut diligatis invicem, sicut dilexi vos, dicit Dominus.

Antiphon 7 1 Co 13:13	Antiphona 7

Let faith, hope and charity,
   these three, remain among you,
but the greatest of these is charity.
 	
V. Now faith, hope and charity,
   these three, remain;
but the greatest of these is charity.
– Let faith, hope and charity...
	Maneant in vobis fides, spes,
	   caritas, tria hæc:
	maior autem horum est caritas.
	
	V. Nunc autem manent fides, spes,
	   caritas, tria hæc:
	maior horum est caritas.
	– Maneant in vobis fides...

After the Washing of Feet, the Priest washes and dries his hands, puts the chasuble back on, and returns to the chair, and from there he directs the Universal Prayer.

The Creed is not said.

The Liturgy of the Eucharist

At the beginning of the Liturgy of the Eucharist, there may be a procession of the faithful in which gifts for the poor may be presented with the bread and wine.

Meanwhile the following, or another appropriate chant, is sung.

Ant. Where true charity is dwelling,
       God is present there.
V. By the love of Christ we have
       been brought together:
V. let us find in him our gladness
       and our pleasure;
V. may we love him and revere him,
       God the living,
V. and in love respect each other
       with sincere hearts.

Ant. Where true charity is dwelling,
       God is present there.
V. So when we as one are gathered
       all together,
V. let us strive to keep our minds
       free of division;
V. may there be an end to malice,
       strife and quarrels,
V. and let Christ our God
       be dwelling here among us.

Ant. Where true charity is dwelling,
       God is present there.
V. May your face thus be our vision,
       bright in glory,
V. Christ our God, with all
       the blessed Saints in heaven:
V. such delight is pure and faultless,
       joy unbounded,
V. which endures through
       countless ages
       world without end. Amen.

Ant. Ubi caritas est vera,
       Deus ibi est.
V. Congregavit nos in unum
       Christi amor.
V. Exsultemus et in
       ipso iucundemur.
V. Timeamus et amemus
       Deum vivum.
V. Et ex corde diligamus
       nos sincero

Ant. Ubi caritas est vera,
       Deus ibi est.
V. Simul ergo cum in
       unum congregamur:
V. Ne nos mente dividamur,
       caveamus.
V. Cessent iurgia maligna,
       cessent lites.
V. Et in medio nostri sit
       Christus Deus.

Ant. Ubi caritas est vera,
       Deus ibi est.
V. Simul quoque cum beatis
       videamus
V. Glorianter vultum tuum,
       Christe Deus:
V. Gaudium, quod est immensum
       atque probum,
V. Sæcula per infinita sæculorum.
       Amen.

Prayer over the Offerings

Grant us, O Lord, we pray,
that we may participate worthily
   in these mysteries,
for whenever the memorial
   of this sacrifice is celebrated
the work of our redemption
   is accomplished.
Through Christ our Lord.

Preface: The Sacrifice and the
Sacrament of Christ.

It is truly right and just,
   our duty and our salvation,
always and everywhere to give
   you thanks,
Lord, holy Father, almighty
   and eternal God,
through Christ our Lord.

For he is the true and eternal Priest,
who instituted the pattern of
   an everlasting sacrifice,
and was the first to offer himself
   as the saving Victim,
commanding us to make this
   offering as his memorial.
As we eat his flesh that was
   sacrificed for us,
we are made strong,
and, as we drink his Blood that was
   poured out for us,
we are washed clean.

And so, with Angels and Archangels,
with Thrones and Dominions,
and with all the hosts and Powers
   of heaven,
we sing the hymn of your glory,
as without end we acclaim:
Holy, Holy, Holy
   Lord God of hosts...

Super oblata

Concede nobis, quæsumus,
   Domine,
hæc digne frequentare mysteria,
quia, quoties huius hostiæ
   commemoratio celebratur,
opus nostræ redemptionis exercetur.
Per Christum Dominum nostrum.

Præfatio: De sacrificia ex de
sacramento Christi.

Vere dignum et iustum est,
   æquum et salutare,
nos tibi semper et ubique
   gratias agere:
Domine, sancte Pater, omnipotens
   æterne Deus:
per Christum Dominum nostrum.

Qui, verus æternusque Sacerdos,
formam sacrificii perennis
   instituens,
hostiam tibi se primus obtulit
   salutarem,
et nos, in sui memoriam,
   præcepit offerre.
Cuius carnem pro nobis
   immolatam
dum sumimus, roboramur,
et fusum pro nobis sanguinem
   dum potamus, abluimur.

Et ideo cum Angelis et Archangelis,
cum Thronis et Dominationibus,
cumque omni militia cælestis
   exercitus,
hymnum gloriæ tuæ canimus,
sine fine dicentes:
Sanctus, Sanctus, Sanctus
   Dominus Deus Sabaoth...

If the Roman Canon is said, the following special forms are used.

Celebrating the most sacred day
on which our Lord Jesus Christ
was handed over for our sake,
and in communion with those
    whose memory we venerate,
especially the glorious
    ever-Virgin Mary,
Mother of our God and Lord,
    Jesus Christ,
and blessed Joseph, her Spouse,
your blessed Apostles and Martyrs,
Peter and Paul, Andrew,
(James, John,
Thomas, James, Philip,
Bartholomew, Matthew,
Simon and Jude;
Linus, Cletus, Clement, Sixtus,
Cornelius, Cyprian,
Lawrence, Chrysogonus,
John and Paul,
Cosmas and Damian)
and all your Saints;
we ask that through their merits
    and prayers,
in all things we may be defended
by your protecting help.
(Through Christ our Lord. Amen.)

Communicantes, et diem
    sacratissimum celebrantes,
quo Dominus noster Iesus Christus
pro nobis est traditus,
sed et memoriam venerantes,
in primis gloriosæ semper
    Virginis Mariæ,
Genetricis eiusdem Dei et Domini
    nostri Iesu Christi:
sed et beati Ioseph,
    eiusdem Virginis Sponsi,
et beatorum Apostolorum ac
    Martyrum tuorum,
Petri et Pauli, Andreæ,
(Iacobi, Ioannis,
Thomæ, Iacobi, Philippi,
Bartholomæi, Matthæi,
Simonis et Thaddæi:
Lini, Cleti, Clementis, Xysti,
Cornelii, Cypriani,
Laurentii, Chrysogoni,
Ioannis et Pauli,
Cosmæ et Damiani)
et omnium Sanctorum tuorum;
quorum meritis precibusque
    concedas,
ut in omnibus protectionis tuæ
    muniamur auxilio.
(Per Christum Dominum nostrum.
    Amen.)

Therefore, Lord, we pray:
graciously accept this oblation of
    our service,
that of your whole family,
which we make to you
as we observe the day
on which our Lord Jesus Christ

Hanc igitur oblationem
    servitutis nostræ,
sed et cunctæ familiæ tuæ,
quam tibi offerimus ob diem,
in qua Dominus noster Iesus Christus
tradidit discipulis suis
Corporis et Sanguinis

handed on the mysteries
   of his Body and Blood
for his disciples to celebrate;
order our days in your peace,
and command that we be delivered
   from eternal damnation
and counted among the flock of
   those you have chosen.
(Through Christ our Lord. Amen.)

sui mysteria celebranda,
quæsumus, Domine,
   ut placatus accipias:
diesque nostros in tua pace disponas,
atque ab æterna damnatione
   nos eripi
et in electorum tuorum iubeas
   grege numerari.
(Per Christum Dominum nostrum.
   Amen.)

Be pleased, O God, we pray,
to bless, acknowledge,
and approve this offering
   in every respect;
make it spiritual and acceptable,
so that it may become for us
the Body and Blood of your most
   beloved Son,
our Lord Jesus Christ.

Quam oblationem tu, Deus,
   in omnibus, quæsumus,
benedictam, adscriptam, ratam,
rationabilem, acceptabilemque
   facere digneris:
ut nobis Corpus et Sanguis fiat
   dilectissimi Filii tui,
Domini nostri Iesu Christi.

On the day before he was to suffer
for our salvation and the salvation
   of all,
that is today,
he took bread in his holy
   and venerable hands,
and with eyes raised to heaven
to you, O God, his almighty Father,
giving you thanks,
   he said the blessing,
broke the bread
and gave it to his disciples, saying:

Qui, pridie quam pro nostra
omniumque salute pateretur,
hoc est hodie,
accepit panem in sanctus ac
   venerabiles manus suas,
et elevatis oculis in cælum
ad te Deum Patrem suum
   omnipotentem,
tibi gratias agens benedixit,
fregit, deditque discipulis suis,
   dicens:

TAKE THIS, ALL OF YOU,
   AND EAT OF IT,
FOR THIS IS MY BODY,
WHICH WILL BE GIVEN UP FOR YOU.

ACCIPITE ET MANDUCATE
   EX HOC OMNES:
HOC EST ENIM CORPUS MEUM,
QUOD PRO VOBIS TRADETUR.

Then follows the remainder of the Roman Canon as usual (see pp.40-45) and the Communion Rite, pp.62ff.

At an appropriate moment during Communion, the Priest entrusts the Eucharist from the table of the altar to Deacons or acolytes or other extraordinary ministers, so that afterwards it may be brought to the sick who are to receive Holy Communion at home.

Communion Antiphon 1 Co 11:24-25	Ant. ad communionem
This is the Body that will be given up for you; this is the Chalice of the new covenant in my Blood, says the Lord; do this, whenever you receive it, in memory of me.	Hoc Corpus, quod pro vobis tradetur: hic calix novi testamenti est in meo Sanguine, dicit Dominus; hoc facite, quotiescumque sumitis, in meam commemorationem.

After the distribution of Communion, the ciborium with hosts for Communion on the following day is left on the altar. The Priest, standing at the chair, says the Prayer after Communion.

Prayer after Communion	Post communionem
Grant, almighty God, that, just as we are renewed by the Supper of your Son in this present age, so we may enjoy his banquet for all eternity. Who lives and reigns for ever and ever.	Concede nobis, omnipotens Deus, ut, sicut Cena Filii tui reficimur temporali, ita satiari mereamur æterna. Per Christum Dominum nostrum.

The Transfer of the Most Blessed Sacrament

After the Prayer after Communion, the Priest puts incense in the thurible while standing, blesses it and then, kneeling, incenses the Blessed Sacrament three times. Then, having put on a white humeral veil, he rises, takes the ciborium, and covers it with the ends of the veil.

A procession is formed in which the Blessed Sacrament, accompanied by torches and incense, is carried through the church to a place of repose prepared in a part of the church or in a chapel suitably decorated. A lay minister with a cross, standing between two other ministers with lighted candles leads off. Others carrying lighted candles follow. Before the Priest carrying the Blessed Sacrament comes the thurifer with a smoking thurible. Meanwhile, the hymn **Pange, lingua** (exclusive of the last two stanzas) or another eucharistic chant is sung.

When the procession reaches the place of repose, the Priest, with the help of the Deacon if necessary, places the ciborium in the tabernacle, the door of which remains open. Then he puts incense in the thurible and, kneeling, incenses the Blessed Sacrament, while **Tantum ergo Sacramentum** or another eucharistic chant is sung. Then the Deacon or the Priest himself places the Sacrament in the tabernacle and closes the door.

After a period of adoration in silence, the Priest and ministers genuflect and return to the sacristy.

At an appropriate time, the altar is stripped and, if possible, the crosses are removed from the church. It is expedient that any crosses which remain in the church be veiled.

Vespers (Evening Prayer) is not celebrated by those who have attended the Mass of the Lord's Supper.

The faithful are invited to continue adoration before the Blessed Sacrament for a suitable length of time during the night, according to local circumstances, but after midnight the adoration should take place without solemnity.

If the celebration of the Passion of the Lord on the following Friday does not take place in the same church, the Mass is concluded in the usual way and the Blessed Sacrament is placed in the tabernacle.

REFLECTION

☩

The festival on which Passover was based was originally a nomad festival at the move from winter pastures in the plains to summer pastures in the hills. A fine lamb was offered to placate the gods, so that they would not harm the rest of the flock; it was eaten at the first full moon of spring, after the spring equinox. Blood on the doorposts of the tents was a sign that the offering had been made. Water is scarce for nomads, so the lamb was roasted, not boiled – cooking pots were packed, anyway! This primitive festival was taken up by the Hebrews to commemorate the great move from Egypt through the desert, and – most of all – the covenant made in the desert of Sinai, when God made Israel his own people. It was celebrated each year, and the blood of the lamb sprinkled over the altar (representing God) and the people signified their union in the covenant.

This feast was taken up by Jesus as the occasion for him to make his own new covenant, fulfilling the promises made by the prophets of a new covenant to replace the old covenant so definitively broken at the time of the Babylonian Exile. Whether Jesus celebrated it on the traditional evening or the day before is unclear; if it was not the conventional day he must have taken this last opportunity to make it his own Passover Festival with his community. Paul gives us the story of this meal, which he himself had received from what was already traditional, hardly a dozen years after the Last Supper, well before the Gospels were written. Jesus himself was the lamb who was to be sacrificed, and his new covenant was sealed, not in blood sprinkled, but in his own blood consumed. It was a 'memorial', that is, an effective re-enactment, actually renewing the act of dedication and union. In today's reading Paul is rebuking the Corinthians for re-enacting this significant moment thoughtlessly, as though it was an ordinary festal meal; they had lost the intention and the seriousness. They were no longer proclaiming the death of Jesus, no longer engaging themselves in the new covenant. It is a dangerous thing to commit oneself to a new covenant sealed by death and leading to new life.

Jesus's extraordinary gesture recorded in the Gospel of John shows us the full meaning of what he was doing. The narrative stresses that Jesus knew what was to come; he was showing his disciples the meaning of the events. By the act of rising from the table and performing the demeaning act of stripping down and washing the feet of his followers, his guests, he was showing the meaning of the dire events to come – Peter's horror says it all, but there was far worse to come. It was a pre-enactment of his great act of serving his community, the new family which he was binding to himself by this new covenant, the foundational act of service in the Church.

As noted above, it is customary to watch at the Altar of Repose after the end of the Mass of the Lord's Supper. We give some texts that may be helpful during this time of Eucharistic Adoration.

A QUARTER HOUR BEFORE THE BLESSED SACRAMENT

To please Me, dear child, it is not necessary to know much; all that is required is to love Me much, to be deeply sorry for ever having offended Me and desirous of being ever faithful to Me in future.

Speak to Me now as you would do to your dearest friend. Tell Me all that now fills your mind and heart. Are there any you wish to commend to Me? Tell Me their names, and tell Me what you would wish Me to do for them. Do not fear, ask for much; I love generous hearts, which, forgetting themselves, wish well to others.

Speak to Me of the poor you wish to comfort; tell Me of the sick that you would wish to see relieved. Ask of Me something for those who have been unkind to you, or who have crossed you. Ask much for them all; commend them with all your heart to Me.

And ask Me many graces for yourself. Are there not many graces you would wish to name that would make you happier in yourself, more useful and pleasing to others, more worthy of the love of Me, the dearest Lord, Master, and Spouse of your soul? Tell Me the whole list of the favours you want of Me. Tell Me them with humility, knowing how poor you are without them, how unable to gain them by yourself; ask for them with much love, that they may make you more pleasing to Me. With all a child's simplicity, tell Me how self-seeking you are, how proud, vain, irritable, how cowardly in sacrifice, how lazy in work, uncertain in your good resolutions, and then ask Me to bless and crown your efforts. Poor child, fear not, blush not at the sight of so many failings; there are Saints in heaven who had the faults you have; they came to Me lovingly, they prayed earnestly to Me, and My grace has made them good and holy in My sight.

You should be Mine, body and soul; fear not, therefore, to ask of Me gifts of body and mind, health, judgement, memory, and success – ask for them for My sake; that God may be glorified in all things. I can grant everything, and never refuse to give what may make a soul dearer to Me and better able to fulfil the will of God. Have you no plans for the future which occupy, perhaps distress, your mind?

Tell Me your hopes, your fears. Is it about your future state? Your position among My creatures? Some good you wish to bring to others? In what shall I help and bless your good will?

And for Me you must have – have you not? – some zeal, some wish to do good to the souls of others. Some, perhaps, who love and care for you, have ceased, almost, to know or care for Me. Shall I give you strength, wisdom and tact, to bring these poor ones close to My heart again? Have you failed in the past? Tell me how you acted; I will show you why you did not gain all you expected; rely on Me, I will help you, and will guide you to lead others to Me.

And what crosses have you, My dear child? Have they been many and heavy ones? Has someone caused you pain? Someone wounded your self-love? slighted you? injured you? Lay your head upon My breast, and tell Me how you suffered. Have you felt that some have been ungrateful to you, and unfeeling towards you? Tell Me all, and in the warmth of My heart you will find strength to forgive and even to forget that they have ever wished to pain you.

And what fears have you, my child? My providence shall comfort you. My love sustain you. I am never away from you, never can abandon you. Are some growing cold in the interest and love they had for you? Pray to Me for them; I will restore them to you if it be better for you and your sanctification.

Have you got some happiness to make known to Me? What happened since you came to Me last, to console you, to gladden and give you joy? What was it? a mark of true friendship you received? a success unexpected and almost unhoped for? a fear suddenly taken away from you? and did you remember the while, that in all it was My will, My love, that brought all that your heart has been so glad to have? It was My hand, My dear child, that guided and prepared all for you. Look to Me now, My child, and say: 'Dear Jesus, I thank you'.

You will soon leave Me now; what promises can you make me? Let them be sincere ones, humble ones, full of love and desire to please Me. Tell Me how carefully you will avoid every occasion of sin, drive from you all that leads to harm, and shun the world – the great deceiver of souls. Promise to be kind to the poor; loving, for My sake, to friends; forgiving to your enemies, and charitable to all, not in word alone and actions, but in your very thoughts. When you have little love for your neighbour, whom you see, you are forgetting Me who am hidden from you.

Love all my Saints; seek the help of your holy patrons. I love to glorify them by giving you much through them. Love, above all, My own sweet glorious Mother – she is your mother; love her, speak to her often, and she will bring you to Me, and for her sake, I will love and bless you more each day.

Return soon to Me again, but come with your heart empty of the world, for I have many more favours to give, more than you can know of; bring your heart so that I may fill it with many gifts of My love.

My peace be with you.

THE LITANY OF THE SACRED HEART

Lord, have mercy.	*Lord, have mercy.*
Christ, have mercy.	*Christ, have mercy.*
Lord, have mercy.	*Lord, have mercy.*
God our Father in Heaven,	*have mercy on us.*
God the Son, Redeemer of the world,	*have mercy on us.*
God, the Holy Spirit,	*have mercy on us.*
Holy Trinity, one God,	*have mercy on us.*
Heart of Jesus, Son of the Eternal Father,	*have mercy on us.*
Heart of Jesus, formed by the Holy Spirit in the womb of the Virgin Mother,	*have mercy on us.*
Heart of Jesus, one with the eternal Word,	*have mercy on us.*
Heart of Jesus, infinite in majesty,	*have mercy on us.*
Heart of Jesus, holy temple of God,	*have mercy on us.*
Heart of Jesus, tabernacle of the Most High,	*have mercy on us.*
Heart of Jesus, house of God and gate of Heaven,	*have mercy on us.*
Heart of Jesus, aflame with love for us,	*have mercy on us.*
Heart of Jesus, source of justice and love,	*have mercy on us.*
Heart of Jesus, full of goodness and love,	*have mercy on us.*
Heart of Jesus, wellspring of all virtue,	*have mercy on us.*
Heart of Jesus, worthy of all praise,	*have mercy on us.*
Heart of Jesus, king and centre of all hearts,	*have mercy on us.*
Heart of Jesus, treasure-house of wisdom and knowledge,	*have mercy on us.*
Heart of Jesus, in whom there dwells the fulness of God,	*have mercy on us.*
Heart of Jesus, in whom the Father is well pleased,	*have mercy on us.*
Heart of Jesus, from whose fulness we have all received,	*have mercy on us.*
Heart of Jesus, desire of the eternal hills,	*have mercy on us.*
Heart of Jesus, patient and full of mercy,	*have mercy on us.*
Heart of Jesus, generous to all who turn to you,	*have mercy on us.*
Heart of Jesus, fountain of life and holiness,	*have mercy on us.*
Heart of Jesus, atonement for our sins,	*have mercy on us.*
Heart of Jesus, overwhelmed with insults,	*have mercy on us.*
Heart of Jesus, broken for our sins,	*have mercy on us.*
Heart of Jesus, obedient even to death,	*have mercy on us.*

Heart of Jesus, pierced by a lance,	*have mercy on us.*
Heart of Jesus, source of all consolation,	*have mercy on us.*
Heart of Jesus, our life and resurrection,	*have mercy on us.*
Heart of Jesus, our peace and reconciliation,	*have mercy on us.*
Heart of Jesus, victim of our sins,	*have mercy on us.*
Heart of Jesus, salvation of all who trust in you,	*have mercy on us.*
Heart of Jesus, hope of all who die in you,	*have mercy on us.*
Heart of Jesus, delight of all the saints,	*have mercy on us.*

Lamb of God, you take away the sins of the world,	*have mercy on us.*
Lamb of God, you take away the sins of the world,	*have mercy on us.*
Lamb of God, you take away the sins of the world,	*have mercy on us.*

Jesus, meek and humble of heart	*Touch our hearts and make them like your own.*

Let us pray.

Father, we rejoice in the gifts of love we have received from the heart of Jesus your Son. Open our hearts to share his life and continue to bless us with his love. We ask this in the name of Jesus the Lord. R. **Amen.**

THE LITANY OF THE MOST PRECIOUS BLOOD

Lord, have mercy.	*Lord, have mercy.*
Christ, have mercy.	*Christ, have mercy.*
Lord, have mercy.	*Lord, have mercy.*

God our Father in heaven,	*have mercy on us.*
God the Son, Redeemer of the world,	*have mercy on us.*
God, the Holy Spirit,	*have mercy on us.*
Holy Trinity, one God,	*have mercy on us.*

Blood of Christ, only Son of the Father,	*save us.*
Blood of Christ, Incarnate Word,	*save us.*
Blood of Christ, of the new and eternal covenant,	*save us.*
Blood of Christ, that spilled to the ground,	*save us.*
Blood of Christ, that flowed at the scourging,	*save us.*
Blood of Christ, dripping from the thorns,	*save us.*
Blood of Christ, shed on the Cross,	*save us.*
Blood of Christ, the price of our redemption,	*save us.*
Blood of Christ, our only claim to pardon,	*save us.*
Blood of Christ, our blessing cup,	*save us.*
Blood of Christ, in which we are washed,	*save us.*

Blood of Christ, torrent of mercy, *save us.*
Blood of Christ, that overcomes evil, *save us.*
Blood of Christ, strength of the martyrs, *save us.*
Blood of Christ, endurance of the saints, *save us.*
Blood of Christ, that makes the barren fruitful, *save us.*
Blood of Christ, protection of the threatened, *save us.*
Blood of Christ, comfort of the weary, *save us.*
Blood of Christ, solace of the mourner, *save us.*
Blood of Christ, hope of the repentant, *save us.*
Blood of Christ, consolation of the dying, *save us.*
Blood of Christ, our peace and refreshment, *save us.*
Blood of Christ, our pledge of life, *save us.*
Blood of Christ, by which we pass to glory, *save us.*
Blood of Christ, most worthy of honour, *save us.*

Lamb of God, you take away the sins of the world, *have mercy on us.*
Lamb of God, you take away the sins of the world, *have mercy on us.*
Lamb of God, you take away the sins of the world, *have mercy on us.*

Lord, you redeemed us by your Blood, *you have made us a Kingdom to serve our God.*

Let us pray.
Father, by the Blood of your Son you have set us free and saved us from death. Continue your work of love within us, that by constantly celebrating the mystery of our salvation we may reach the eternal life it promises. We ask this through Christ our Lord. R. **Amen.**

THE LITANY OF THE HOLY NAME OF JESUS

Lord, have mercy. *Lord, have mercy.*
Christ, have mercy. *Christ, have mercy.*
Lord, have mercy. *Lord, have mercy.*

God our Father in heaven, *have mercy on us.*
God the Son, Redeemer of the world, *have mercy on us.*
God, the Holy Spirit, *have mercy on us.*
Holy Trinity, one God, *have mercy on us.*

Jesus, Son of the living God, *have mercy on us.*
Jesus, splendour of the Father, *have mercy on us.*
Jesus, brightness of everlasting light, *have mercy on us.*
Jesus, king of glory, *have mercy on us.*

Jesus, dawn of justice,	*have mercy on us.*
Jesus, Son of the Virgin Mary,	*have mercy on us.*
Jesus, worthy of our love,	*have mercy on us.*
Jesus, worthy of our wonder,	*have mercy on us.*
Jesus, mighty God,	*have mercy on us.*
Jesus, father of the world to come,	*have mercy on us.*
Jesus, prince of peace,	*have mercy on us.*
Jesus, all-powerful,	*have mercy on us.*
Jesus, pattern of patience,	*have mercy on us.*
Jesus, model of obedience,	*have mercy on us.*
Jesus, gentle and humble of heart,	*have mercy on us.*
Jesus, lover of chastity,	*have mercy on us.*
Jesus, lover of us all,	*have mercy on us.*
Jesus, God of peace,	*have mercy on us.*
Jesus, author of life,	*have mercy on us.*
Jesus, model of goodness,	*have mercy on us.*
Jesus, seeker of souls,	*have mercy on us.*
Jesus, our God,	*have mercy on us.*
Jesus, our refuge,	*have mercy on us.*
Jesus, father of the poor,	*have mercy on us.*
Jesus, treasure of the faithful,	*have mercy on us.*
Jesus, Good Shepherd,	*have mercy on us.*
Jesus, the true light,	*have mercy on us.*
Jesus, eternal wisdom,	*have mercy on us.*
Jesus, infinite goodness,	*have mercy on us.*
Jesus, our way and our life,	*have mercy on us.*
Jesus, joy of angels,	*have mercy on us.*
Jesus, king of the patriarchs,	*have mercy on us.*
Jesus, teacher of apostles,	*have mercy on us.*
Jesus, master of evangelists,	*have mercy on us.*
Jesus, courage of martyrs,	*have mercy on us.*
Jesus, light of confessors,	*have mercy on us.*
Jesus, purity of virgins,	*have mercy on us.*
Jesus, crown of all saints,	*have mercy on us.*
Lord, be merciful.	*Jesus, save your people.*
From all evil,	*Jesus, save your people.*
From every sin,	*Jesus, save your people.*

From the snares of the devil,	*Jesus, save your people.*
From your anger,	*Jesus, save your people.*
From the spirit of infidelity,	*Jesus, save your people.*
From everlasting death,	*Jesus, save your people.*
From neglect of your Holy Spirit,	*Jesus, save your people.*

By the mystery of your Incarnation,	*Jesus, save your people.*
By your birth,	*Jesus, save your people.*
By your childhood,	*Jesus, save your people.*
By your hidden life,	*Jesus, save your people.*
By your public ministry,	*Jesus, save your people.*
By your agony and crucifixion,	*Jesus, save your people.*
By your abandonment,	*Jesus, save your people.*
By your grief and sorrow,	*Jesus, save your people.*
By your death and burial,	*Jesus, save your people.*
By your rising to new life,	*Jesus, save your people.*
By your return in glory to the Father,	*Jesus, save your people.*
By your gift of the Holy Eucharist,	*Jesus, save your people.*
By your joy and glory,	*Jesus, save your people.*

Christ, hear us.	*Christ, hear us.*
Lord Jesus, hear our prayer	*Lord Jesus, hear our prayer.*

Lamb of God, you take away the sins of the world,	*have mercy on us.*
Lamb of God, you take awaythe sins of the world,	*have mercy on us.*
Lamb of God, you take away the sins of the world,	*have mercy on us.*

Let us pray.
Lord, may we who honour the holy name of Jesus enjoy his friendship in
this life and be filled with eternal joy in the Kingdom where he lives and
reigns for ever and ever. R. **Amen.**

THE LITANY OF THE MOST BLESSED SACRAMENT

Lord, have mercy.	*Lord, have mercy.*
Christ, have mercy.	*Christ, have mercy.*
Lord, have mercy.	*Lord, have mercy.*

God our Father in heaven,	*have mercy on us.*
God the Son, Redeemer of the world,	*have mercy on us.*
God, the Holy Spirit,	*have mercy on us.*
Holy Trinity, one God,	*have mercy on us.*

Jesus, Eternal High Priest of the Eucharistic Sacrifice,   *have mercy on us.*
Jesus, Divine Victim on the Altar for our salvation,   *have mercy on us.*
Jesus, hidden under the appearance of bread,   *have mercy on us.*
Jesus, dwelling in the tabernacles of the world,   *have mercy on us.*
Jesus, really, truly and substantially
    present in the Blessed Sacrament,   *have mercy on us.*
Jesus, abiding in your fulness,
    Body, Blood, Soul and Divinity,   *have mercy on us.*
Jesus, Bread of Life,   *have mercy on us.*
Jesus, Bread of Angels,   *have mercy on us.*
Jesus, with us always until the end of the world,   *have mercy on us.*

Sacred Host, summit and source
    of all worship and Christian life,   *have mercy on us.*
Sacred Host, sign and cause of the unity of the Church,   *have mercy on us.*
Sacred Host, adored by countless angels,   *have mercy on us.*
Sacred Host, spiritual food,   *have mercy on us.*

Sacred Host, Sacrament of love,   *have mercy on us.*
Sacred Host, bond of charity,   *have mercy on us.*
Sacred Host, greatest aid to holiness,   *have mercy on us.*
Sacred Host, gift and glory of the priesthood,   *have mercy on us.*
Sacred Host, in which we partake of Christ,   *have mercy on us.*
Sacred Host, in which the soul is filled with grace,   *have mercy on us.*
Sacred Host, in which we are given
    a pledge of future glory,   *have mercy on us.*

Blessed be Jesus in the Most Holy Sacrament of the Altar.
Blessed be Jesus in the Most Holy Sacrament of the Altar.
Blessed be Jesus in the Most Holy Sacrament of the Altar.

For those who do not believe
    in your Eucharistic presence,   *have mercy on us.*
For those who are indifferent
    to the Sacrament of your love,   *have mercy on us.*
For those who have offended you
    in the Holy Sacrament of the Altar,   *have mercy on us.*

That we may show fitting reverence
    when entering your holy temple,   *we beseech you, hear us.*

That we may make suitable preparation before approaching the altar,	*we beseech you, hear us.*
That we may receive you frequently in Holy Communion with real devotion and true humility,	*we beseech you, hear us.*
That we may never neglect to thank you for so wonderful a blessing,	*we beseech you, hear us.*
That we may cherish time spent in silent prayer before you,	*we beseech you, hear us.*
That we may grow in knowledge of this Sacrament of sacraments,	*we beseech you, hear us.*
That all priests may have a profound love of the Holy Eucharist,	*we beseech you, hear us.*
That they may celebrate the Holy Sacrifice of the Mass in accordance with its sublime dignity,	*we beseech you, hear us.*
That we may be comforted and sanctified with Holy Viaticum at the hour of our death,	*we beseech you, hear us.*
That we may see you one day face to face in Heaven,	*we beseech you, hear us.*
Lamb of God, you take away the sins of the world,	*spare us, O Lord.*
Lamb of God, you take away the sins of the world,	*graciously hear us, O Lord.*
Lamb of God, you take away the sins of the world,	*have mercy on us, O Lord.*

V. O Sacrament Most Holy, O Sacrament Divine,
R. All praise and all thanksgiving be every moment thine.

Let us pray.
Most merciful Father,
you continue to draw us to yourself
through the Eucharistic Mystery.
Grant us fervent faith in this Sacrament of love,
in which Christ the Lord himself is contained, offered and received.
We make this prayer through the same Christ our Lord. R. **Amen.**

(by St Julian Peter Eymard)

FRIDAY OF THE PASSION OF THE LORD
(GOOD FRIDAY)

The liturgy applies to Jesus's descent into the night of death the words of Psalm 23[24]: "Lift up your heads, O gates; be lifted up, O ancient doors!" The gates of death are closed, no one can return from there. There is no key for those iron doors. But Christ has the key. His Cross opens wide the gates of death, the stern doors. They are barred no longer. His Cross, his radical love, is the key that opens them. The love of the One who, though God, became man in order to die – this love has the power to open those doors. This love is stronger than death.

(Pope Benedict XVI)

On this and the following day, by a most ancient tradition, the Church does not celebrate the Sacraments at all, except for Penance and the Anointing of the Sick.

On this day, Holy Communion is distributed to the faithful only within the celebration of the Lord's Passion; but it may be brought at any hour of the day to the sick who cannot participate in this celebration.

The altar should be completely bare: without a cross, without candles and without cloths.

The Celebration of the Passion of the Lord

On the afternoon of this day, about three o'clock (unless a later hour is chosen for a pastoral reason), there takes place the celebration of the Lord's Passion consisting of three parts, namely, the Liturgy of the Word, the Adoration of the Cross, and Holy Communion.

The Priest and the Deacon, if a Deacon is present, wearing red vestments as for Mass, go to the altar in silence and, after making a reverence to the altar, prostrate themselves or, if appropriate, kneel and pray in silence for a while. All others kneel.

Then the Priest, with the ministers, goes to the chair where, facing the people, who are standing, he says, with hands extended, one of the following prayers, omitting the invitation **Let us pray**.

Prayer

Remember your mercies, O Lord,
and with your eternal protection
    sanctify your servants,
for whom Christ your Son,
by the shedding of his Blood,
established the Paschal Mystery.
Who lives and reigns
    for ever and ever.
R. Amen.

Or:

O God, who by the Passion
    of Christ your Son, our Lord,
abolished the death inherited
    from ancient sin
by every succeeding generation,
grant that just as,
    being conformed to him,
we have borne by the law of nature
the image of the man of earth,
so by the sanctification of grace
we may bear the image of the Man
    of heaven.
Through Christ our Lord.
R. Amen.

Oratio

Reminiscere miserationum
    tuarum, Domine,
et famulos tuos æterna
    protectione sanctifica,
pro quibus Christus, Filius tuus,
per suum cruorem instituit
    paschale mysterium.
Qui vivit et regnat
    in sæcula sæculorum.
R. Amen.

Vel:

Deus, qui peccati veteris
    hereditariam mortem,
in qua posteritatis genus
    omne successerat,
Christi Filii tui, Domini nostri,
    passione solvisti,
da, ut conformes eidem facti,
sicut imaginem terreni hominis
naturæ necessitate portavimus,
ita imaginem cælestis
gratiæ sanctificatione portemus.
Per Christum Dominum nostrum.
R. Amen.

FIRST PART:

The Liturgy of the Word

FIRST READING

A reading from the prophet Isaiah   52:13-53:12
He was pierced through our faults.

See, my servant will prosper,
he shall be lifted up, exalted, rise to great heights.

As the crowds were appalled on seeing him
 – so disfigured did he look
that he seemed no longer human –
so will the crowds be astonished at him,

and kings stand speechless before him;
for they shall see something never told
and witness something never heard before:
'Who could believe what we have heard,
and to whom has the power of the Lord been revealed?'

Like a sapling he grew up in front of us,
like a root in arid ground.
Without beauty, without majesty (we saw him),
no looks to attract our eyes;
a thing despised and rejected by men,
a man of sorrows and familiar with suffering,
a man to make people screen their faces;
he was despised and we took no account of him.

And yet ours were the sufferings he bore,
ours the sorrows he carried.
But we, we thought of him as someone punished,
struck by God, and brought low.
Yet he was pierced through for our faults,
crushed for our sins.
On him lies a punishment that brings us peace,
and through his wounds we are healed.

We had all gone astray like sheep,
each taking his own way,
and the Lord burdened him
with the sins of all of us.
Harshly dealt with, he bore it humbly,
he never opened his mouth,
like a lamb that is led to the slaughter-house,
like a sheep that is dumb before its shearers
never opening its mouth.

By force and by law he was taken;
would anyone plead his cause?
Yes, he was torn away from the land of the living;
for our faults struck down in death.
They gave him a grave with the wicked,
a tomb with the rich,
though he had done no wrong
and there had been no perjury in his mouth.
The Lord has been pleased to crush him with suffering.

If he offers his life in atonement,
he shall see his heirs, he shall have a long life
and through him what the Lord wishes will be done.

His soul's anguish over
he shall see the light and be content.
By his sufferings shall my servant justify many,
taking their faults on himself.

Hence I will grant whole hordes for his tribute,
he shall divide the spoil with the mighty,
for surrendering himself to death
and letting himself be taken for a sinner,
while he was bearing the faults of many
and praying all the time for sinners.

The word of the Lord.

Responsorial Psalm   Ps 30:2,6,12-13,15-17,25. R. Lk 23:46

R. **Father, into your hands I commend my spirit.**

In you, O Lord, I take refuge.
Let me never be put to shame.
In your justice, set me free.
Into your hands I commend my spirit.
It is you who will redeem me, Lord. R.

In the face of all my foes
I am a reproach,
an object of scorn to my neighbours
and of fear to my friends. R.

Those who see me in the street
run far away from me.
I am like a dead man, forgotten in men's hearts,
like a thing thrown away. R.

But as for me, I trust in you, Lord,
I say: 'You are my God.'
My life is in your hands, deliver me
from the hands of those who hate me. R.

Let your face shine on your servant.
Save me in your love.
Be strong, let your heart take courage,
all who hope in the Lord. R.

SECOND READING

A reading from the letter to the Hebrews   4:14-16; 5:7-9

He learnt to obey through suffering and became for all who obey him the source of eternal salvation.

Since in Jesus, the Son of God, we have the supreme high priest who has gone through to the highest heaven, we must never let go of the faith that we have professed. For it is not as if we had a high priest who was incapable of feeling our weaknesses with us; but we have one who has been tempted in every way that we are, though he is without sin. Let us be confident, then, in approaching the throne of grace, that we shall have mercy from him and find grace when we are in need of help.

During his life on earth, he offered up prayer and entreaty, aloud and in silent tears, to the one who had the power to save him out of death, and he submitted so humbly that his prayer was heard. Although he was Son, he learnt to obey through suffering; but having been made perfect, he became for all who obey him the source of eternal salvation.

The word of the Lord.

Gospel Acclamation   Ph 2:8-9

R. **Glory and praise to you, O Christ!**
Christ was humbler yet,
even accepting death, death on a cross.
But God raised him high
and gave him the name which is above all names.
R. **Glory and praise to you, O Christ!**

GOSPEL

The symbols in the following passion narrative represent:

N Narrator   J Jesus   O Other single speaker
C Crowd, or more than one speaker

The passion of our Lord Jesus Christ according to John   18:1-19:42

N   Jesus left with his disciples and crossed the Kedron valley. There was a garden there, and he went into it with his disciples. Judas the traitor knew the place well, since Jesus had often met his disciples there, and he brought the cohort to this place together with a detachment of guards sent by the chief priests and the Pharisees, all with lanterns and torches and weapons. Knowing everything that was going to happen to him, Jesus then came forward and said,

J   Who are you looking for?

N   They answered,

C   Jesus the Nazarene.

N   He said,

J   I am he.

N   Now Judas the traitor was standing among them. When Jesus said, 'I am he', they moved back and fell to the ground. He asked them a second time,

J   Who are you looking for?

N   They said,

C   Jesus the Nazarene.

N   Jesus replied,

J   I have told you that I am he. If I am the one you are looking for, let these others go.

N   This was to fulfil the words he has spoken: 'Not one of those you gave me have I lost.'

     Simon Peter, who carried a sword, drew it and wounded the high priest's servant, cutting off his right ear. The servant's name was Malchus. Jesus said to Peter,

J   Put your sword back in its scabbard; am I not to drink the cup that the Father has given me?

N   The cohort and its captain and the Jewish guards seized Jesus and bound him. They took him first to Annas, because Annas was the father-in-law of Caiaphas, who was high priest that year. It was Caiaphas who had suggested to the Jews, 'It is better for one man to die for the people.'

     Simon Peter, with another disciple, followed Jesus. This disciple, who was known to the high priest, went with Jesus into the high priest's palace, but Peter stayed outside the door. So the other disciple, the one known to the high priest, went out, spoke to the woman who was keeping the door and brought Peter in. The maid on duty at the door said to Peter,

O   Aren't you another of that man's disciples?

N   He answered,

O   I am not.

N   Now it was cold, and the servants and guards had lit a charcoal fire and were standing there warming themselves; so Peter stood there too, warming himself with the others.

     The high priest questioned Jesus about his disciples and his teaching. Jesus answered,

J   I have spoken openly for all the world to hear; I have always taught in the synagogue and in the Temple where all the Jews meet together: I have said nothing in secret. But why ask me? Ask my hearers what I taught: they know what I said.

N   At these words, one of the guards standing by gave Jesus a slap in the face, saying,

O   Is that the way to answer the high priest?

N   Jesus replied,

J   If there is something wrong in what I said, point it out; but if there is no offence in it, why do you strike me?

N   Then Annas sent him, still bound, to Caiaphas, the high priest. As Simon Peter stood there warming himself, someone said to him,

O   Aren't you another of his disciples?

N   He denied it saying,

O   I am not.

N   One of the high priest's servants, a relation of the man whose ear Peter had cut off, said,

O   Didn't I see you in the garden with him?

N   Again Peter denied it, and at once a cock crew.

They then led Jesus from the house of Caiaphas to the Praetorium. It was now morning. They did not go into the Praetorium themselves or they would be defiled and unable to eat the passover. So Pilate came outside to them and said,

O   What charge do you bring against this man?

N   They replied,

C   If he were not a criminal, we should not be handing him over to you.

N   Pilate said,

O   Take him yourselves, and try him by your own Law.

N   The Jews answered,

C   We are not allowed to put a man to death.

N   This was to fulfil the words Jesus had spoken indicating the way he was going to die.

So Pilate went back into the Praetorium and called Jesus to him, and asked,

O   Are you the king of Jews?

N   Jesus replied,

J   Do you ask this of your own accord, or have others spoken to you about me?

N   Pilate answered,

O   Am I a Jew? It is your own people and the chief priests who have handed you over to me: what have you done?

N   Jesus replied,

J   Mine is not a kingdom of this world; if my kingdom were of this world, my men would have fought to prevent me being surrendered to the Jews. But my kingdom is not of this kind.

N   Pilate said,

O   So you are the king then?

N   Jesus answered,

J   It is you who say it. Yes, I am a king. I was born for this; I came into the world for this; to bear witness to the truth, and all who are on the side of truth listen to my voice.

N   Pilate said,

O   Truth? What is that?

N   And with that he went out again to the Jews and said,

O   I find no case against him. But according to a custom of yours I should release one prisoner at the Passover; would you like me, then, to release the king of Jews?

N   At this they shouted:

C   Not this man, but Barabbas.

N   Barabbas was a brigand.

Pilate then had Jesus taken away and scourged; and after this, the soldiers twisted some thorns into a crown and put it on his head, and dressed him in a purple robe. They kept coming up to him and saying,

C   Hail, king of the Jews!

N   and they slapped him in the face.

Pilate came outside again and said to them,

O   Look, I am going to bring him out to you to let you see that I find no case.

N   Jesus then came out wearing the crown of thorns and the purple robe. Pilate said,

O   Here is the man.

N   When they saw him the chief priests and the guards shouted,

C   Crucify him! Crucify him!

N   Pilate said,

O   Take him yourselves and crucify him: I can find no case against him

N   The Jews replied,

C   We have a Law, and according to the Law he ought to die, because he has claimed to be the son of God.

N When Pilate heard them say this his fears increased. Re-entering the Praetorium, he said to Jesus,

O Where do you come from?

N But Jesus made no answer. Pilate then said to him,

O Are you refusing to speak to me? Surely you know I have power to release you and I have power to crucify you?

N Jesus replied,

J You would have no power over me if it had not been given you from above; that is why the one who handed me over to you has the greater guilt.

N From that moment Pilate was anxious to set him free, but the Jews shouted,

C If you set him free you are no friend of Caesar's; anyone who makes himself king is defying Caesar.

N Hearing these words, Pilate had Jesus brought out, and seated himself on the chair of judgement at a place called the Pavement, in Hebrew Gabbatha. It was Passover Preparation Day, about the sixth hour. Pilate said to the Jews,

O Here is your king.

N They said,

C Take him away, take him away. Crucify him!

N Pilate said,

O Do you want me to crucify your king?

N The chief priests answered,

C We have no king except Caesar.

N So in the end Pilate handed him over to them to be crucified.

They then took charge of Jesus, and carrying his own cross he went out of the city to the place of the skull, or, as it was called in Hebrew, Golgotha, where they crucified him with two others, one on either side with Jesus in the middle. Pilate wrote out a notice and had it fixed to the cross; it ran: 'Jesus the Nazarene, King of the Jews.' This notice was read by many of the Jews, because the place where Jesus was crucified was not far from the city, and the writing was in Hebrew, Latin and Greek. So the Jewish chief priests said to Pilate,

C You should not write 'King of the Jews', but 'This man said: I am King of the Jews'.

N Pilate answered,

O What I have written, I have written.

N When the soldiers had finished crucifying Jesus they took his clothing and divided it into four shares, one for each soldier. His undergarment was seamless, woven in one piece from neck to hem; so they said to one another,

C   Instead of tearing it, let's throw dice to decide who is to have it.

N   In this way the words of scripture were fulfilled:

> They shared out my clothing among them.
> They cast lots for my clothes.

This is exactly what the soldiers did.

Near the cross of Jesus stood his mother and his mother's sister, Mary the wife of Clopas, and Mary of Magdala. Seeing his mother and the disciple he loved standing near her, Jesus said to his mother,

J   Woman, this is your son.

N   Then to the disciple he said,

J   This is your mother.

N   And from that moment the disciple made a place for her in his home.

After this, Jesus knew that everything had now been completed, and to fulfil the scripture perfectly he said:

J   I am thirsty.

N   A jar full of vinegar stood there, so putting a sponge soaked in vinegar on a hyssop stick they held it up to his mouth. After Jesus had taken the vinegar he said,

J   It is accomplished;

N   and bowing his head he gave up the spirit.

All kneel and pause a moment.

N   It was Preparation Day, and to prevent the bodies remaining on the cross during the sabbath – since that sabbath was a day of special solemnity – the Jews asked Pilate to have the legs broken and the bodies taken away. Consequently the soldiers came and broke the legs of the first man who had been crucified with him and then of the other. When they came to Jesus, they found that he was already dead, and so instead of breaking his legs one of the soldiers pierced his side with a lance; and immediately there came out blood and water. This is the evidence of one who saw it – trustworthy evidence, and he knows he speaks the truth – and he gives it so that you may believe as well. Because all this happened to fulfil the words of scripture:

> Not one bone of his will be broken,

and again, in another place scripture says:

> They will look on the one whom they have pierced.

After this, Joseph of Arimathaea, who was a disciple of Jesus – though a secret one because he was afraid of the Jews – asked Pilate to let him remove the body of Jesus. Pilate gave permission, so they came and took it away. Nicodemus came as well – the same one who had first come to Jesus at night – time – and he brought a mixture of myrrh and aloes, weighing about a hundred pounds. They took the body of Jesus and wrapped it with the spices in linen cloths, following the Jewish burial custom. At the place where he had been crucified there was a garden, and in the garden a new tomb in which no one had yet been buried. Since it was the Jewish Day of Preparation and the tomb was near at hand, they laid Jesus there.

The Gospel of the Lord.

After the reading of the Lord's Passion, the Priest gives a brief homily and, at its end, the faithful may be invited to spend a short time in prayer.

The Solemn Intercessions

The Liturgy of the Word concludes with the Solemn Intercessions, which take place in this way: the Deacon, if a Deacon is present, or if he is not, a lay minister, stands at the ambo, and sings or says the invitation in which the intention is expressed. Then all pray in silence for a while, and afterwards the Priest, standing at the chair or, if appropriate, at the altar, with hands extended, sings or says the prayer.

The faithful may remain either kneeling or standing throughout the entire period of the prayers.

Before the Priest's prayer, in accord with tradition, it is permissible to use the Deacon's invitations Let us kneel – Let us stand, (Flectamus genua – Levate), with all kneeling for silent prayer.

The Conferences of Bishops may provide other invitations to introduce the prayer of the Priest.

In a situation of grave public need, the Diocesan Bishop may permit or order the addition of a special intention.

The prayer is sung in the simple tone or, if the invitations Let us kneel – Let us stand (Flectamus genua – Levate) are used, in the solemn tone.

I. For Holy Church

Let us pray, dearly beloved,
    for the holy Church of God,
that our God and Lord be pleased
    to give her peace,
to guard her and to unite her
    throughout the whole world
and grant that, leading our life
    in tranquillity and quiet,
we may glorify God
    the Father almighty.

I. Pro sancta Ecclesia

Oremus, dilectissimi nobis,
    pro Ecclesia sancta Dei,
ut eam Deus et Dominus noster
pacificare, adunare
    et custodire dignetur
toto orbe terrarum,
detque nobis, quietam et tranquillam
    vitam degentibus,
glorificare Deum
    Patrem omnipotentem.

Prayer in silence. Then the Priest says:

Almighty ever-living God,
who in Christ revealed your glory
    to all the nations,
watch over the works of your mercy,
that your Church, spread
    throughout all the world,
may persevere with steadfast faith
    in confessing your name.
Through Christ our Lord.
R. Amen.

Omnipotens sempiterne Deus,
qui gloriam tuam omnibus
    in Christo gentibus revelasti:
custodi opera misericordiæ tuæ,
ut Ecclesia tua, toto orbe diffusa,
stabili fide in confessione
    tui nominis perseveret.
Per Christum Dominum nostrum.
R. Amen.

II. For the Pope

Let us pray also for our most
    Holy Father Pope N.,
that our God and Lord,
who chose him for the
    Order of Bishops,
may keep him safe and unharmed
    for the Lord's holy Church,
to govern the holy People of God.

II. Pro Papa

Oremus et pro beatissimo
    Papa nostro N.,
ut Deus et Dominus noster,
qui elegit eum
    in ordine episcopatus,
salvum atque incolumem custodiat
    Ecclesiæ suæ sanctæ,
ad regendum populum
    sanctum Dei.

Prayer in silence. Then the Priest says:

Almighty ever-living God,
by whose decree all things
    are founded,
look with favour on our prayers
and in your kindness protect
    the Pope chosen for us,
that, under him,
    the Christian people,
governed by you their maker,
may grow in merit by reason
    of their faith.
Through Christ our Lord.
R. Amen.

Omnipotens sempiterne Deus,
cuius iudicio universa fundantur,
respice propitius ad preces nostras,
et electum nobis Antistitem
    tua pietate conserva,
ut christiana plebs,
    quæ te gubernatur auctore,
sub ipso Pontifice,
    fidei suæ meritis augeatur.
Per Christum Dominum nostrum.
R. Amen.

III. For all orders and degrees of the faithful

Let us pray also for our Bishop N.,
for all Bishops, Priests,
 and Deacons of the Church
and for the whole
 of the faithful people.

Prayer in silence. Then the Priest says:

Almighty ever-living God,
by whose Spirit the whole body
 of the Church
is sanctified and governed,
hear our humble prayer
 for your ministers,
that, by the gift of your grace,
all may serve you faithfully.
Through Christ our Lord.
R. Amen.

IV. For catechumens

Let us pray also
 for (our) catechumens,
that our God and Lord
may open wide the ears
 of their inmost hearts
and unlock the gates of his mercy,
that, having received forgiveness
 of all their sins
through the waters of rebirth,
they, too, may be one with Christ
 Jesus our Lord.

Prayer in silence. Then the Priest says:

Almighty ever-living God,
who make your Church ever
 fruitful with new offspring,
increase the faith and understanding
 of (our) catechumens,
that, reborn in the font of Baptism,

III. Pro omnibus ordinibus gradibusque fidelium

Oremus et pro Episcopo nostro N.,
pro omnibus Episcopis, presbyteris,
 diaconis Ecclesiæ,
et universa plebe fidelium.

Omnipotens sempiterne Deus,
cuius Spiritu totum corpus Ecclesiæ
sanctificatur et regitur,
exaudi nos pro ministris
 tuis supplicantes,
ut, gratiæ tuæ munere, ab omnibus
 tibi fideliter serviatur.
Per Christum Dominum nostrum.
R. Amen.

IV. Pro catechumenis

Oremus et pro
 catechumenis (nostris),
ut Deus et Dominus noster
adaperiat aures
 præcordiorum ipsorum
ianuamque misericordiæ,
ut, per lavacrum regenerationis
accepta remissione
 omnium peccatorum,
et ipsi inveniantur in Christo Iesu
 Domino nostro.

Omnipotens sempiterne Deus,
qui Ecclesiam tuam nova semper
 prole fecundas,
auge fidem et intellectum
 catechumenis (nostris),
ut, renati fonte baptismatis,

they may be added to the number
   of your adopted children.
Through Christ our Lord.
R. Amen.

adoptionis tuæ filiis aggregentur.
Per Christum Dominum nostrum.
R. Amen.

V. For the unity of Christians

V. Pro unitate Christianorum

Let us pray also for all our brothers
   and sisters who believe in Christ,
that our God and Lord may
   be pleased,
as they live the truth,
to gather them together and keep
   them in his one Church.

Oremus et pro universis fratribus
   in Christum credentibus,
ut Deus et Dominus noster eos,
   veritatem facientes,
in una Ecclesia sua congregare
   et custodire dignetur.

Prayer in silence. Then the Priest says:

Almighty ever-living God,
who gather what is scattered
and keep together what you
   have gathered,
look kindly on the flock of your Son,
that those whom one Baptism
   has consecrated
may be joined together by integrity
   of faith
and united in the bond of charity.
Through Christ our Lord.
R. Amen.

Omnipotens sempiterne Deus,
qui dispersa congregas
   et congregata conservas,
ad gregem Filii tui placatus intende,
ut, quos unum baptisma sacravit,
eos et fidei iungat integritas
et vinculum societ caritatis.
Per Christum Dominum nostrum.
R. Amen.

VI. For the Jewish people

VI. Pro Iudæis

Let us pray also for the Jewish people,
to whom the Lord our God
   spoke first,
that he may grant them to advance
   in love of his name
and in faithfulness to his covenant.

Oremus et pro Iudæis,
ut, ad quos prius locutus est
   Dominus Deus noster,
eis tribuat in sui nominis amore
et in sui fœderis fidelitate proficere.

Prayer in silence. Then the Priest says:

Almighty ever-living God,
who bestowed your promises on
   Abraham and his descendants,

Omnipotens sempiterne Deus,
qui promissiones tuas Abrahæ
   eiusque semini contulisti,

graciously hear the prayers
of your Church,
that the people you first made
your own
may attain the fullness
of redemption.
Through Christ our Lord.
R. Amen.

Ecclesiæ tuæ preces
clementer exaudi,
ut populus acquisitionis prioris
ad redemptionis mereatur
plenitudinem pervenire.
Per Christum Dominum nostrum.
R. Amen.

VII. For those who do not believe in Christ

VII. Pro iis qui Christum non credunt

Let us pray also for those who
do not believe in Christ,
that, enlightened by the Holy Spirit,
they, too, may enter on the way
of salvation.

Oremus et pro iis qui in Christum
non credunt,
ut, luce Sancti Spiritus illustrati,
viam salutis et ipsi valeant introire.

Prayer in silence. Then the Priest says:

Almighty ever-living God,
grant to those who do not
confess Christ
that, by walking before you
with a sincere heart,
they may find the truth,
and that we ourselves, being
constant in mutual love
and striving to understand more
fully the mystery of your life,
may be made more perfect witnesses
to your love in the world.
Through Christ our Lord.
R. Amen.

Omnipotens sempiterne Deus,
fac ut qui Christum
non confitentur,
coram te sincero corde ambulantes,
inveniant veritatem,
nosque, mutuo proficientes
semper amore
et ad tuæ vitæ mysterium plenius
percipiendum sollicitos,
perfectiores effice tuæ testes
caritatis in mundo.
Per Christum Dominum nostrum.
R. Amen.

VIII. For those who do not believe in God

VIII. Pro iis qui in Deum non credunt

Let us pray also for those who
do not acknowledge God,
that, following what is right
in sincerity of heart,
they may find the way
to God himself.

Oremus et pro iis qui Deum
non agnoscunt,
ut, quæ recta sunt sincero
corde sectantes,
ad ipsum Deum
pervenire mereantur.

Prayer in silence. Then the Priest says:

Almighty ever-living God,
who created all people
to seek you always by desiring you
and, by finding you, come to rest,
grant, we pray,
that, despite every harmful obstacle,
all may recognise the signs
   of your fatherly love
and the witness of the good works
done by those who believe in you,
and so in gladness confess you,
the one true God and Father
   of our human race.
Through Christ our Lord.
R. Amen.

Omnipotens sempiterne Deus,
qui cunctos homines condidisti,
ut te semper desiderando quærerent
et inveniendo quiescerent,
præsta, quæsumus,
ut inter noxia quæque obstacula
omnes, tuæ signa pietatis
et in te credentium testimonium
bonorum operum percipientes,
te solum verum Deum nostrique
   generis Patrem
gaudeant confiteri.
Per Christum Dominum nostrum.
R. Amen.

IX. For those in public office

Let us pray also for those
   in public office,
that our God and Lord
may direct their minds and hearts
   according to his will
for the true peace and freedom of all.

IX. Pro rempublicam moderantibus

Oremus et pro omnibus
   rempublicam moderantibus,
ut Deus et Dominus noster
mentes et corda eorum secundum
   voluntatem suam dirigat
ad veram omnium pacem
   et libertatem.

Prayer in silence. Then the Priest says:

Almighty ever-living God,
in whose hand lies every
   human heart
and the rights of peoples,
look with favour, we pray,
on those who govern
   with authority over us,
that throughout the whole world,
the prosperity of peoples,
the assurance of peace,
and freedom of religion
may through your gift
   be made secure.
Through Christ our Lord.
R. Amen.

Omnipotens sempiterne Deus,
in cuius manu sunt hominum
   corda et iura populorum,
respice benignus ad eos,
   qui nos in potestate moderantur,
ut ubique terrarum populorum
   prosperitas,
pacis securitas et religionis libertas,
te largiente, consistant.
Per Christum Dominum nostrum.
R. Amen.

X. For those in tribulation

Let us pray, dearly beloved,
to God the Father almighty,
that he may cleanse the world
    of all errors,
banish disease, drive out hunger,
unlock prisons, loosen fetters,
granting to travellers safety,
    to pilgrims return,
health to the sick,
    and salvation to the dying.

Prayer in silence. Then the Priest says:

Almighty ever-living God,
comfort of mourners,
    strength of all who toil,
may the prayers of those who cry out
    in any tribulation
come before you,
that all may rejoice,
because in their hour of need
your mercy was at hand.
Through Christ our Lord.
R. Amen.

X. Pro tribulatis

Oremus, dilectissimi nobis,
    Deum Patrem omnipotentem,
ut cunctis mundum
    purget erroribus,
morbos auferat, famem depellat,
aperiat carceres, vincula solvat,
viatoribus securitatem,
    peregrinantibus reditum,
infirmantibus sanitatem
atque morientibus
    salutem indulgeat.

Omnipotens sempiterne Deus,
mæstorum consolatio,
    laborantium fortitudo,
perveniant ad te preces
de quacumque
    tribulatione clamantium,
ut omnes sibi in necessitatibus suis
misericordiam tuam
    gaudeant affuisse.
Per Christum Dominum nostrum.
R. Amen.

SECOND PART:

THE ADORATION OF THE HOLY CROSS

After the Solemn Intercessions, the solemn Adoration of the Holy Cross takes place. Of the two forms of the showing of the Cross presented here, the more appropriate one, according to pastoral needs, should be chosen.

The Showing of the Holy Cross

First Form

The Deacon accompanied by ministers, or another suitable minister, goes to the sacristy, from which, in procession, accompanied by two ministers with lighted candles, he carries the Cross, covered with a violet veil, through the church to the middle of the sanctuary.

The Priest, standing before the altar and facing the people, receives the Cross, uncovers a little of its upper part and elevates it while beginning the **Ecce lignum**

Crucis (Behold the wood of the Cross). He is assisted in singing by the Deacon or, if need be, by the choir. All respond, **Come, let us adore**. At the end of the singing, all kneel and for a brief moment adore in silence, while the Priest stands and holds the Cross raised.

Behold the wood of the Cross, on which hung the salvation of the world. R. Come, let us adore.	Ecce lignum Crucis, in quo salus mundi pependit. R. Venite, adoremus.

Then the Priest uncovers the right arm of the Cross and again, raising up the Cross, begins, **Behold the wood of the Cross** and everything takes place as above.

Finally, he uncovers the Cross entirely and, raising it up, he begins the invitation **Behold the wood of the Cross** a third time and everything takes place like the first time.

Second Form

The Priest or the Deacon accompanied by ministers, or another suitable minister, goes to the door of the church, where he receives the unveiled Cross, and the ministers take lighted candles; then the procession sets off through the church to the sanctuary. Near the door, in the middle of the church, and before the entrance of the sanctuary, the one who carries the Cross elevates it, singing, **Behold the wood of the Cross,** to which all respond, **Come, let us adore**. After each response all kneel and for a brief moment adore in silence, as above.

The Adoration of the Holy Cross

Then, accompanied by two ministers with lighted candles, the Priest or the Deacon carries the Cross to the entrance of the sanctuary or to another suitable place and there puts it down or hands it over to the ministers to hold. Candles are placed on the right and left sides of the Cross.

For the Adoration of the Cross, first the Priest Celebrant alone approaches, with the chasuble and his shoes removed, if appropriate. Then the clergy, the lay ministers, and the faithful approach, moving as if in procession, and showing reverence to the Cross by a simple genuflection or by some other sign appropriate to the usage of the region, for example, by kissing the Cross.

Only one Cross should be offered for adoration. If, because of the large number of people, it is not possible for all to approach individually, the Priest, after some of the clergy and faithful have adored, takes the Cross and, standing in the middle before the altar, invites the people in a few words to adore the Holy Cross and afterwards holds the Cross elevated higher for a brief time, for the faithful to adore it in silence.

While the adoration of the Holy Cross is taking place, the antiphon **Crucem tuam adoramus** (We adore your Cross, O Lord), the Reproaches, the hymn **Crux fidelis** (Faithful Cross) or other suitable chants are sung, during which all who have already adored the Cross remain seated.

Chants to be Sung
during the Adoration of the Holy Cross

Ant. We adore your Cross, O Lord,
we praise and glorify your
holy Resurrection,
for behold, because of the wood
of a tree
joy has come to the whole world.

Ant. Crucem tuam
adoramus, Domine,
et sanctam resurrectionem tuam
laudamus et glorificamus:
ecce enim propter lignum
venit gaudium in universo mundo.

Cf. Ps 66:2

May God have mercy on us
and bless us;
may he let his face shed its light
upon us
and have mercy on us.

Deus misereatur nostri,
et benedicat nobis:
illuminet vultum suum super nos,
et misereatur nostri.

And the antiphon is repeated:
We adore...

Crucem tuam...

THE REPROACHES

Parts assigned to one of the two choirs separately are indicated by the numbers 1 (first choir) and 2 (second choir); parts sung by both choirs together are marked: 1 and 2. Some of the verses may also be sung by two cantors.

1 and 2 My people,
what have I done to you?
Or how have I grieved you?
Answer me!
1 Because I led you out of the land
of Egypt,
you have prepared a Cross
for your Saviour.

1 et 2 Popule meus,
quid feci tibi?
Aut in quo contristavi te?
Responde mihi!
1 Quia eduxi te de terra Ægypti:
parasti Crucem Salvatori tuo.

1 Hagios o Theos,
2 Holy is God,
1 Hagios Ischyros,
2 Holy and Mighty,
1 Hagios Athanatos,
eleison himas.
2 Holy and Immortal One,
have mercy on us.

1 Hagios o Theos.
2 Sanctus Deus.
1 Hagios Ischyros.
2 Sanctus Fortis.
1 Hagios Athanatos,
eleison himas.
2 Sanctus Immortalis,
miserere nobis.

1 and 2 Because I led you out
 through the desert forty years
and fed you with manna and
 brought you into a land of plenty,
you have prepared a Cross
 for your Saviour.

1 Hagios o Theos,
2 Holy is God,
1 Hagios Ischyros,
2 Holy and Mighty,
1 Hagios Athanatos, eleison himas.
2 Holy and Immortal One,
  have mercy on us.

1 and 2 What more should I have
 done for you and have not done?
Indeed, I planted you as my most
 beautiful chosen vine
and you have turned very bitter
 for me,
for in my thirst you gave me
 vinegar to drink
and with a lance you pierced your
 Saviour's side.

1 Hagios o Theos,
2 Holy is God,
1 Hagios Ischyros,
2 Holy and Mighty,
1 Hagios Athanatos,
  eleison himas.
2 Holy and Immortal One, have
  mercy on us.

1 et 2 Quia eduxi te per desertum
 quadraginta annis,
et manna cibavi te,
et introduxi te in terram
 satis bonam:
parasti Crucem Salvatori tuo.

1 Hagios o Theos.
2 Sanctus Deus.
1 Hagios Ischyros.
2 Sanctus Fortis.
1 Hagios Athanatos, eleison himas.
2 Sanctus Immortalis,
  miserere nobis.

1 et 2 Quid ultra debui facere tibi,
 et non feci?
Ego quidem plantavi te
vineam electam
 meam speciosissimam:
et tu facta es mihi nimis amara:
aceto namque sitim meam potasti,
et lancea perforasti latus
 Salvatori tuo.

1 Hagios o Theos.
2 Sanctus Deus.
1 Hagios Ischyros.
2 Sanctus Fortis.
1 Hagios Athanatos,
  eleison himas.
2 Sanctus Immortalis,
  miserere nobis.

II

Cantors:
I scourged Egypt for your sake
 with its firstborn sons,
and you scourged me and handed
 me over.

Cantores:
Ego propter te flagellavi Ægyptum
cum primogenitis suis:
et tu me flagellatum tradidisti.

1 and 2 repeat:

My people, what have I done to you?
Or how have I grieved you?
Answer me!

Cantors:

I led you out from Egypt as Pharaoh
     lay sunk in the Red Sea,
and you handed me over
     to the chief priests.

1 and 2 repeat:

My people...

Cantors:

I opened up the sea before you,
and you opened my side with a lance.

1 and 2 repeat:

My people...

Cantors:

I went before you in a pillar of cloud,
and you led me into Pilate's palace.

1 and 2 repeat:

My people...

Cantors:

I fed you with manna in the desert,
and on me you rained blows
     and lashes.

1 and 2 repeat:

My people...

Cantors:

I gave you saving water
     from the rock to drink,
and for drink you gave me gall
     and vinegar.

1 and 2 repeat:

My people...

1 et 2 repetunt:

Popule meus, quid feci tibi?
Aut in quo contristavi te?
Responde mihi!

Cantores:

Ego eduxi te de Ægypto,
demerso Pharaone in Mare Rubrum:
et tu me tradidisti
     principibus sacerdotum.

1 et 2 repetunt:

Popule meus...

Cantores:

Ego ante te aperui mare:
et tu aperuisti lancea latus meum.

1 et 2 repetunt:

Popule meus...

Cantores:

Ego ante te præivi in columna nubis:
et tu me duxisti ad prætorium Pilati.

1 et 2 repetunt:

Popule meus...

Cantores:

Ego te pavi manna per desertum:
et tu me cecidisti alapis et flagellis.

1 et 2 repetunt:

Popule meus...

Cantores:

Ego te potavi aqua salutis de petra:
et tu me potasti felle et aceto.

1 et 2 repetunt:

Popule meus...

Cantors:

I struck down for you the kings
    of the Canaanites,
and you struck my head with a reed.

1 and 2 repeat:

My people...

Cantors:

I put in your hand a royal sceptre,
and you put on my head
    a crown of thorns.

1 and 2 repeat:

My people...

Cantors:

I exalted you with great power,
and you hung me on the scaffold
    of the Cross.

1 and 2 repeat:

My people...

Cantores:

Ego propter te Chananæorum
    reges percussi:
et tu percussisti arundine
    caput meum.

1 et 2 repetunt:

Popule meus...

Cantores:

Ego dedi tibi sceptrum regale:
et tu dedisti capiti meo spineam
    coronam.

1 et 2 repetunt:

Popule meus...

Cantores:

Ego te exaltavi magna virtute:
et tu me suspendisti
    in patibulo Crucis.

1 et 2 repetunt:

Popule meus...

HYMN

All:

Faithful Cross the Saints rely on,
Noble tree beyond compare!
Never was there such a scion,
Never leaf or flower so rare.
Sweet the timber, sweet the iron,
Sweet the burden that they bear!

Cantors:

Sing, my tongue, in exultation
Of our banner and device!
Make a solemn proclamation
Of a triumph and its price:
How the Saviour of creation
Conquered by his sacrifice!

Omnes:

Crux fidelis, inter omnes
    arbor una nobilis,
Nulla talem silva profert,
    flore, fronde, germine!
Dulce lignum dulci clavo
    dulce pondus sustinens!

Cantores:

Pange, lingua, gloriosi
    prœlium certaminis,
Et super crucis tropæo
    dic triumphum nobilem,
Qualiter Redemptor orbis
    immolatus vicerit.

All:

Faithful Cross the Saints rely on,
Noble tree beyond compare!
Never was there such a scion,
Never leaf or flower so rare.

Cantors:

For, when Adam first offended,
Eating that forbidden fruit,
Not all hopes of glory ended
With the serpent at the root:
Broken nature would be mended
By a second tree and shoot.

All:

Sweet the timber, sweet the iron,
Sweet the burden that they bear!

Cantors:

Thus the tempter was outwitted
By a wisdom deeper still:
Remedy and ailment fitted,
Means to cure and means to kill;
That the world might be acquitted,
Christ would do his Father's will.

All:

Faithful Cross the Saints rely on,
Noble tree beyond compare!
Never was there such a scion,
Never leaf or flower so rare.

Cantors:

So the Father, out of pity
For our self-inflicted doom,
Sent him from the heavenly city
When the holy time had come:
He, the Son and the Almighty,
Took our flesh in Mary's womb.

All:

Sweet the timber, sweet the iron,
Sweet the burden that they bear!

Omnes:

Crux fidelis, inter omnes
    arbor una nobilis,
Nulla talem silva profert,
    flore, fronde, germine!

Cantores:

De parentis protoplasti
    fraude factor condolens,
Quando pomi noxialis
    morte morsu corruit,
Ipse lignum tunc notavit,
    damna ligni ut solveret.

Omnes:

Dulce lignum dulci clavo
    dulce pondus sustinens!

Cantores:

Hoc opus nostræ salutis
    ordo depoposcerat,
Multiformis perditoris
    arte ut artem falleret,
Et medelam ferret inde,
    hostis unde læserat.

Omnes:

Crux fidelis, inter omnes
    arbor una nobilis,
Nulla talem silva profert,
    flore, fronde, germine!

Cantores:

Quando venit ergo sacri
    plenitudo temporis,
Missus est ab arce Patris
    Natus, orbis conditor,
Atque ventre virginali
    carne factus prodiit.

Omnes:

Dulce lignum dulci clavo
    dulce pondus sustinens!

Cantors:
Hear a tiny baby crying,
Founder of the seas and strands;
See his virgin Mother tying
Cloth around his feet and hands;
Find him in a manger lying
Tightly wrapped in swaddling-bands!

All:
Faithful Cross the Saints rely on,
Noble tree beyond compare!
Never was there such a scion,
Never leaf or flower so rare.

Cantors:
So he came, the long-expected,
Not in glory, not to reign;
Only born to be rejected,
Choosing hunger, toil and pain,
Till the scaffold was erected
And the Paschal Lamb was slain.

All:
Sweet the timber, sweet the iron,
Sweet the burden that they bear!

Cantors:
No disgrace was too abhorrent:
Nailed and mocked and
    parched he died;
Blood and water, double warrant,
Issue from his wounded side,
Washing in a mighty torrent
Earth and stars and oceantide.

All:
Faithful Cross the Saints rely on,
Noble tree beyond compare!
Never was there such a scion,
Never leaf or flower so rare.

Cantores:
Vagit infans inter arta
    conditus præsepia,
Membra pannis involuta
    Virgo Mater alligat,
Et manus pedesque et crura
    stricta cingit fascia.

Omnes:
Crux fidelis, inter omnes
    arbor una nobilis,
Nulla talem silva profert,
    flore, fronde, germine!

Cantores:
Lustra sex qui iam peracta,
    tempus implens corporis,
se volente, natus ad hoc,
    passioni deditus,
agnus in crucis levatur
    immolandus stipite.

Omnes:
Dulce lignum dulci clavo
    dulce pondus sustinens!

Cantores:
En acetum, fel, arundo,
    sputa, clavi, lancea;
Mite corpus perforatur,
    sanguis unde profluit;
Terra, pontus, astra, mundus
    quo lavantur flumine!

Omnes:
Crux fidelis, inter omnes
    arbor una nobilis,
Nulla talem silva profert,
    flore, fronde, germine!

Cantors:

Lofty timber,
   smooth your roughness,
Flex your boughs for blossoming;
Let your fibres lose their toughness,
Gently let your tendrils cling;
Lay aside your native gruffness,
Clasp the body of your King!

All:

Sweet the timber, sweet the iron,
Sweet the burden that they bear!

Cantors:

Noblest tree of all created,
Richly jewelled and embossed:
Post by Lamb's blood consecrated;
Spar that saves the tempest-tossed;
Scaffold-beam which, elevated,
Carries what the world has cost!

All:

Faithful Cross the Saints rely on,
Noble tree beyond compare!
Never was there such a scion,
Never leaf or flower so rare.

Cantores:

Flecte ramos, arbor alta,
   tensa laxa viscera,
Et rigor lentescat ille,
   quem dedit nativitas,
Ut superni membra Regis
   miti tendas stipite.

Omnes:

Dulce lignum dulci clavo
   dulce pondus sustinens!

Cantores:

Sola digna tu fuisti
   ferre sæcli pretium
Atque portum præparare
   nauta mundo naufrago,
Quem sacer cruor perunxit
   fusus Agni corpore.

Omnes:

Crux fidelis, inter omnes
   arbor una nobilis,
Nulla talem silva profert,
   flore, fronde, germine!

The following conclusion is never to be omitted:

All:

Wisdom, power, and adoration
To the blessed Trinity
For redemption and salvation
Through the Paschal Mystery,
Now, in every generation,
And for all eternity. Amen.

Omnes:

Æqua Patri Filioque,
   inclito Paraclito,
Sempiterna sit beatæ
   Trinitati gloria;
cuius alma nos redemit
   atque servat gratia. Amen.

In accordance with local circumstances or popular traditions and if it is pastorally appropriate, the **Stabat Mater** may be sung, as found in the *Graduale Romanum*, or another suitable chant in memory of the compassion of the Blessed Virgin Mary.

When the adoration has been concluded, the Cross is carried by the Deacon or a minister to its place at the altar. Lighted candles are placed around or on the altar or near the Cross.

THIRD PART:

Holy Communion

A cloth is spread on the altar, and a corporal and the Missal put in place. Meanwhile the Deacon or, if there is no Deacon, the Priest himself, putting on a humeral veil, brings the Blessed Sacrament back from the place of repose to the altar by a shorter route, while all stand in silence. Two ministers with lighted candles accompany the Blessed Sacrament and place their candlesticks around or upon the altar.

When the Deacon, if a Deacon is present, has placed the Blessed Sacrament upon the altar and uncovered the ciborium, the Priest goes to the altar and genuflects.

Then the Priest, with hands joined, says aloud:

At the Saviour's command and formed by divine teaching, we dare to say:	Præceptis salutaribus moniti, et divina institutione formati, audemus dicere:

The Priest, with hands extended says, and all present continue:

Our Father, who art in heaven,
hallowed be thy name;
thy kingdom come,
thy will be done
on earth as it is in heaven.
Give us this day our daily bread,
and forgive us our trespasses,
as we forgive those who trespass
    against us;
and lead us not into temptation,
but deliver us from evil.
	Pater noster, qui es in cælis:
	sanctificetur nomen tuum;
	adveniat regnum tuum;
	fiat voluntas tua, sicut in cælo,
	    et in terra.
	Panem nostrum cotidianum
	    da nobis hodie;
	et dimitte nobis debita nostra,
	sicut et nos dimittimus
	    debitoribus nostris;
	et ne nos inducas in tentationem;
	sed libera nos a malo.

With hands extended, the Priest continues alone:

Deliver us, Lord, we pray,
    from every evil,
graciously grant peace in our days,
that, by the help of your mercy,
we may be always free from sin
and safe from all distress,
as we await the blessed hope
and the coming of our Saviour,
    Jesus Christ.
	Libera nos, quæsumus, Domine,
	    ab omnibus malis,
	da propitius pacem in diebus nostris,
	ut, ope misericordiæ tuæ adiuti,
	et a peccato simus semper liberi
	et ab omni perturbatione securi:
	exspectantes beatam spem
	et adventum Salvatoris nostri
	    Iesu Christi.

He joins his hands.

The people conclude the prayer, acclaiming:

For the kingdom,	Quia tuum est regnum,
the power and the glory are yours	et potestas,
now and for ever.	et gloria in sæcula.

Then the Priest, with hands joined, says quietly:

May the receiving of your Body	Perceptio Corporis tui,
and Blood,	Domine Iesu Christe,
Lord Jesus Christ,	non mihi proveniat in iudicium
not bring me to judgement	et condemnationem:
and condemnation,	sed pro tua pietate prosit mihi
but through your loving mercy	ad tutamentum mentis et corporis,
be for me protection in mind	et ad medelam percipiendam.
and body	
and a healing remedy.	

The Priest then genuflects, takes a particle, and, holding it slightly raised over the ciborium, while facing the people, says aloud:

Behold the Lamb of God,	Ecce Agnus Dei, ecce qui tollit
behold him who takes away	peccata mundi.
the sins of the world.	Beati qui ad cenam
Blessed are those called	Agni vocati sunt.
to the supper of the Lamb.	

And together with the people he adds once:

Lord, I am not worthy	Domine, non sum dignus,
that you should enter under my roof,	ut intres sub tectum meum,
but only say the word	sed tantum dic verbo,
and my soul shall be healed.	et sanabitur anima mea.

And facing the altar, he reverently consumes the Body of Christ, saying quietly:

| May the Body of Christ keep me | Corpus Christi custodiat me |
| safe for eternal life. | in vitam æternam. |

He then proceeds to distribute Communion to the faithful. During Communion, Psalm 21 or another appropriate chant may be sung.

When the distribution of Communion has been completed, the ciborium is taken by the Deacon or another suitable minister to a place prepared outside the church or, if circumstances so require, it is placed in the tabernacle.

Then the Priest says: **Let us pray,** and, after a period of sacred silence, if circumstances so suggest, has been observed, he says the Prayer after Communion.

Almighty ever-living God,
who have restored us to life
by the blessed Death
   and Resurrection of your Christ,
preserve in us the work
   of your mercy,
that, by partaking of this mystery,
we may have a life unceasingly
   devoted to you.
Through Christ our Lord.
R. Amen.

Omnipotens sempiterne Deus,
qui nos Christi tui beata morte
   et resurrectione reparasti,
conserva in nobis opus
   misericordiæ tuæ,
ut huius mysterii participatione
perpetua devotione vivamus.
Per Christum Dominum nostrum.
R. Amen.

For the Dismissal the Deacon or, if there is no Deacon, the Priest himself, may say the invitation **Bow down for the blessing**.

Then the Priest, standing facing the people and extending his hands over them, says this Prayer over the People:

May abundant blessing, O Lord,
   we pray,
descend upon your people,
who have honoured the Death
   of your Son
in the hope of their resurrection:
may pardon come,
comfort be given,
holy faith increase,
and everlasting redemption
   be made secure.
Through Christ our Lord.
R. Amen.

Super populum tuum,
   quæsumus, Domine,
qui mortem Filii tui in spe suæ
   resurrectionis recoluit,
benedictio copiosa descendat,
indulgentia veniat,
   consolatio tribuatur,
fides sancta succrescat,
   redemptio sempiterna firmetur.
Per Christum Dominum nostrum.
R. Amen.

And all, after genuflecting to the Cross, depart in silence.

After the celebration, the altar is stripped, but the Cross remains on the altar with two or four candlesticks.

Vespers (Evening Prayer) is not celebrated by those who have been present at the solemn afternoon liturgical celebration.

REFLECTION

✠

John's narrative of the Passion is different from that of the synoptic Gospels in important respects. Some of these differences are matters of emphasis, others spring from a set of different facts. After Caiaphas's decision no Jewish trial scene before the High Priest, no meeting of a Sanhedrin to prepare a charge to put before Pilate, was necessary. Instead John gives an interrogation before Annas, the ex-High Priest and father-in-law of Caiaphas. The trial before Pilate may well be built on the same incident as that of the synoptics, but in John it is highly elaborated for theological reasons.

The Johannine account is not the story of a condemned criminal being dragged to the disgraceful and tortured death reserved for slaves. Jesus is the majestic king, who proceeds royally to his triumph in death. There is no painful prayer for release in Gethsemane. From the beginning it is stressed that Jesus is fully aware of what is to happen. Before he can be arrested his captors repeatedly fall to the ground in an involuntary gesture of reverence at Jesus' pronouncement of the divine name, "I am". Jesus commands them to let his followers go, and is taken only when he gives the word (18:11). The humiliating elements of the other accounts, such as buffeting, spitting and the challenge to prophesy, have disappeared. Jesus is emphatically declared king in the three great world languages by the very man who condemns him to death (19:20-22). John even notes that the proclamation was publicly acknowledged by "many of the Jews".

Not only is Jesus king; he continues his role as revealer and judge as well. In the interview with Annas it is Jesus who challenges and questions the High Priest, reiterating his own teaching which he has given for all the world to hear. Similarly at the trial before Pilate, Jesus questions the governor and shows his control, until Pilate collapses with the feeble evasion, "What is truth?" – a humiliating self-condemnation in this gospel of truth. The judgement reaches its climax when the Jewish leaders, in a formal and balanced scene, condemn themselves before Jesus: he is enthroned on the judgement seat as judge and crowned – with thorns – as king, still wearing the royal purple robe of his mockery, while they deny the very existence of Judaism by declaring, "We have no king but Caesar" (19:15). If the God of Israel is not universal king, then Israel has no point or purpose.

The final scene has special significance. Jesus carries his own cross, unaided, and is enthroned on it – no agonising details of nailing and hoisting – between two attendants. There is no final psalm quotation of seeming despair (as in Mark and Matthew) or of resignation (as in Luke), no wordless "great cry" as Jesus expires. In John Jesus prepares the community of the future. In contrast to the other Gospels, Mary and the Beloved Disciple stand at the foot of the cross and are entrusted to each other's care to constitute the first Christian community, the woman and the man, the mother and the ideal disciple. This is cemented by the gift of the Spirit, as Jesus – with typical Johannine ambiguity – "gave over his spirit". Does this mean "breathed his last" or "gave them the Holy Spirit"? Only then does Jesus consent to die, with the words, "It is fulfilled".

HOLY SATURDAY

On Holy Saturday the Church waits at the Lord's tomb in prayer and fasting, meditating on his Passion and Death and on his Descent into Hell, and awaiting his Resurrection.

The Church abstains from the Sacrifice of the Mass, with the sacred table left bare, until after the solemn Vigil, that is, the anticipation by night of the Resurrection, when the time comes for paschal joys, the abundance of which overflows to occupy fifty days.

Holy Communion may only be given on this day as Viaticum.

MORNING PRAYER FOR HOLY SATURDAY

Mass is not celebrated on Holy Saturday. The Church does however continue to pray the Divine Office. We give below the texts of Morning Prayer (Lauds) from the Divine Office, together with one of the long readings from the Office of Readings; this may be a helpful way to enter into the liturgical rhythm of this day of waiting.

V. O Lord, open our lips.
R. **And we shall praise your name.**

Glory be...

Invitatory ant. **Christ the Lord suffered for us and was buried.
Come, let us adore him.**

Psalm 94

Come, ring out our joy to the Lord;
hail the God who saves us.
Let us come before him, giving thanks,
with songs let us hail the Lord. Ant.

A mighty God is the Lord,
a great king above all gods.
In his hand are the depths of the earth;
the heights of the mountains are his.
To him belongs the sea, for he made it
and the dry land shaped by his hands. Ant.

Come in; let us bow and bend low;
let us kneel before the God who made us
for he is our God and we
the people who belong to his pasture,
the flock that is led by his hand. Ant.

O that today you would listen to his voice!
"Harden not your hearts as at Meribah,
as on that day at Massah in the desert
when your fathers put me to the test;
when they tried me, though they saw my work. Ant.

For forty years I was wearied of these people
and I said: 'Their hearts are astray,
these people do not know my ways.'
Then I took an oath in my anger:
'Never shall they enter my rest.'" Ant.

Glory be...

Ant. **Christ the Lord suffered for us and was buried. Come, let us adore him.**

Hymn

> O loving wisdom of our God!
> When all was sin and shame,
> a second Adam to the fight
> and to the rescue came.

> O generous love! that he, who smote
> in Man for man the foe,
> the double agony in Man
> for man should undergo;

> And in the garden secretly,
> and on the cross on high,
> should teach his brethren, and inspire
> to suffer and to die.

> Praise to the Holiest in the height,
> and in the depth be praise,
> in all his words most wonderful,
> most sure in all his ways.

Psalmody

Ant. 1 **They will mourn for him as for an only son, since it is the innocent one of the Lord who has been slain.**

Psalm 63 (64)

> Hear my voice, O God, as I complain,
> guard my life from dread of the foe.
> Hide me from the band of the wicked,
> from the throng of those who do evil.

> They sharpen their tongues like swords;
> they aim bitter words like arrows
> to shoot at the innocent from ambush,
> shooting suddenly and recklessly.

> They scheme their evil course;
> they conspire to lay secret snares.
> They say: "Who will see us?
> Who can search out our crimes?"

He will search who searches the mind
and knows the depths of the heart.
God has shot then with his arrow
and dealt them sudden wounds.
Their own tongue has brought them to ruin
and all who see them mock.

Then all men will fear;
they will tell what God has done.
They will understand God's deeds.
The just will rejoice in the Lord
and fly to him for refuge.
All the upright hearts will glory.

Glory be...

Ant. **They will mourn for him as for an only son, since it is the innocent one of the Lord who has been slain.**

Ant. 2 **Save my soul from the gates of hell, Lord.**

Canticle: Is 38:10-14,17-20

I said, in the noontide of my days I must depart;
I am consigned to the gates of Sheol
for the rest of my years.

I said, I shall not see the Lord
in the land of the living;
I shall look upon man no more
among the inhabitants of the world.

My dwelling is plucked up and removed from me
like a shepherd's tent;
like a weaver, I have rolled up my life;
he cuts me off from the loom;

From day to night you bring me to an end;
I cry for help until morning;
like a lion he breaks all my bones;
from day to night you bring me to an end.

Like a swallow or a crane I clamour,
I moan like a dove.
My eyes are weary with looking upward.
O Lord I am oppressed; be my security.

Lo, it was for my welfare
that I had great bitterness;
but you have held back my life
from the pit of destruction
for you have cast all my sins
behind your back.

For Sheol cannot thank you,
death cannot praise you;
those who go down to the pit
cannot hope for your faithfulness.

The living, the living, he thanks you
as I do this day;
the father makes known to the children
your faithfulness.

The Lord will save me
and we will sing to stringed instruments
all the days of our life,
at the house of the Lord.

Glory be...

Ant. **Save my soul from the gates of hell, Lord.**

Ant. 3 **I was dead and now I am to live for ever and ever,
and I hold the keys of death and of hell.**

Psalm 150

Praise God in his holy place,
praise him in his mighty heavens.
Praise him for his powerful deeds,
praise his surpassing greatness.

O praise him with sound of trumpet,
praise him with lute and harp.
Praise him with timbrel and dance,
praise him with strings and pipes.

O praise him with resounding cymbals,
praise him with clashing of cymbals.
Let everything that lives and that breathes
give praise to the Lord.

Glory be...

Ant. **I was dead and now I am to live for ever and ever,
and I hold the keys of death and of hell.**

Scripture Reading   Ho 6:1-3a
Come, let us return to the Lord. He has torn us to pieces but he will heal
us; he has struck us down, but he will bandage our wounds; after a day or
two he will bring us back to life, on the third day he will raise us and we
shall live in his presence.

In place of the short responsory the following antiphon is said:
Christ humbled himself for us, and, in obedience, accepted death, even
death on a cross. Therefore God raised him to the heights and gave him
the name which is above all other names.

The Benedictus
Ant. **Save us, Saviour of the world. By the cross and the shedding of
your blood you have redeemed us. Come to help us, Lord, our God.**

Blessed be the Lord, the God of Israel!
He has visited his people and redeemed them.

He has raised up for us a mighty saviour
in the house of David his servant,
as he promised by the lips of holy men,
those who were his prophets from of old.

A saviour who would free us from our foes,
from the hands of all who hate us.
So his love for our fathers is fulfilled
and his holy covenant remembered.

He swore to Abraham our father to grant us,
that freed from fear, and saved from the hands of our foes,
we might serve him in holiness and justice
all the days of our life in his presence.

As for you, little child,
you shall be called a prophet of God, the Most High.
You shall go ahead of the Lord
to prepare his ways before him,

To make known to his people their salvation,
through forgiveness of all their sins,
the loving-kindness of the heart of our God
who visits us like the dawn from on high.

He will give light to those in darkness,
those who dwell in the shadow of death,
and guide us into the way of peace.

Glory be...

Ant. **Save us, Saviour of the world. By the cross and the shedding of your blood you have redeemed us. Come to help us, Lord, our God.**

Intercessions

Let us pray to our Redeemer, who suffered for us, was buried, and rose from the dead.

R. **Lord, have mercy on us.**

Christ, our Lord, you saw your mother standing by the cross; – may we share your saving passion in our time of suffering. R.

Christ ,our Saviour, you died like a grain of wheat falling into the ground; – gather us to yourself in the harvest of redemption. R.

Christ, our shepherd, lying in the tomb you were hidden from men; – teach us to love our real life, which is hidden with you in God. R.

Christ, the new Adam, you went down in to the world of the dead to free the just; – may those who have died in sin hear your voice and live. R.

Son of the living God, we were buried with you in baptism; – let us rise with you, alive to God for ever. R.

Our Father...

Concluding Prayer

Almighty, ever-living God, whose Only-begotten Son
    descended to the realm of the dead,
and rose from there to glory,
grant that your faithful people,
who were buried with him in baptism,
may, by his resurrection, obtain eternal life.
(We make our prayer) through our Lord Jesus Christ, your Son,
    who lives and reigns with you and the Holy Spirit,
    world without end.

R. **Amen.**

If a Priest or Deacon is present, then:
The Lord be with you.
R. **And with your spirit.**

May almighty God bless you, the Father,
  and the Son, and the Holy Spirit.
R. **Amen.**

Go in the peace of Christ.
R. **Thanks be to God.**

If no Priest or Deacon is present or in recitation on one's own:
The Lord bless us, and keep us from all evil,
  and bring us to everlasting life.
R. **Amen.**

From an Ancient Homily for Holy Saturday
(from the Office of Readings)

What is happening? Today there is a great silence over the earth, a great silence, and stillness, a great silence because the King sleeps; the earth was in terror and was still, because God slept in the flesh and raised up those who were sleeping from the ages. God has died in the flesh, and the underworld has trembled.

Truly he goes to seek out our first parent like a lost sheep; he wishes to visit those who sit in darkness and in the shadow of death. He goes to free the prisoner Adam and his fellow-prisoner Eve from their pains, he who is God, and Adam's son.

The Lord goes in to them holding his victorious weapon, his cross. When Adam, the first created man, sees him, he strikes his breast in terror and calls out to all: 'My Lord be with you all.' And Christ in reply says to Adam: 'And with your spirit.' And grasping his hand he raises him up, saying: 'Awake, O sleeper, and arise from the dead, and Christ shall give you light.

'I am your God, who for your sake became your son, who for you and your descendants now speak and command with authority those in prison: Come forth, and those in darkness: Have light, and those who sleep: Rise.

'I command you: Awake, sleeper, I have not made you to be held a prisoner in the underworld. Arise from the dead; I am the life of the dead. Arise, O man, work of my hands, arise, you who were fashioned in my image. Rise, let us go hence; for you in me and I in you, together we are one undivided person.

'For you, I your God became your son; for you, I the Master took on your form; that of slave; for you, I who am above the heavens came on earth and under the earth; for you, man, I became as a man without help, free among the dead; for you, who left a garden, I was handed over to Jews from a garden and crucified in a garden.

'Look at the spittle on my face, which I received because of you, in order to restore you to that first divine inbreathing at creation. See the blows on my cheeks, which I accepted in order to refashion your distorted form to my own image.

'See the scourging of my back, which I accepted in order to disperse the load of your sins which was laid upon your back. See my hands nailed to the tree for a good purpose, for you, who stretched out your hand to the tree for an evil one.

'I slept on the cross and a sword pierced my side, for you, who slept in paradise and brought forth Eve from your side. My side healed the pain of your side; my sleep will release you from your sleep in Hades; my sword has checked the sword which was turned against you.

'But arise, let us go hence. The enemy brought you out of the land of paradise; I will reinstate you, no longer in paradise, but on the throne of heaven. I denied you the tree of life, which was a figure, but now I myself am united to you, I who am life. I posted the cherubim to guard you as they would slaves; now I make the cherubim worship you as they would God.

'The cherubim throne has been prepared, the bearers are ready and waiting, the bridal chamber is in order, the food is provided, the everlasting houses and rooms are in readiness; the treasures of good things have been opened; the kingdom of heaven has been prepared before the ages.'

EASTER SUNDAY OF THE RESURRECTION OF THE LORD

THE EASTER VIGIL IN THE HOLY NIGHT

During the Easter Vigil, the Church reads the account of creation as a prophecy. In the resurrection, we see the most sublime fulfilment of what this text describes as the beginning of all things. God says once again: "Let there be light!" The resurrection of Jesus is an eruption of light. Death is conquered, the tomb is thrown open. The Risen One himself is Light, the Light of the world. With the resurrection, the Lord's day enters the nights of history. Beginning with the resurrection, God's light spreads throughout the world and throughout history. Day dawns. This Light alone – Jesus Christ – is the true light, something more than the physical phenomenon of light. He is pure Light: God himself, who causes a new creation to be born in the midst of the old, transforming chaos into cosmos.

(Pope Benedict XVI)

By most ancient tradition, this is the night of keeping vigil for the Lord (Ex 12:42), in which, following the Gospel admonition (Lk 12:35-37), the faithful, carrying lighted lamps in their hands, should be like those looking for the Lord when he returns, so that at his coming he may find them awake and have them sit at his table.

Of this night's Vigil, which is the greatest and most noble of all solemnities, there is to be only one celebration in each church. It is arranged, moreover, in such a way that after the Lucernarium and Easter Proclamation (which constitutes the first part of this Vigil), Holy Church meditates on the wonders the Lord God has done for his people from the beginning, trusting in his word and promise (the second part, that is, the Liturgy of the Word) until, as day approaches, with new members reborn in Baptism (the third part), the Church is called to the table the Lord has prepared for his people, the memorial of his Death and Resurrection until he comes again (the fourth part).

The entire celebration of the Easter Vigil must take place during the night, so that it begins after nightfall and ends before daybreak on the Sunday.

The Mass of the Vigil, even if it is celebrated before midnight, is a paschal Mass of the Sunday of the Resurrection.

Anyone who participates in the Mass of the night may receive Communion again at Mass during the day. A Priest who celebrates or concelebrates the Mass of the night may again celebrate or concelebrate Mass during the day.

The Easter Vigil takes the place of the Office of Readings.

The Priest is usually assisted by a Deacon. If, however, there is no Deacon, the duties of his Order, except those indicated below, are assumed by the Priest Celebrant or by a concelebrant.

The Priest and Deacon vest as at Mass, in white vestments.

Candles should be prepared for all who participate in the Vigil. The lights of the church are extinguished.

FIRST PART:

THE SOLEMN BEGINNING OF THE VIGIL OR LUCERNARIUM

The Blessing of the Fire and Preparation of the Candle

A blazing fire is prepared in a suitable place outside the church. When the people are gathered there, the Priest approaches with the ministers, one of whom carries the paschal candle. The processional cross and candles are not carried.

Where, however, a fire cannot be lit outside the church, the rite is carried out as below.

The Priest and faithful sign themselves while the Priest says: **In the name of the Father, and of the Son, and of the Holy Spirit**, and then he greets the assembled people in the usual way and briefly instructs them about the night vigil in these or similar words:

Dear brethren (brothers and sisters), on this most sacred night, in which our Lord Jesus Christ passed over from death to life, the Church calls upon her sons and daughters, scattered throughout the world, to come together to watch and pray. If we keep the memorial of the Lord's paschal solemnity in this way, listening to his word and celebrating his mysteries, then we shall have the sure hope of sharing his triumph over death and living with him in God.	Fratres carissimi, hac sacratissima nocte, in qua Dominus noster Iesus Christus de morte transivit ad vitam, Ecclesia invitat filios dispersos per orbem terrarum, ut ad vigilandum et orandum conveniant. Si ita memoriam egerimus Paschatis Domini, audientes verbum et celebrantes mysteria eius, spem habebimus participandi triumphum eius de morte et vivendi cum ipso in Deo.

Then the Priest blesses the fire, saying with hands extended:

Let us pray.	Oremus.

O God, who through your Son bestowed upon the faithful the fire of your glory, sanctify ✠ this new fire, we pray, and grant that, by these paschal celebrations, we may be so inflamed with heavenly desires, that with minds made pure we may attain festivities of unending splendour. Through Christ our Lord. R. Amen.	Deus, qui per Filium tuum claritatis tuæ ignem fidelibus contulisti, novum hunc ignem ✠ sanctifica, et concede nobis, ita per hæc festa paschalia cælestibus desideriis inflammari, ut ad perpetuæ claritatis puris mentibus valeamus festa pertingere. Per Christum Dominum nostrum. R. Amen.

After the blessing of the new fire, one of the ministers brings the paschal candle to the Priest, who cuts a cross into the candle with a stylus. Then he makes the Greek letter Alpha above the cross, the letter Omega below, and the four numerals of the current year between the arms of the cross, saying meanwhile:

1. Christ yesterday and today	1. Christus heri et hodie
2. the Beginning and the End	2. Principium et Finis
3. the Alpha	3. Alpha
4. and the Omega	4. et Omega
5. All time belongs to him	5. Ipsius sunt tempora
6. and all the ages	6. et sæcula
7. To him be glory and power	7. Ipsi gloria et imperium
8. through every age and for ever. Amen.	8. per universa æternitatis sæcula. Amen.

When the cutting of the cross and of the other signs has been completed, the Priest may insert five grains of incense into the candle in the form of a cross, meanwhile saying:

1. By his holy	1. Per sua sancta vulnera
2. and glorious wounds,	2. gloriosa
3. may Christ the Lord	3. custodiat
4. guard us	4. et conservet nos
5. and protect us. Amen.	5. Christus Dominus. Amen.

Where, because of difficulties that may occur, a fire is not lit, the blessing of fire is adapted to the circumstances. When the people are gathered in the church as on other occasions, the Priest comes to the door of the church, along with the ministers carrying the paschal candle. The people, insofar as is possible, turn to face the Priest.

The greeting and address take place as above; then the fire is blessed and the candle is prepared, as above.

The Priest lights the paschal candle from the new fire, saying:

May the light of Christ rising in glory dispel the darkness of our hearts and minds.	**Lumen Christi gloriose resurgentis dissipet tenebras cordis et mentis.**

As regards the preceding elements, Conferences of Bishops may also establish other forms more adapted to the culture of the different peoples.

Procession

When the candle has been lit, one of the ministers takes burning coals from the fire and places them in the thurible, and the Priest puts incense into it in the usual way. The Deacon or, if there is no Deacon, another suitable minister, takes the paschal candle and a procession forms. The thurifer with the smoking thurible precedes the Deacon or other minister who carries the paschal candle. After them follows the Priest with the ministers and the people, all holding in their hands unlit candles.

At the door of the church the Deacon, standing and raising up the candle, sings:

The Light of Christ. | **Lumen Christi.**

And all reply:

Thanks be to God. | **Deo gratias.**

The Priest lights his candle from the flame of the paschal candle.

Then the Deacon moves forward to the middle of the church and, standing and raising up the candle, sings a second time:

The Light of Christ. | **Lumen Christi.**

And all reply:

Thanks be to God. | **Deo gratias.**

All light their candles from the flame of the paschal candle and continue in procession.

When the Deacon arrives before the altar, he stands facing the people, raises up the candle and sings a third time:

The Light of Christ. | **Lumen Christi.**

And all reply:

Thanks be to God. | **Deo gratias.**

Then the Deacon places the paschal candle on a large candlestand prepared next to the ambo or in the middle of the sanctuary.

And lights are lit throughout the church, except for the altar candles.

The Easter Proclamation (Exsultet)

Arriving at the altar, the Priest goes to his chair, gives his candle to a minister, puts incense into the thurible and blesses the incense as at the Gospel at Mass. The Deacon goes to the Priest and saying, **Your blessing, Father**, asks for and receives a blessing from the Priest, who says in a low voice:

May the Lord be in your heart
   and on your lips,
that you may proclaim his paschal
   praise worthily and well,
in the name of the Father and of
   the Son, ✠ and of the Holy Spirit.

The Deacon replies: **Amen.**

Dominus sit in corde tuo
   et in labiis tuis,
ut digne et competenter annunties
suum paschale præconium:
in nomine Patris, et Filii,
   ✠ et Spiritus Sancti.

Amen.

This blessing is omitted if the Proclamation is made by someone who is not a Deacon.

The Deacon, after incensing the book and the candle, proclaims the Easter Proclamation (Exsultet) at the ambo or at a lectern, with all standing and holding lighted candles in their hands.

The Easter Proclamation may be made, in the absence of a Deacon, by the Priest himself or by another concelebrating Priest. If, however, because of necessity, a lay cantor sings the Proclamation, the words **Therefore, dearest friends** up to the end of the invitation are omitted, along with the greeting **The Lord be with you**.

The Proclamation may also be sung in the shorter form p.213.

Longer Form of the Easter Proclamation

Exult, let them exult,
   the hosts of heaven,
exult, let Angel ministers
   of God exult,
let the trumpet of salvation
sound aloud our mighty
   King's triumph!
Be glad, let earth be glad,
   as glory floods her,
ablaze with light from her
   eternal King,
let all corners of the earth be glad,
knowing an end to gloom
   and darkness.

Exsultet iam angelica
   turba cælorum:
exsultent divina mysteria:
et pro tanti Regis victoria tuba
   insonet salutaris.

Gaudeat et tellus tantis
   irradiata fulgoribus:
et, æterni Regis splendore illustrata,
totius orbis se sentiat
   amisisse caliginem.

Rejoice, let Mother Church
    also rejoice,
arrayed with the lightning
    of his glory,
let this holy building shake with joy,
filled with the mighty voices
    of the peoples.

(Therefore, dearest friends,
standing in the awesome glory
    of this holy light,
invoke with me, I ask you,
the mercy of God almighty,
that he, who has been pleased
    to number me,
though unworthy, among the Levites,
may pour into me his light
    unshadowed,
that I may sing this candle's
    perfect praises.)

(V. The Lord be with you.
R. And with your spirit.)
V. Lift up your hearts.
R. We lift them up to the Lord.
V. Let us give thanks to the Lord
    our God.
R. It is right and just.
It is truly right and just,
with ardent love of mind and heart
and with devoted service of our voice,
to acclaim our God invisible,
    the almighty Father,
and Jesus Christ, our Lord, his Son,
    his Only Begotten.

Who for our sake paid Adam's debt
    to the eternal Father,
and, pouring out his own dear Blood,
wiped clean the record of our
    ancient sinfulness.

Lætetur et mater Ecclesia,
tanti luminis adornata fulgoribus:
et magnis populorum vocibus hæc
    aula resultet.

(Quapropter astantes vos,
    fratres carissimi,
ad tam miram huius sancti
    luminis claritatem,
una mecum, quæso,
Dei omnipotentis
    misericordiam invocate.
Ut, qui me non meis meritis
intra Levitarum numerum dignatus
    est aggregare,
luminis sui claritatem infundens,
cerei huius laudem
    implere perficiat.)

(V. Dominus vobiscum.
R. Et cum spiritu tuo.)
V. Sursum corda.
R. Habemus ad Dominum.
V. Gratias agamus Domino
    Deo nostro.
R. Dignum et iustum est.
Vere dignum et iustum est,
invisibilem Deum
    Patrem omnipotentem
Filiumque eius Unigenitum,
Dominum nostrum
    Iesum Christum,
toto cordis ac mentis affectu
    et vocis ministerio personare.

Qui pro nobis æterno Patri Adæ
    debitum solvit,
et veteris piaculi cautionem
    pio cruore detersit.

These then are the feasts of Passover,
in which is slain the Lamb,
   the one true Lamb,
whose Blood anoints the doorposts
   of believers.

This is the night,
when once you led our forebears,
   Israel's children,
from slavery in Egypt
and made them pass dry-shod
   through the Red Sea.

This is the night
that with a pillar of fire
banished the darkness of sin.

This is the night
that even now, throughout the world,
sets Christian believers apart
   from worldly vices
and from the gloom of sin,
leading them to grace
and joining them to his holy ones.

This is the night,
when Christ broke the prison-bars
   of death
and rose victorious
   from the underworld.

Our birth would have been no gain,
had we not been redeemed.
O wonder of your humble care for us!
O love, O charity beyond all telling,
to ransom a slave you gave away
   your Son!

O truly necessary sin of Adam,
destroyed completely by the Death
   of Christ!

Hæc sunt enim festa paschalia,
in quibus verus ille Agnus occiditur,
cuius sanguine postes
   fidelium consecrantur.

Hæc nox est,
in qua primum patres nostros,
filios Israel eductos de Ægypto,
Mare Rubrum sicco vestigio
   transire fecisti.

Hæc igitur nox est,
quæ peccatorum tenebras columnæ
   illuminatione purgavit.

Hæc nox est,
quæ hodie per universum mundum
   in Christo credentes,
a vitiis sæculi et caligine
   peccatorum segregatos,
reddit gratiæ, sociat sanctitati.

Hæc nox est,
in qua, destructis vinculis mortis,
Christus ab inferis victor ascendit.

Nihil enim nobis nasci profuit,
   nisi redimi profuisset.
O mira circa nos tuæ pietatis
   dignatio!
O inæstimablilis dilectio caritatis:
ut servum redimeres,
   Filium tradidisti!

O certe necessarium
   Adæ peccatum,
quod Christi morte deletum est!

O happy fault
that earned so great,
 so glorious a Redeemer!

O truly blessed night,
worthy alone to know the time
 and hour
when Christ rose
 from the underworld!

This is the night
of which it is written:
The night shall be as bright as day,
dazzling is the night for me,
and full of gladness.

The sanctifying power of this night
dispels wickedness,
 washes faults away,
restores innocence to the fallen,
 and joy to mourners,
drives out hatred, fosters concord,
 and brings down the mighty.

On this, your night of grace,
 O holy Father,
accept this candle, a solemn offering,
the work of bees and of your
 servants' hands,
an evening sacrifice of praise,
this gift from your most holy Church.

But now we know the praises
 of this pillar,
which glowing fire ignites
 for God's honour,
a fire into many flames divided,
yet never dimmed by sharing
 of its light,
for it is fed by melting wax,
drawn out by mother bees
to build a torch so precious.

O felix culpa,
quæ talem ac tantum meruit
 habere Redemptorem!

O vere beata nox,
quæ sola meruit scire tempus
 et horam,
in qua Christus ab inferis resurrexit!

Hæc nox est, de qua scriptum est:
Et nox sicut dies illuminabitur:
et nox illuminatio mea
 in deliciis meis.

Huius igitur sanctificatio noctis
 fugat scelera, culpas lavat:
et reddit innocentiam lapsis
 et mæstis lætitiam.
Fugat odia, concordiam parat
 et curvat imperia.

In huius igitur noctis gratia,
suscipe, sancte Pater, laudis huius
 sacrificium vespertinum,
quod tibi in hac cerei
 oblatione sollemni,
per ministrorum manus
de operibus apum,
 sacrosancta reddit Ecclesia.

Sed iam columnæ huius
 præconia novimus,
quam in honorem Dei rutilans
 ignis accendit.
Qui, licet sit divisus in partes,
mutuati tamen luminis detrimenta
 non novit.
Alitur enim liquantibus ceris,
quas in substantiam pretiosæ
 huius lampadis
apis mater eduxit.

O truly blessed night,
when things of heaven are wed
   to those of earth,
and divine to the human.

Therefore, O Lord,
we pray you that this candle,
hallowed to the honour of
   your name,
may persevere undimmed,
to overcome the darkness
   of this night.
Receive it as a pleasing fragrance,
and let it mingle with
   the lights of heaven.
May this flame be found still burning
by the Morning Star:
the one Morning Star who never sets,
Christ your Son,
who, coming back
   from death's domain,
has shed his peaceful light
   on humanity,
and lives and reigns
   for ever and ever.
R. Amen.

O vere beata nox,
in qua terrenis cælestia,
   humanis divina iunguntur!

Oramus ergo te, Domine,
ut cereus iste in honorem tui
   nominis consecratus,
ad noctis huius
   caliginem destruendam,
indeficiens perseveret.

Et in odorem suavitatis acceptus,
supernis luminaribus misceatur.
Flammas eius lucifer
   matutinus inveniat:

Ille, inquam, lucifer,
   qui nescit occasum:
Christus Filius tuus,
qui, regressus ab inferis, humano
   generi serenus illuxit,
et vivit et regnat
   in sæcula sæculorum.
R. Amen.

Shorter Form of the Easter Proclamation

Exult, let them exult,
   the hosts of heaven,
exult, let Angel ministers
   of God exult,
let the trumpet of salvation
sound aloud our mighty
   King's triumph!
Be glad, let earth be glad, as glory
   floods her,
ablaze with light from her
   eternal King,
let all corners of the earth be glad,
knowing an end to gloom
   and darkness.

Exsultet iam angelica
   turba cælorum:
exsultent divina mysteria:
et pro tanti Regis victoria tuba
   insonet salutaris.

Gaudeat et tellus tantis
   irradiata fulgoribus:
et, æterni Regis splendore illustrata,
totius orbis se sentiat
   amisisse caliginem.

Rejoice, let Mother Church
    also rejoice,
arrayed with the lightning
    of his glory,
let this holy building shake with joy,
filled with the mighty voices
    of the peoples.

Lætetur et mater Ecclesia,
tanti luminis adornata fulgoribus:
et magnis populorum vocibus hæc
    aula resultet.

(V. The Lord be with you.
R. And with your spirit.)
V. Lift up your hearts.
R. We lift them up to the Lord.
V. Let us give thanks to the Lord
    our God.
R. It is right and just.

(V. Dominus vobiscum.
R. Et cum spiritu tuo.)
V. Sursum corda.
R. Habemus ad Dominum.
V. Gratias agamus Domino
    Deo nostro.
R. Dignum et iustum est.

It is truly right and just,
with ardent love of mind and heart
and with devoted service of our voice,
to acclaim our God invisible,
    the almighty Father,
and Jesus Christ, our Lord, his Son,
    his Only Begotten.

Vere dignum et iustum est,
invisibilem Deum
    Patrem omnipotentem
Filiumque eius Unigenitum,
Dominum nostrum
    Iesum Christum,
toto cordis ac mentis affectu
    et vocis ministerio personare.

Who for our sake paid Adam's debt
    to the eternal Father,
and, pouring out his own dear Blood,
wiped clean the record
    of our ancient sinfulness.

Qui pro nobis æterno Patri Adæ
    debitum solvit,
et veteris piaculi cautionem pio
    cruore detersit.

These then are the feasts of Passover,
in which is slain the Lamb,
    the one true Lamb,
whose Blood anoints the doorposts
    of believers.

Hæc sunt enim festa paschalia,
in quibus verus ille
    Agnus occiditur,
cuius sanguine postes
    fidelium consecrantur.

This is the night,
when once you led our forebears,
    Israel's children,
from slavery in Egypt
and made them pass dry-shod
    through the Red Sea.

Hæc nox est,
in qua primum patres nostros,
    filios Israel
eductos de Ægypto,
Mare Rubrum sicco vestigio
    transire fecisti.

This is the night
that with a pillar of fire
banished the darkness of sin.

This is the night
that even now, throughout the world,
sets Christian believers apart
     from worldly vices
and from the gloom of sin,
leading them to grace
and joining them to his holy ones.

This is the night,
when Christ broke the prison-bars
     of death
and rose victorious
     from the underworld.

O wonder of your humble care for us!
O love, O charity beyond all telling,
to ransom a slave you gave away
     your Son!

O truly necessary sin of Adam,
destroyed completely by the Death
     of Christ!

O happy fault
that earned so great,
     so glorious a Redeemer!

The sanctifying power of this night
dispels wickedness,
     washes faults away,
restores innocence to the fallen,
     and joy to mourners.

O truly blessed night,
when things of heaven are wed
     to those of earth,
and divine to the human.

On this, your night of grace,
     O holy Father,
accept this candle, a solemn offering,
the work of bees and of your

Hæc igitur nox est,
quæ peccatorum tenebras columnæ
     illuminatione purgavit.

Hæc nox est,
quæ hodie per universum mundum
     in Christo credentes,
a vitiis sæculi et caligine
peccatorum segregatos,
reddit gratiæ, sociat sanctitati.

Hæc nox est,
in qua, destructis vinculis mortis,
Christus ab inferis victor ascendit.

O mira circa nos tuæ
     pietatis dignatio!
O inæstimablilis dilectio caritatis:
ut servum redimeres,
     Filium tradidisti!

O certe necessarium Adæ peccatum,
quod Christi morte deletum est!

O felix culpa,
quæ talem ac tantum meruit
     habere Redemptorem!

Huius igitur sanctificatio noctis
     fugat scelera, culpas lavat:
et reddit innocentiam lapsis
     et mæstis lætitiam.

O vere beata nox,
in qua terrenis cælestia,
     humanis divina iunguntur!

In huius igitur noctis gratia,
suscipe, sancte Pater, laudis huius
     sacrificium vespertinum,
quod tibi in hac cerei

servants' hands,
an evening sacrifice of praise,
this gift from your most
    holy Church.

Therefore, O Lord,
we pray you that this candle,
hallowed to the honour
    of your name,
may persevere undimmed,
to overcome the darkness
    of this night.
Receive it as a pleasing fragrance,
and let it mingle with the lights
    of heaven.
May this flame be found
    still burning
by the Morning Star:
the one Morning Star who never sets,
Christ your Son,
who, coming back from
    death's domain,
has shed his peaceful light
    on humanity,
and lives and reigns
    for ever and ever.
℞. Amen.

oblatione sollemni,
per ministrorum manus
de operibus apum,
    sacrosancta reddit Ecclesia.

Oramus ergo te, Domine,
ut cereus iste in honorem tui
    nominis consecratus,
ad noctis huius
    caliginem destruendam,
indeficiens perseveret.
Et in odorem suavitatis acceptus,
supernis luminaribus misceatur.
Flammas eius lucifer
    matutinus inveniat:
Ille, inquam, lucifer,
    qui nescit occasum:
Christus Filius tuus,
qui, regressus ab inferis,
    humano generi serenus illuxit,
et vivit et regnat
    in sæcula sæculorum.
℞. Amen.

SECOND PART:

The Liturgy of the Word

In this Vigil, the mother of all Vigils, nine readings are provided, namely seven from the Old Testament and two from the New (the Epistle and Gospel), all of which should be read whenever this can be done, so that the character of the Vigil, which demands an extended period of time, may be preserved.

Nevertheless, where more serious pastoral circumstances demand it, the number of readings from the Old Testament may be reduced, always bearing in mind that the reading of the Word of God is a fundamental part of this Easter Vigil. At least three readings should be read from the Old Testament, both from the Law and from the Prophets, and their respective Responsorial Psalms should be sung. Never, moreover, should the reading of chapter 14 of Exodus with its canticle be omitted.

After setting aside their candles, all sit. Before the readings begin, the Priest instructs the people in these or similar words:

Dear brethren (brothers and sisters), now that we have begun
  our solemn Vigil,
let us listen with quiet hearts
  to the Word of God.
Let us meditate on how God in
  times past saved his people
and in these, the last days, has sent
  us his Son as our Redeemer.
Let us pray that our God may
  complete this paschal work
  of salvation
by the fullness of redemption.

Vigiliam sollemniter ingressi,
  fratres carissimi,
quieto corde nunc verbum
  Dei audiamus.
Meditemur, quomodo Deus
  populum suum
elapsis temporibus salvum fecerit,
et novissime nobis Filium suum
  miserit Redemptorem.
Oremus, ut Deus noster hoc
  paschale salvationis opus
ad plenam redemptionem perficiat.

Then the readings follow. A reader goes to the ambo and proclaims the reading. Afterwards a psalmist or a cantor sings or says the Psalm with the people making the response. Then all rise, the Priest says, **Let us pray** and, after all have prayed for a while in silence, he says the prayer corresponding to the reading. In place of the Responsorial Psalm a period of sacred silence may be observed, in which case the pause after **Let us pray** is omitted.

FIRST READING

A reading from the book of Genesis   1:1-2:2

God saw all he made, and indeed it was very good.

[In the beginning God created the heavens and the earth.] Now the earth was a formless void, there was darkness over the deep, and God's spirit hovered over the water.

God said, 'Let there be light,' and there was light. God saw that light was good, and God divided light from darkness. God called light 'day', and darkness he called 'night'. Evening came and morning came: the first day.

God said, 'Let there be a vault in the waters to divide the waters in two.' And so it was. God made the vault, and it divided the waters above the vault from the waters under the vault. God called the vault 'heaven'. Evening came and morning came: the second day.

God said, 'Let the waters under heaven come together into a single mass, and let dry land appear.' And so it was. God called the dry land 'earth' and the mass of waters 'seas', and God saw that it was good.

God said, 'Let the earth produce vegetation: seed-bearing plants, and fruit trees bearing fruit with their seed inside, on the earth.' And so it was.

The earth produced vegetation: plants bearing seed in their several kinds, and trees bearing fruit with their seed inside in their several kinds. God saw that it was good. Evening came and morning came: the third day.

God said, 'Let there be lights in the vault of heaven to divide day from night, and let them indicate festivals, days and years. Let them be lights in the vault of heaven to shine on the earth.' And so it was. God made the two great lights: the greater light to govern the day, the smaller light to govern the night, and the stars. God set them in the vault of heaven to shine on the earth, to govern the day and the night and to divide light from darkness. God saw that it was good. Evening came and morning came: the fourth day.

God said, 'Let the waters teem with living creatures, and let birds fly above the earth within the vault of heaven.' And so it was. God created great sea-serpents and every kind of living creature with which the waters teem, and every kind of winged creature. God saw that it was good. God blessed them, saying, 'Be fruitful, multiply, and fill the waters of the seas, and let the birds multiply upon the earth.' Evening came and morning came: the fifth day.

God said, 'Let the earth produce every kind of living creature: cattle, reptiles, and every kind of wild beast.' And so it was. God made every kind of wild beast, every kind of cattle, and every kind of land reptile. God saw that it was good.

[God said, 'Let us make man in our own image, in the likeness of ourselves, and let them be masters of the fish of the sea, the birds of heaven, the cattle, all the wild beasts and all the reptiles that crawl upon the earth.'

God created man in the image of himself,
in the image of God he created him,
male and female he created them.

God blessed them, saying to them, 'Be fruitful, multiply, fill the earth and conquer it. Be masters of the fish of the sea, the birds of heaven and all living animals on the earth.' God said, 'See, I give you all the seed-bearing plants that are upon the whole earth, and all the trees with seed-bearing fruit; this shall be your food. To all wild beasts, all birds of heaven and all living reptiles on the earth I give all the foliage of plants for food.' And so it was. God saw all he had made, and indeed it was very good. Evening came and morning came: the sixth day.

Thus heaven and earth were completed with all their array. On the seventh day God completed the work he had been doing. He rested on the seventh day after all the work he had been doing.

The word of the Lord.]

Shorter Form, verses 1, 26-31. Read between [ ]

Responsorial Psalm   Ps 103:1-2,5-6,10,12-14,24,35. R. Cf. v.30

R. **Send forth your spirit, O Lord,**
   and renew the face of the earth.
   Bless the Lord, my soul!
   Lord God, how great you are,
   clothed in majesty and glory,
   wrapped in light as in a robe! R.

   You founded the earth on its base,
   to stand firm from age to age.
   You wrapped it with the ocean like a cloak:
   the waters stood higher than the mountains. R.

   You make springs gush forth in the valleys:
   they flow in between the hills.
   On their banks dwell the birds of heaven;
   from the branches they sing their song. R.

   From your dwelling you water the hills;
   earth drinks its fill of your gift.
   You make the grass grow for the cattle
   and the plants to serve man's needs. R.

   How many are your works, O Lord!
   In wisdom you have made them all.
   The earth is full of your riches.
   Bless the Lord, my soul! R.

Alternative Psalm   Ps 32:4-7,12-13,20,22. R. v.5

R. **The Lord fills the earth with his love.**

   The word of the Lord is faithful
   and all his works to be trusted.
   The Lord loves justice and right
   and fills the earth with his love. R.

   By his word the heavens were made,
   by the breath of his mouth all the stars.
   He collects the waves of the ocean;
   he stores up the depths of the sea. R.

   They are happy, whose God is the Lord,
   the people he has chosen as his own.
   From the heavens the Lord looks forth,
   he sees all the children of men. R.

Our soul is waiting for the Lord.
The Lord is our help and our shield.
May your love be upon us, O Lord,
as we place all our hope in you. R.

R. **The Lord fills the earth with his love.**

Prayer

Let us pray.

Almighty ever-living God,
who are wonderful in the ordering
    of all your works,
may those you have
    redeemed understand
that there exists nothing
    more marvellous
than the world's creation
    in the beginning
except that, at the end of the ages,
Christ our Passover
    has been sacrificed.
Who lives and reigns
    for ever and ever.
R. Amen.

Or, On the creation of man:

O God, who wonderfully created
    human nature
and still more wonderfully
    redeemed it,
grant us, we pray,
to set our minds against
    the enticements of sin,
that we may merit to attain
    eternal joys.
Through Christ our Lord.
R. Amen.

Oremus.

Omnipotens sempiterne Deus,
qui es in omnium operum tuorum
    dispensatione mirabilis,
intellegant redempti tui,
    non fuisse excellentius,
quod initio factus est mundus,
quam quod in fine sæculorum
Pascha nostrum immolatus
    est Christus.
Qui vivit et regnat
    in sæcula sæculorum.
R. Amen.

Deus, qui mirabiliter creasti hominem
et mirabilius redemisti,
da nobis, quæsumus,
contra oblectamenta peccati mentis
    ratione persistere,
ut mereamur ad æterna
    gaudia pervenire.
Per Christum Dominum nostrum.
R. Amen.

SECOND READING

A reading from the book of Genesis   22:1-18

The sacrifice of Abraham, our father in faith.

[God put Abraham to the test. 'Abraham, Abraham,' he called. 'Here I am'
he replied. 'Take your son,' God said 'your only child Isaac, whom you

love, and go to the land of Moriah. There you shall offer him as a burnt offering, on a mountain I will point out to you.']

Rising early next morning Abraham saddled his ass and took with him two of his servants and his son Isaac. He chopped wood for the burnt offering and started on his journey to the place God had pointed out to him. On the third day Abraham looked up and saw the place in the distance. Then Abraham said to his servants, 'Stay here with the donkey. The boy and I will go over there; we will worship and come back to you.'

Abraham took the wood for the burnt offering, loaded it on Isaac, and carried in his own hands the fire and the knife. Then the two of them set out together. Isaac spoke to his father Abraham, 'Father' he said. 'Yes, my son' he replied. 'Look,' he said 'here are the fire and the wood, but where is the lamb for the burnt offering?' Abraham answered, 'My son, God himself will provide the lamb for the burnt offering.' Then the two of them went on together.

[When they arrived at the place God had pointed out to him, Abraham built an altar there, and arranged the wood. Then he bound his son Isaac and put him on the altar on top of the wood. Abraham stretched out his hand and seized the knife to kill his son.

But the angel of the Lord called to him from heaven. 'Abraham, Abraham' he said. 'I am here' he replied. 'Do not raise your hand against the boy' the angel said. 'Do not harm him, for now I know you fear God. You have not refused me your son, your only son.' Then looking up, Abraham saw a ram caught by its horns in a bush. Abraham took the ram and offered it as a burnt-offering in place of his son.] Abraham called this place 'The Lord provides', and hence the saying today: On the mountain the Lord provides.

[The angel of the Lord called Abraham a second time from heaven. 'I swear by my own self – it is the Lord who speaks – because you have done this, because you have not refused me your son, your only son, I will shower blessings on you, I will make your descendants as many as the stars of heaven and the grains of sand on the seashore. Your descendants shall gain possession of the gates of their enemies. All the nations of the earth shall bless themselves by your descendants, as a reward for your obedience.

The word of the Lord.]

Shorter Form, verses 1-2,9-13,15-18. Read between [ ]

Responsorial Psalm   Ps 15:5,8-11, R. v.1

R. **Preserve me, God, I take refuge in you.**

> O Lord, it is you who are my portion and cup;
> it is you yourself who are my prize.
> I keep the Lord ever in my sight:
> since he is at my right hand, I shall stand firm. R.

> And so my heart rejoices, my soul is glad;
> even my body shall rest in safety.
> For you will not leave my soul among the dead,
> nor let your beloved know decay. R.

> You will show me the path of life,
> the fullness of joy in your presence,
> at your right hand happiness for ever. R.

Prayer

Let us pray.

O God, supreme Father
   of the faithful,
who increase the children
   of your promise
by pouring out the grace
   of adoption
throughout the whole world
and who through the Paschal Mystery
make your servant Abraham father
   of nations,
as once you swore,
grant, we pray,
that your peoples may enter worthily
into the grace to which you call them.
Through Christ our Lord.
R. Amen.

Oremus.

Deus, Pater summe fidelium,
qui promissionis tuæ filios diffusa
   adoptionis gratia
in toto terrarum orbe multiplicas,
et per paschale sacramentum
Abraham puerum tuum
universarum, sicut iurasti,
   gentium efficis patrem,
da populis tuis digne ad gratiam
   tuæ vocationis intrare.
Per Christum Dominum nostrum.
R. Amen.

The following reading must always be read.

THIRD READING

A reading from book of Exodus   14:15-15:1

The sons of Israel went on dry ground right into the sea.

The Lord said to Moses, 'Why do you cry to me so? Tell the sons of Israel to march on. For yourself, raise your staff and stretch out your hand over the sea and part it for the sons of Israel to walk through the sea on dry ground. I for my part will make the heart of the Egyptians so stubborn that they will follow them. So shall I win myself glory at the expense of Pharaoh, of all his army, his chariots, his horsemen. And when I have won glory for myself, at the expense of Pharaoh and his chariots and his army, the Egyptians will learn that I am the Lord.'

Then the angel of the Lord, who marched at the front of the army of Israel, changed station and moved to their rear. The pillar of cloud changed station from the front to the rear of them, and remained there. It came between the camp of the Egyptians and the camp of Israel. The cloud was dark, and the night passed without the armies drawing any closer the whole night long. Moses stretched out his hand over the sea. The Lord drove back the sea with a strong easterly wind all night, and he made dry land of the sea. The waters parted and the sons of Israel went on dry ground right into the sea, walls of water to right and to left of them. The Egyptians gave chase: after them they went, right into the sea, all Pharaoh's horses, his chariots, and his horsemen. In the morning watch, the Lord looked down on the army of the Egyptians from the pillar of fire and of cloud, and threw the army into confusion. He so clogged their chariot wheels that they could scarcely make headway. 'Let us flee from the Israelites,' the Egyptians cried 'the Lord is fighting for them against the Egyptians!' 'Stretch out your hand over the sea,' the Lord said to Moses 'that the waters may flow back on the Egyptians and their chariots and their horsemen.' Moses stretched out his hand over the sea and, as day broke, the sea returned to its bed. The fleeing Egyptians marched right into it, and the Lord overthrew the Egyptians in the very middle of the sea. The returning waters overwhelmed the chariots and the horsemen of Pharaoh's whole army, which had followed the Israelites into the sea; not a single one of them was left. But the sons of Israel had marched through the sea on dry ground, walls of water to right and to left of them. That day, the Lord rescued Israel from the Egyptians, and Israel saw the Egyptians lying dead on the shore. Israel witnessed the great act that the Lord had performed against the Egyptians, and the people venerated the Lord; they put their faith in the Lord and in Moses, his servant.

It was then that Moses and the sons of Israel sang this song in honour of the Lord:

The choir takes up the Responsorial Psalm immediately.

Responsorial Psalm   Ex 15:1-6,17-18. R. v.1

R. **I will sing to the Lord, glorious his triumph!**

I will sing to the Lord, glorious his triumph!
Horse and rider he has thrown into the sea!
The Lord is my strength, my song, my salvation.
This is my God and I extol him,
my father's God and I give him praise. R.

The Lord is a warrior! The Lord is his name.
The chariots of Pharaoh he hurled into the sea,
the flower of his army is drowned in the sea.
The deeps hide them; they sank like a stone. R.

Your right hand, Lord, glorious in its power,
your right hand, Lord, has shattered the enemy.
In the greatness of your glory you crushed the foe. R.

You will lead your people and plant them on your mountain,
the place, O Lord, where you have made your home,
the sanctuary, Lord, which your hands have made.
The Lord will reign for ever and ever. R.

Prayer

Let us pray.

O God, whose ancient wonders
remain undimmed in splendour
    even in our day,
for what you once bestowed
    on a single people,
freeing them from
    Pharaoh's persecution
by the power of your right hand,
now you bring about as the salvation
    of the nations
through the waters of rebirth,
grant, we pray,
    that the whole world
may become children of Abraham
and inherit the dignity
    of Israel's birthright.
Through Christ our Lord.
R. Amen.

Oremus.

Deus, cuius antiqua miracula
etiam nostris temporibus
    coruscare sentimus,
dum, quod uni populo
a persecutione Pharaonis liberando
dexteræ tuæ potentia contulisti,
id in salutem gentium
per aquam regenerationis operaris,
præsta, ut in Abrahæ filios
et in Israeliticam dignitatem
totius mundi transeat plenitudo.
Per Christum Dominum nostrum.
R. Amen.

Or:

O God, who by the light
    of the New Testament
have unlocked the meaning
of wonders worked in former times,
so that the Red Sea prefigures
    the sacred font
and the nation delivered from slavery
foreshadows the Christian people,
grant, we pray, that all nations,
obtaining the privilege of Israel
    by merit of faith,
may be reborn by partaking
    of your Spirit.
Through Christ our Lord.
R. Amen.

Vel:

Deus, qui primis temporibus
impleta miracula novi testamenti
    luce reserasti,
ut et Mare Rubrum forma sacri
    fontis exsisteret,
et plebs a servitute liberata
christiani populi
    sacramenta præferret,
da, ut omnes gentes,
Israelis privilegium merito
    fidei consecutæ,
Spiritus tui participatione
    regenerentur.
Per Christum Dominum nostrum.
R. Amen.

FOURTH READING

A reading from the prophet Isaiah   54:5-14

With everlasting love the Lord your redeemer has taken pity on you.

Now your creator will be your husband,
his name, the Lord of hosts;
your redeemer will be the Holy One of Israel,
he is called the God of the whole earth.
Yes, like a forsaken wife, distressed in spirit,
the Lord calls you back.
Does a man cast off the wife of his youth?
says your God.

I did forsake you for a brief moment,
but with great love will I take you back.
In excess of anger, for a moment
I hid my face from you.
But with everlasting love I have taken pity on you,
says the Lord, your redeemer.

I am now as I was in the days of Noah
when I swore that Noah's waters
should never flood the world again.
So now I swear concerning my anger with you
and the threats I made against you;

for the mountains may depart,

the hills be shaken,
but my love for you will never leave you;
and my covenant of peace with you will never be shaken,
says the Lord who takes pity on you.

Unhappy creature, storm-tossed, disconsolate,
see, I will set your stones on carbuncles
and your foundations on sapphires.
I will make rubies your battlements,
your gates crystal,
and your entire wall precious stones.
Your sons will all be taught by the Lord.
The prosperity of your sons will be great.
You will be founded on integrity;
remote from oppression, you will have nothing to fear;
remote from terror, it will not approach you.

The word of the Lord.

Responsorial Psalm

Ps 29:2,4-6,11-13. R. v.2

R. **I will praise you, Lord, you have rescued me.**

I will praise you, Lord, you have rescued me
and have not let my enemies rejoice over me.
O Lord, you have raised my soul from the dead,
restored me to life from those who sink into the grave. R.

Sing psalms to the Lord, you who love him,
give thanks to his holy name.
His anger lasts but a moment; his favour through life.
At night there are tears, but joy comes with dawn. R.

The Lord listened and had pity.
The Lord came to my help.
For me you have changed my mourning into dancing,
O Lord my God, I will thank you for ever. R.

Prayer

Let us pray.
Almighty ever-living God,
surpass, for the honour of your name,
what you pledged to the Patriarchs
    by reason of their faith,
and through sacred adoption increase
    the children of your promise,

Oremus.
Omnipotens sempiterne Deus,
multiplica in honorem nominis tui
quod patrum fidei spopondisti,
et promissionis filios sacra
    adoptione dilata,
ut, quod priores sancti non

so that what the Saints of old never doubted would come to pass your Church may now see in great part fulfilled.
Through Christ our Lord. R. Amen.

dubitaverunt futurum,
Ecclesia tua magna ex parte iam cognoscat impletum.
Per Christum Dominum nostrum.
R. Amen.

Alternatively, other prayers may be used from among those which follow the readings that have been omitted.

FIFTH READING

A reading from the prophet Isaiah   55:1-11

Come to me and your soul will live, and I will make an everlasting covenant with you.

Thus says the Lord:

Oh, come to the water all you who are thirsty;
though you have no money, come!
Buy corn without money, and eat,
and, at no cost, wine and milk.
Why spend money on what is not bread,
your wages on what fails to satisfy?
Listen, listen to me, and you will have good things to eat
and rich food to enjoy.
Pay attention, come to me;
and your soul will live.

With you I will make an everlasting covenant
out of the favours promised to David.
See, I have made of you a witness to the peoples,
a leader and a master of the nations.
See, you will summon a nation you never knew,
those unknown will come hurrying to you,
for the sake of the Lord your God,
of the Holy One of Israel who will glorify you.

Seek the Lord while he is still to be found,
call to him while he is still near.
Let the wicked man abandon his way,
the evil man his thoughts.
Let him turn back to the Lord who will take pity on him,
to our God who is rich in forgiving;
for my thoughts are not your thoughts,
my ways not your ways – it is the Lord who speaks.
Yes, the heavens are as high above earth
as my ways are above your ways,
my thoughts above your thoughts.

Yes, as the rain and the snow come down from the heavens and do not return without watering the earth, making it yield and giving growth to provide seed for the sower and bread for the eating, so the word that goes from my mouth does not return to me empty, without carrying out my will and succeeding in what it was sent to do.

The word of the Lord.

Responsorial Psalm   Is 12:2-6. R. v.3

R. **With joy you will draw water from the wells of salvation.**

> Truly God is my salvation,
> I trust, I shall not fear.
> For the Lord is my strength, my song,
> he became my saviour.
> With joy you will draw water
> from the wells of salvation. R.

> Give thanks to the Lord, give praise to his name!
> Make his mighty deeds known to the peoples,
> declare the greatness of his name. R.

> Sing a psalm to the Lord
> for he has done glorious deeds,
> make them known to all the earth!
> People of Zion, sing and shout for joy
> for great in your midst is the Holy One of Israel. R.

Prayer

Let us pray.

Almighty ever-living God,
sole hope of the world,
who by the preaching
    of your Prophets
unveiled the mysteries
    of this present age,
graciously increase the longing
    of your people,
for only at the prompting
    of your grace
do the faithful progress in any
    kind of virtue.
Through Christ our Lord.
R. Amen.

Oremus.

Omnipotens sempiterne Deus,
spes unica mundi,
qui prophetarum tuorum præconio
præsentium temporum
    declarasti mysteria,
auge populi tui vota placatus,
quia in nullo fidelium
    nisi ex tua inspiratione
    proveniunt quarumlibet
    incrementa virtutum.
Per Christum Dominum nostrum.
R. Amen.

SIXTH READING

A reading from the prophet Baruch   3:9-15,32-4:4

In the radiance of the Lord make your way to light.

Listen, Israel, to commands that bring life;
hear, and learn what knowledge means.
Why, Israel, why are you in the country of your enemies,
growing older and older in an alien land,
sharing defilement with the dead,
reckoned with those who go to Sheol?
Because you have forsaken the fountain of wisdom.
Had you walked in the way of God,
you would have lived in peace for ever.
Learn where knowledge is, where strength,
where understanding, and so learn
where length of days is, where life,
where the light of the eyes and where peace.
But who has found out where she lives,
who has entered her treasure house?

But the One who knows all knows her,
he has grasped her with his own intellect,
he has set the earth firm for ever
and filled it with four-footed beasts,
he sends the light – and it goes,
he recalls it – and trembling it obeys;
the stars shine joyfully at their set times:
when he calls them, they answer, 'Here we are';
they gladly shine for their creator.
It is he who is our God,
no other can compare with him.
He has grasped the whole way of knowledge,
and confided it to his servant Jacob,
to Israel his well-beloved;
so causing her to appear on earth
and move among men.

This is the book of the commandments of God,
the Law that stands for ever;
those who keep her live,
those who desert her die.
Turn back, Jacob, seize her,

in her radiance make your way to light:
do not yield your glory to another,
your privilege to a people not your own.
Israel, blessed are we:
what pleases God has been revealed to us.

   The word of the Lord.

Responsorial Psalm   Ps 18:8-11. R. Jn 6:69

R. **You have the message of eternal life, O Lord.**

   The law of the Lord is perfect,
   it revives the soul.
   The rule of the Lord is to be trusted,
   it gives wisdom to the simple. R.

   The precepts of the Lord are right,
   they gladden the heart.
   The command of the Lord is clear,
   it gives light to the eyes. R.

   The fear of the Lord is holy,
   abiding for ever.
   The decrees of the Lord are truth
   and all of them just. R.

   They are more to be desired than gold,
   than the purest of gold
   and sweeter are they than honey,
   than honey from the comb. R.

Prayer

Let us pray.

O God, who constantly increase
     your Church
by your call to the nations,
graciously grant
to those you wash clean
     in the waters of Baptism
the assurance of your
     unfailing protection.
Through Christ our Lord.
R. Amen.

Oremus.

Deus, qui Ecclesiam tuam
semper gentium
     vocatione multiplicas,
concede propitius,
ut, quos aqua baptismatis abluis,
continua protectione tuearis.
Per Christum Dominum nostrum.
R. Amen.

SEVENTH READING

A reading from the prophet Ezekiel   36:16-28

I shall pour clean water over you, and I shall give you a new heart.

The word of the Lord was addressed to me as follows: 'Son of man, the members of the House of Israel used to live in their own land, but they defiled it by their conduct and actions. I then discharged my fury at them because of the blood they shed in their land and the idols with which they defiled it. I scattered them among the nations and dispersed them in foreign countries. I sentenced them as their conduct and actions deserved. And now they have profaned my holy name among the nations where they have gone, so that people say of them, "These are the people of the Lord; they have been exiled from his land." But I have been concerned about my holy name, which the House of Israel has profaned among the nations where they have gone. And so, say to the House of Israel, "The Lord says this: I am not doing this for your sake, House of Israel, but for the sake of my holy name, which you have profaned among the nations where you have gone. I mean to display the holiness of my great name, which has been profaned among the nations, which you have profaned among them. And the nations will learn that I am the Lord – it is the Lord who speaks – when I display my holiness for your sake before their eyes. Then I am going to take you from among the nations and gather you together from all the foreign countries, and bring you home to your own land. I shall pour clean water over you and you will be cleansed; I shall cleanse you of all your defilement and all your idols. I shall give you a new heart, and put a new spirit in you; I shall remove the heart of stone from your bodies and give you a heart of flesh instead. I shall put my spirit in you, and make you keep my laws and sincerely respect my observances. You will live in the land which I gave your ancestors. You shall be my people and I will be your God."'

The word of the Lord.

Responsorial Psalm   Pss 41:3,5; 42:3,4. R. Ps 41:1

R. **Like the deer that yearns for running streams,**
so my soul is yearning for you, my God.

My soul is thirsting for God.
the God of my life;
when can I enter and see
the face of God? R.

These things I will remember
as I pour out my soul:
how I would lead the rejoicing crowd
into the house of God,
amid cries of gladness and thanksgiving,
the throng wild with joy. R.

O send forth your light and your truth;
let these be my guide.
Let them bring me to your holy mountain
to the place where you dwell. R.

And I will come to the altar of God,
the God of my joy.
My redeemer, I will thank you on the harp,
O God, my God. R.

R. **Like the deer that yearns for running streams,
so my soul is yearning for you, my God.**

If a Baptism takes place the Responsorial Psalm which follows the Fifth Reading
(see p.228) is used, or Psalm 50 as follows.

Responsorial Psalm   Ps 50:12-15,18,19. R. v.12

R. **A pure heart create for me, O God.**

A pure heart create for me, O God,
put a steadfast spirit within me.
Do not cast me away from your presence,
nor deprive me of your holy spirit. R.

Give me again the joy of your help;
with a spirit of fervour sustain me,
that I may teach transgressors your ways
and sinners may return to you. R.

For in sacrifice you take no delight,
burnt offering from me you would refuse,
my sacrifice, a contrite spirit.
A humbled, contrite heart you will not spurn. R.

Prayer

Let us pray. | Oremus.

O God of unchanging power
and eternal light,
look with favour on the wondrous
mystery of the whole Church

Deus, incommutabilis virtus
et lumen æternum,
respice propitius ad totius
Ecclesiæ mirabile sacramentum,

and serenely accomplish the work
of human salvation,
which you planned from all eternity;
may the whole world know and see
that what was cast down is raised up,
what had become old is made new,
and all things are restored
   to integrity through Christ,
just as by him they came into being.
Who lives and reigns
   for ever and ever.
R. Amen.

Or:

O God, who by the pages
   of both Testaments
instruct and prepare us to celebrate
   the Paschal Mystery,
grant that we may comprehend
   your mercy,
so that the gifts we receive
   from you this night
may confirm our hope of the gifts
   to come.
Through Christ our Lord.
R. Amen.

et opus salutis humanæ
perpetuæ dispositionis effectu
tranquillius operare;
totusque mundus experiatur
   et videat
deiecta erigi, inveterata renovari
et per ipsum Christum redire
   omnia in integrum,
a quo sumpsere principium.
Qui vivit et regnat
   in sæcula sæculorum.
R. Amen.

Vel:

Deus, qui nos ad celebrandum
   paschale sacramentum
utriusque Testamenti
   paginis instruis,
da nobis intellegere
   misericordiam tuam,
ut ex perceptione
   præsentium munerum
firma sit exspectatio futurorum.
Per Christum Dominum nostrum.
R. Amen.

After the last reading from the Old Testament with its Responsorial Psalm and its
prayer, the altar candles are lit, and the Priest intones the hymn **Gloria in excelsis
Deo** (**Glory to God in the highest**), which is taken up by all, while bells are rung,
according to local custom.

The complete musical setting of the Latin text is found in the *Graduale Romanum*.

When the hymn is concluded, the Priest says the Collect in the usual way.

Collect

Let us pray.

O God, who make this most sacred
   night radiant
with the glory
   of the Lord's Resurrection,
stir up in your Church a spirit
   of adoption,

Collecta

Oremus.

Deus, qui hanc
   sacratissimam noctem
gloria dominicæ
   resurrectionis illustras,
excita in Ecclesia tua
   adoptionis spiritum,

so that, renewed in body and mind, we may render you undivided service. Through our Lord Jesus Christ, your Son, who lives and reigns with you in the unity of the Holy Spirit, one God, for ever and ever.	ut, corpore et mente renovati, puram tibi exhibeamus servitutem. Per Dominum nostrum Iesum Christum Filium tuum, qui tecum vivit et regnat in unitate Spiritus Sancti, Deus, per omnia sæcula sæculorum.

FIRST READING

A reading from the letter of St Paul to the Romans   6:3-11

Christ, having been raised from the dead, will never die again.

When we were baptised in Christ Jesus we were baptised in his death; in other words, when we were baptised we went into the tomb with him and joined him in death, so that as Christ was raised from the dead by the Father's glory, we too might live a new life.

If in union with Christ we have imitated his death, we shall also imitate him in his resurrection. We must realise that our former selves have been crucified with him to destroy this sinful body and to free us from the slavery of sin. When a man dies, of course, he has finished with sin.

But we believe that having died with Christ we shall return to life with him: Christ, as we know, having been raised from the dead will never die again. Death has no power over him any more. When he died, he died, once for all, to sin, so his life now is life with God; and in that way, you too must consider yourselves to be dead to sin but alive for God in Christ Jesus.

The word of the Lord.

After the Epistle has been read, all rise, then the Priest solemnly intones the **Alleluia** three times, raising his voice by a step each time, with all repeating it. If necessary, the psalmist intones the **Alleluia**.

Responsorial Psalm   Ps 117:1-2,16-17,22-23

R. **Alleluia, alleluia, alleluia!**
    Give thanks to the Lord for he is good,
    for his love has no end.
    Let the sons of Israel say:
    'His love has no end.' R.

    The Lord's right hand has triumphed;
    his right hand raised me.
    I shall not die, I shall live
    and recount his deeds. R.

The stone which the builders rejected
has become the corner stone.
This is the work of the Lord,
a marvel in our eyes. R.

The Priest, in the usual way, puts incense in the thurible and blesses the Deacon. At the Gospel lights are not carried, but only incense.

GOSPEL

YEAR A

A reading from the holy Gospel according to Matthew   28:1-10
He has risen from the dead and now he is going before you into Galilee.

After the sabbath, and towards dawn on the first day of the week, Mary of Magdala and the other Mary went to visit the sepulchre. And all at once there was a violent earthquake, for the angel of the Lord, descending from heaven, came and rolled away the stone and sat on it. His face was like lightning, his robe white as snow. The guards were so shaken, so frightened of him, that they were like dead men. But the angel spoke; and he said to the women, 'There is no need for you to be afraid. I know you are looking for Jesus, who was crucified. He is not here, for he has risen, as he said he would. Come and see the place where he lay, then go quickly and tell his disciples, "He has risen from the dead and now he is going before you to Galilee; it is there you will see him." Now I have told you.' Filled with awe and great joy, the women came quickly away from the tomb and ran to tell the disciples.

And there, coming to meet them, was Jesus. 'Greetings' he said. And the women came up to him and, falling down before him, clasped his feet. Then Jesus said to them, 'Do not be afraid; go and tell my brothers that they must leave for Galilee; they will see me there.'

The Gospel of the Lord.

YEAR B

A reading from the holy Gospel according to Mark   16:1-7
Jesus of Nazareth, who was crucified, has risen.

When the sabbath was over, Mary of Magdala, Mary the mother of James, and Salome, bought spices with which to go and anoint him. And very early in the morning on the first day of the week they went to the tomb, just as the sun was rising.

They had been saying to one another, 'Who will roll away the stone for us from the entrance to the tomb?' But when they looked they could see that the stone – which was very big – had already been rolled back. On entering the tomb they saw a young man in a white robe seated on the right-hand side, and they were struck with amazement. But he said to them, 'There is no need for alarm. You are looking for Jesus of Nazareth, who was crucified: he has risen, he is not here. See, here is the place where they laid him. But you must go and tell his disciples and Peter, "He is going before you to Galilee; it is there you will see him, just as he told you."'

The Gospel of the Lord.

YEAR C

A reading from the holy Gospel according to Luke   24:1-12

Why look among the dead for someone who is alive?

On the first day of week, at the first sign of dawn, the women went to the tomb with the spices they had prepared. They found that the stone had been rolled away from the tomb, but on entering discovered that the body of the Lord Jesus was not there. As they stood there not knowing what to think, two men in brilliant clothes suddenly appeared at their side. Terrified, the women lowered their eyes. But the two men said to them, 'Why look among the dead for someone who is alive? He is not here; he has risen. Remember what he told you when he was still in Galilee: that the Son of Man had to be handed over into the power of sinful men and be crucified, and rise again on the third day?' And they remembered his words.

When the women returned from the tomb they told all this to the Eleven and to all the others. The women were Mary of Magdala, Joanna, and Mary the mother of James. The other women with them also told the apostles, but this story of theirs seemed pure nonsense, and they did not believe them.

Peter, however, went running to the tomb. He bent down and saw the binding cloths, but nothing else; he then went back home, amazed at what had happened.

The Gospel of the Lord.

After the Gospel, the Homily, even if brief, is not to be omitted.

THIRD PART:

Baptismal Liturgy

After the Homily the Baptismal Liturgy begins. The Priest goes with the ministers to the baptismal font, if this can be seen by the faithful. Otherwise a vessel with water is placed in the sanctuary.

Catechumens, if there are any, are called forward and presented by their godparents in front of the assembled Church or, if they are small children, are carried by their parents and godparents.

Then, if there is to be a procession to the baptistery or to the font, it forms immediately. A minister with the paschal candle leads off, and those to be baptised follow him with their godparents, then the ministers, the Deacon, and the Priest. During the procession, the Litany is sung. When the Litany is completed, the Priest gives the address.

If, however, the Baptismal Liturgy takes place in the sanctuary, the Priest immediately makes an introductory statement in these or similar words.

If there are candidates to be baptised:

Dearly beloved,
with one heart and one soul,
   let us by our prayers
come to the aid of these our brothers
   and sisters in their blessed hope,
so that, as they approach the font
   of rebirth,
the almighty Father may bestow
   on them
all his merciful help.
	Precibus nostris, carissimi,
	fratrum nostrorum beatam spem
	   unanimes adiuvemus,
	ut Pater omnipotens ad fontem
	   regenerationis euntes
	omni misericordiæ suæ
	   auxilio prosequatur.

If the font is to be blessed, but no one is to be baptised:

Dearly beloved,
let us humbly invoke upon
   this font
the grace of God the almighty Father,
that those who from it are born anew
may be numbered among the
   children of adoption in Christ.
	Dei Patris omnipotentis gratiam,
	   carissimi,
	super hunc fontem
	   supplices invocemus,
	ut qui ex eo renascentur
	adoptionis filiis in
	   Christo aggregentur.

The Litany

The Litany is sung by two cantors, with all standing (because it is Easter Time) and responding.

If, however, there is to be a procession of some length to the baptistery, the Litany is sung during the procession; in this case, those to be baptised are called forward before the procession begins, and the procession takes place led by the paschal candle, followed by the catechumens with their godparents, then the ministers, the Deacon, and the Priest. The address should occur before the Blessing of Water.

If no one is to be baptised and the font is not to be blessed, the Litany is omitted, and the Blessing of Water takes place at once.

In the Litany the names of some Saints may be added, especially the Titular Saint of the church and the Patron Saints of the place and of those to be baptised.

Lord, have mercy.		Kyrie, eleison.	
	Lord, have mercy.		*Kyrie, eleison.*
Christ, have mercy.		Christe, eleison.	
	Christ, have mercy.		*Christe, eleison.*
Lord, have mercy.		Kyrie, eleison.	
	Lord have mercy.		*Kyrie, eleison.*
Holy Mary,		Sancta Maria,	
Mother of God,	*pray for us.*	Mater Dei,	*ora pro nobis.*
Saint Michael,	*pray for us.*	Sancte Michael,	*ora pro nobis.*
Holy Angels of God,	*pray for us.*	Sancti Angeli Dei,	*orate pro nobis.*
Saint John the Baptist,	*pray for us.*	Sancte Ioannes	
Saint Joseph,	*pray for us.*	Baptista,	*ora pro nobis.*
Saint Peter and		Sancte Ioseph,	*ora pro nobis.*
Saint Paul,	*pray for us.*	Sancti Petre et Paule,	*orate pro nobis.*
Saint Andrew,	*pray for us.*	Sancte Andrea,	*ora pro nobis.*
Saint John,	*pray for us.*	Sancte Ioannes,	*ora pro nobis.*
Saint Mary Magdalene,	*pray for us.*	Sancta Maria	
		Magdalena,	*ora pro nobis.*
Saint Stephen,	*pray for us.*	Sancte Stephane,	*ora pro nobis.*
Saint Ignatius of		Sancte Ignati	
Antioch,	*pray for us.*	Antiochene,	*ora pro nobis.*
Saint Lawrence,	*pray for us.*	Sancte Laurenti,	*ora pro nobis.*
Saint Perpetua and		Sanctæ Perpetua	
Saint Felicity,	*pray for us.*	et Felicitas,	*orate pro nobis.*
Saint Agnes,	*pray for us.*	Sancta Agnes,	*ora pro nobis.*
Saint Gregory,	*pray for us.*	Sancte Gregori,	*ora pro nobis.*
Saint Augustine,	*pray for us.*	Sancte Augustine,	*ora pro nobis.*

Saint Athanasius,	*pray for us.*
Saint Basil,	*pray for us.*
Saint Martin,	*pray for us.*
Saint Benedict,	*pray for us.*
Saint Francis and	
Saint Dominic,	*pray for us.*
Saint Francis Xavier,	*pray for us.*
Saint John Vianney,	*pray for us.*
Saint Catherine	
of Siena,	*pray for us.*
Saint Teresa of Jesus,	*pray for us.*
All holy men and women,	
Saints of God,	*pray for us.*

Lord, be merciful
      Lord, deliver us, we pray.

From all evil,
      Lord, deliver us, we pray.

From every sin,
      Lord, deliver us, we pray.

From everlasting death,
      Lord, deliver us, we pray.

By your Incarnation,
      Lord, deliver us, we pray.

By your Death and Resurrection,
      Lord, deliver us, we pray.

By the out-pouring of the Holy
   Spirit,   *Lord, deliver us, we pray.*

Be merciful to us sinners,
      Lord we ask you to hear our prayer.

If there are candidates to be baptised

Bring these chosen ones to new birth
   through the grace of Baptism,
      Lord, we ask you, hear our prayer.

Sancte Athanasi,	*ora pro nobis.*
Sancte Basili,	*ora pro nobis.*
Sancte Martine,	*ora pro nobis.*
Sancte Benedicte,	*ora pro nobis.*
Sancti Francisce	
et Dominice,	*orate pro nobis.*
Sancte Francisce	
(Xavier),	*ora pro nobis.*
Sancte Ioannes	
Maria (Vianney),	*ora pro nobis.*
Sancta Catharina	
(Senensis),	*ora pro nobis.*
Sancta Teresia a Iesu,	*ora pro nobis.*
Omnes Sancti	
et Sanctæ Dei,	*orate pro nobis.*

Propitius esto,   *libera nos, Domine.*

Ab omni malo,   *libera nos, Domine.*

Ab omni peccato,
      libera nos, Domine.

A morte perpetua,
      libera nos, Domine.

Per incarnationem tuam,
      libera nos, Domine.

Per mortem et
   resurrectionem tuam,
      libera nos, Domine.

Per effusionem Spiritus Sancti,
      libera nos, Domine.

Peccatores,   *te rogamus, audi nos.*

Ut hos electos per gratiam
   Baptismi regenerare digneris
      te rogamus, audi nos.

If there is no one to be baptised:

Make this font holy by your grace
    for the new birth of your children,
        Lord, we ask you, hear our prayer.

Ut hunc fontem,
    regenerandis tibi filiis,
      gratia tua sanctificare digneris
           te rogamus, audi nos.

Jesus, Son of the Living God,
    Lord, we ask you, hear our prayer.

Iesu, Fili Dei vivi,
           te rogamus, audi nos.

Christ, hear us.   *Christ, hear us.*
Christ, graciously hear us.
        Christ graciously hear us.

Christe, audi nos. *Christe, audi nos.*
Christe, exaudi nos.
           Christe, exaudi nos.

If there are candidates to be baptised, the Priest, with hands extended, says the following prayer:

Almighty ever-living God,
be present by the mysteries of your
    great love
and send forth the spirit of adoption
to create the new peoples
brought to birth for you in the font
    of Baptism,
so that what is to be carried out
    by our humble service
may be brought to fulfilment
    by your mighty power.
Through Christ our Lord.
R. Amen.

Omnipotens sempiterne Deus,
adesto magnæ pietatis
    tuæ sacramentis,
et ad recreandos novos populos,
quos tibi fons baptismatis parturit,
spiritum adoptionis emitte,
ut, quod nostræ humilitatis
    gerendum est ministerio,
virtutis tuæ impleatur effectu.
Per Christum Dominum nostrum.
R. Amen.

Blessing of Baptismal Water

The Priest then blesses the baptismal water, saying the following prayer with hands extended:

O God, who by invisible power
accomplish a wondrous effect
through sacramental signs
and who in many ways have
    prepared water, your creation,
to show forth the grace of Baptism;

Deus, qui invisibili potentia
per sacramentorum signa
    mirabilem operaris effectum,
et creaturam aquæ multis
    modis præparasti,
ut baptismi gratiam demonstraret;

O God, whose Spirit
in the first moments
   of the world's creation
hovered over the waters,
so that the very substance of water
would even then take to itself
   the power to sanctify;

O God, who by the outpouring
   of the flood
foreshadowed regeneration,
so that from the mystery of one
   and the same element of water
would come an end to vice
   and a beginning of virtue;

O God, who caused the children
   of Abraham
to pass dry-shod through the Red Sea,
so that the chosen people,
set free from slavery to Pharaoh,
would prefigure the people
   of the baptised;

O God, whose Son,
baptised by John in the waters
   of the Jordan,
was anointed with the Holy Spirit,
and, as he hung upon the Cross,
gave forth water from his side
   along with blood,
and after his Resurrection,
   commanded his disciples:
'Go forth, teach all nations,
   baptising them
in the name of the Father and of the
   Son and of the Holy Spirit',
look now, we pray, upon the face
   of your Church
and graciously unseal for her
   the fountain of Baptism.

Deus, cuius Spiritus
super aquas inter ipsa mundi
   primordia ferebatur,
ut iam tunc virtutem sanctificandi
aquarum natura conciperet;

Deus, qui regenerationis speciem
in ipsa diluvii effusione signasti,
ut unius eiusdemque
   elementi mysterio
et finis esset vitiis et origo virtutum;

Deus, qui Abrahæ filios
per Mare Rubrum sicco vestigio
   transire fecisti,
ut plebs, a Pharaonis
   servitute liberata,
populum baptizatorum
   præfiguraret;

Deus, cuius Filius, in aqua Iordanis
   a Ioanne baptizatus,
Sancto Spiritu est inunctus,
et, in cruce pendens,
una cum sanguine aquam de latere
   suo produxit,
ac, post resurrectionem suam,
   discipulis iussit:

'Ite, docete omnes gentes,
   baptizantes eos
in nomine Patris et Filii
   et Spiritus Sancti':
respice in faciem Ecclesiæ tuæ,
eique dignare fontem
   baptismatis aperire.

May this water receive
   by the Holy Spirit
the grace of your Only Begotten Son,
so that human nature,
   created in your image,
and washed clean through
   the Sacrament of Baptism
from all the squalor of the life of old,
may be found worthy to rise
   to the life of newborn children
through water and the Holy Spirit.

Sumat hæc aqua Unigeniti tui
   gratiam de Spiritu Sancto,
ut homo, ad imaginem
   tuam conditus,
sacramento baptismatis
a cunctis squaloribus
   vetustatis ablutus,
in novam infantiam
ex aqua et Spiritu Sancto
   resurgere mereatur.

And, if appropriate, lowering the paschal candle into the water either once or three times, he continues:

May the power of the Holy Spirit,
O Lord, we pray,
come down through your Son
into the fullness of this font,

Descendat, quæsumus, Domine,
in hanc plenitudinem fontis
per Filium tuum virtus
   Spiritus Sancti,

and, holding the candle in the water, he continues:

so that all who have been buried
   with Christ
by Baptism into death
may rise again to life with him.
Who lives and reigns with you
   in the unity of the Holy Spirit,
one God, for ever and ever.
R. **Amen.**

ut omnes, cum Christo consepulti
per baptismum in mortem,
ad vitam cum ipso resurgant.
Qui tecum vivit et regnat
   in unitate Spiritus Sancti,
Deus, per omnia sæcula sæculorum.
R. **Amen.**

Then the candle is lifted out of the water, as the people acclaim:

Springs of water, bless the Lord;
praise and exalt him above all
   for ever.

Benedicite, fontes, Domino,
laudate et superexaltate eum
   in sæcula.

After the blessing of baptismal water and the acclamation of the people, the Priest, standing, puts the prescribed questions to the adults and the parents or godparents of the children, as is set out in the respective Rites of the Roman Ritual, in order for them to make the required renunciation.

If the anointing of the adults with the Oil of Catechumens has not taken place beforehand, as part of the immediately preparatory rites, it occurs at this moment.

Then the Priest questions the adults individually about the faith and, if there are children to be baptised, he requests the triple profession of faith from all the parents and godparents together, as is indicated in the respective Rites.

Where many are to be baptised on this night, it is possible to arrange the rite so that, immediately after the response of those to be baptised and of the godparents and the parents, the Celebrant asks for and receives the renewal of baptismal promises of all present.

When the interrogation is concluded, the Priest baptises the adult elect and the children.

After the Baptism, the Priest anoints the infants with chrism. A white garment is given to each, whether adults or children. Then the Priest or Deacon receives the paschal candle from the hand of the minister, and the candles of the newly baptised are lighted. For infants the rite of Ephphetha is omitted.

Afterwards, unless the baptismal washing and the other explanatory rites have occurred in the sanctuary, a procession returns to the sanctuary, formed as before, with the newly baptised or the godparents or parents carrying lighted candles. During this procession, the baptismal canticle **Vidi aquam** (**I saw water**) or another appropriate chant is sung.

If adults have been baptised, the Bishop or, in his absence, the Priest who has conferred Baptism, should at once administer the Sacrament of Confirmation to them in the sanctuary, as is indicated in the Roman Pontifical or Roman Ritual.

The Blessing of Water

If no one present is to be baptised and the font is not to be blessed, the Priest introduces the faithful to the blessing of water, saying:

Dear brothers and sisters, let us humbly beseech the Lord our God to bless this water he has created, which will be sprinkled upon us as a memorial of our Baptism. May he graciously renew us, that we may remain faithful to the Spirit whom we have received.	Dominum Deum nostrum, fratres carissimi, suppliciter exoremus, ut hanc creaturam aquæ benedicere dignetur, super nos aspergendam in nostri memoriam baptismi. Ipse autem nos adiuvare dignetur, ut Spiritui, quem accepimus, fideles maneamus.

And after a brief pause in silence, he proclaims the following prayer, with hands extended:

Lord our God,
in your mercy be present
    to your people
who keep vigil on this most
    sacred night,
and, for us who recall the wondrous
    work of our creation
and the still greater work
    of our redemption,
graciously bless this water.
For you created water to make
    the fields fruitful
and to refresh and cleanse our bodies.
You also made water the instrument
    of your mercy:
for through water you freed
    your people from slavery
and quenched their thirst
    in the desert;
through water the Prophets
    proclaimed the new covenant
you were to enter upon
    with the human race;
and last of all,
through water, which Christ made
    holy in the Jordan,
you have renewed our
    corrupted nature
in the bath of regeneration.
Therefore, may this water be for us
a memorial of the Baptism
    we have received,
and grant that we may share
in the gladness of our brothers
    and sisters,
who at Easter have received
    their Baptism.
Through Christ our Lord.
R. Amen.

Domine Deus noster,
populo tuo hac nocte
    sacratissima vigilanti
adesto propitius;
et nobis, mirabile nostræ
    creationis opus,
sed et redemptionis nostræ
    mirabilius, memorantibus,
hanc aquam benedicere tu dignare.

Ipsam enim tu fecisti,
ut et arva fecunditate donaret,
et levamen corporibus nostris
    munditiamque præberet.

Aquam etiam tuæ ministram
    misericordiæ condidisti;
nam per ipsam solvisti tui
    populi servitutem
illiusque sitim in deserto sedasti;
per ipsam novum fœdus
    nuntiaverunt prophetæ,
quod eras cum hominibus initurus;
per ipsam denique, quam Christus
    in Iordane sacravit,
corruptam naturæ
    nostræ substantiam
in regenerationis lavacro renovasti.

Sit igitur hæc aqua nobis suscepti
    baptismatis memoria,
et cum fratribus nostris,
    qui sunt in Paschate baptizati,
gaudia nos tribuas sociare.
Per Christum Dominum nostrum.
R. Amen.

The Renewal of Baptismal Promises

When the Rite of Baptism (and Confirmation) has been completed or, if this has not taken place, after the blessing of water, all stand, holding lighted candles in their hands, and renew the promise of baptismal faith, unless this has already been done together with those to be baptised.

The Priest addresses the faithful in these or similar words:

Dear brethren (brothers and sisters), through the Paschal Mystery we have been buried with Christ in Baptism, so that we may walk with him in newness of life. And so, now that our Lenten observance is concluded, let us renew the promises of Holy Baptism, by which we once renounced Satan and his works and promised to serve God in the holy Catholic Church. And so I ask you:

Per paschale mysterium, fratres carissimi, in baptismo consepulti sumus cum Christo, ut cum eo in novitate vitæ ambulemus. Quapropter, quadragesimali observatione absoluta, sancti baptismatis promissiones renovemus, quibus olim Satanæ et operibus eius abrenuntiavimus, et Deo in sancta Ecclesia catholica servire promisimus. Quapropter:

Priest: Do you renounce Satan?
All: **I do.**

Sacerdos: Abrenutiatis Satanæ?
Omnes: **Abrenuntio.**

Priest: And all his works?
All: **I do.**

Sacerdos: Et omnibus operibus eius?
Omnes: **Abrenuntio.**

Priest: And all his empty show?
All: **I do.**

Sacerdos: Et omnibus pompis eius?
Omnes: **Abrenuntio.**

Or:

Vel:

Priest: Do you renounce sin, so as to live in the freedom of the children of God?
All: **I do.**

Sacerdos: Abrenuntiatis peccato, ut in libertate filiorum Dei vivatis?
Omnes: **Abrenuntio.**

Priest: Do you renounce the lure of evil, so that sin may have no mastery over you?
All: **I do.**

Sacerdos: Abrenuntiatis seductionibus iniquitatis, ne pecccatum vobis dominetur?
Omnes: **Abrenuntio.**

Priest: Do you renounce Satan,
the author and prince of sin?
All: **I do.**

Sacerdos: Abrenuntiatis Satanæ,
qui est auctor et princeps peccati?
Omnes: **Abrenuntio.**

If the situation warrants, this second formula may be adapted by Conferences of Bishops according to local needs.

Then the Priest continues:

Priest: Do you believe in God,
the Father almighty,
Creator of heaven and earth?
All: **I do.**

Sacerdos: Creditis in Deum Patrem
    omnipotentem,
creatorem cæli et terræ?
Omnes: **Credo.**

Priest: Do you believe in Jesus
    Christ, his only Son, our Lord,
who was born of the Virgin Mary,
suffered death and was buried,
rose again from the dead
and is seated at the right hand
    of the Father?
All: **I do.**

Sacerdos: Creditis in Iesum
    Christum, Filium eius unicum,
Dominum nostrum,
natum ex Maria Virgine,
passum et sepultum,
    qui a mortuis resurrexit
    et sedet ad dexteram Patris?
Omnes: **Credo.**

Priest: Do you believe
    in the Holy Spirit,
the holy Catholic Church,
the communion of saints,
the forgiveness of sins,
the resurrection of the body,
and life everlasting?
All: **I do.**

Sacerdos: Creditis in Spiritum
    Sanctum,
sanctam Ecclesiam catholicam,
sanctorum communionem,
remissionem peccatorum,
carnis resurrectionem et
vitam æternam?
Omnes: **Credo.**

And the Priest concludes:

And may almighty God, the Father
    of our Lord Jesus Christ,
who has given us new birth by water
    and the Holy Spirit
and bestowed on us forgiveness
    of our sins,
keep us by his grace,
in Christ Jesus our Lord,
for eternal life.
All: **Amen.**

Et Deus omnipotens, Pater Domini
    nostri Iesu Christi,
qui nos regeneravit ex aqua
    et Spiritu Sancto,
quique nobis dedit
    remissionem peccatorum,
ipse nos custodiat gratia sua,
in Christo Iesu Domino nostro,
in vitam æternam.
Omnes: **Amen.**

The Priest sprinkles the people with the blessed water, while all sing:

Antiphon

I saw water flowing 　　from the Temple, from its right-hand side, alleluia; and all to whom this water 　　came were saved and shall say: Alleluia, alleluia.	Vidi aquam egredientem 　　de templo, a latere dextro, alleluia; et omnes, ad quos pervenit aqua 　　ista, salvi facti sunt et dicent: Alleluia, alleluia.

Another chant that is baptismal in character may also be sung.

Meanwhile the newly baptised are led to their place among the faithful.

If the blessing of baptismal water has not taken place in the baptistery, the Deacon and the ministers reverently carry the vessel of water to the font.

If the blessing of the font has not occurred, the blessed water is put aside in an appropriate place.

After the sprinkling, the Priest returns to the chair where, omitting the Creed, he directs the Universal Prayer, in which the newly baptised participate for the first time.

FOURTH PART:
The Liturgy of the Eucharist

The Priest goes to the altar and begins the Liturgy of the Eucharist in the usual way. It is desirable that the bread and wine be brought forward by the newly baptised or, if they are children, by their parents or godparents.

Prayer over the Offerings	Super oblata
Accept, we ask, O Lord, the prayers of your people with the sacrificial offerings, that what has begun 　　in the paschal mysteries may, by the working of your power, bring us to the healing of eternity. Through Christ our Lord.	Suscipe, quæsumus, Domine, 　　preces populi tui cum oblationibus hostiarum, ut, paschalibus initiata mysteriis, ad æternitatis nobis medelam, 　　te operante, proficiant. Per Christum Dominum nostrum.

Preface: The Paschal Mystery	Præfatio: De mysterio paschali
It is truly right and just, our duty 　　and our salvation, at all times to acclaim you, O Lord, but (on this night / on this day) 　　above all to laud you yet more gloriously,	Vere dignum et iustum est, æquum 　　et salutare: Te quidem, Domine, omni tempore 　　confiteri, sed in hac potissimum nocte (die) 　　gloriosius prædicare,

when Christ our Passover has been sacrificed.

For he is the true Lamb
who has taken away the sins of the world;
by dying he has destroyed our death,
and by rising, restored our life.

Therefore, overcome with paschal joy,
every land, every people exults in your praise
and even the heavenly Powers, with the angelic hosts,
sing together the unending hymn of your glory, as they acclaim:
**Holy, Holy, Holy
Lord God of hosts...**

cum Pascha nostrum immolatus est Christus.

Ipse enim verus est Agnus
qui abstulit peccata mundi.
Qui mortem nostram moriendo destruxit,
et vitam resurgendo reparavit.

Quapropter, profusis paschalibus gaudiis,
totus in orbe terrarum mundus exsultat.
Sed et supernæ virtutes atque angelicæ potestates
hymnum gloriæ tuæ concinunt, sine fine dicentes:
**Sanctus, Sanctus, Sanctus
Dominus Deus Sabaoth...**

In the Eucharistic Prayer, a commemoration is made of the baptised and their godparents in accord with the formulas which are found in the Roman Missal and Roman Ritual for each of the Eucharistic Prayers.

Before the **Ecce Agnus Dei** (**Behold the Lamb of God**), the Priest may briefly address the newly baptised about receiving their first Communion and about the excellence of this great mystery, which is the climax of Initiation and the centre of the whole of Christian life.

It is desirable that the newly baptised receive Holy Communion under both kinds, together with their godfathers, godmothers, and Catholic parents and spouses, as well as their lay catechists. It is even appropriate that, with the consent of the Diocesan Bishop, where the occasion suggests this, all the faithful be admitted to Holy Communion under both kinds.

Communion Antiphon   1 Co 5:7-8

Christ our Passover
  has been sacrificed;
therefore let us keep the feast
with the unleavened bread
  of purity and truth, alleluia.

Psalm 117 may appropriately be sung.

Prayer after Communion

Pour out on us, O Lord,
  the Spirit of your love,
and in your kindness make those
  you have nourished
by this paschal Sacrament
one in mind and heart.
Through Christ our Lord.

Solemn Blessing

May almighty God bless you
through today's Easter Solemnity
and, in his compassion,
defend you from every assault of sin.
R. Amen.

And may he, who restores you
  to eternal life
in the Resurrection
  of his Only Begotten,
endow you with the prize
  of immortality.
R. Amen.

Now that the days of the Lord's
  Passion have drawn to a close,
may you who celebrate
  the gladness of the Paschal Feast
come with Christ's help,
  and exulting in spirit,
to those feasts that are celebrated
  in eternal joy.
R. Amen.

Ant. ad communionem

Pascha nostrum immolatus
  est Christus;
itaque epulemur in azymis
  sinceritatis et veritatis, alleluia.

Post communionem

Spiritum nobis, Domine,
  tuæ caritatis infunde,
ut, quos sacramentis
  paschalibus satiasti,
tua facias pietate concordes.
Per Christum Dominum nostrum.

Benedictio sollemnis

Benedicat vos omnipotens Deus,
hodierna interveniente
  sollemnitate paschali,
et ab omni miseratus defendat
  incursione peccati.
R. Amen.

Et qui ad æternam vitam
in Unigeniti sui resurrectione
  vos reparat,
vos præmiis
  immortalitatis adimpleat.
R. Amen.

Et qui, expletis passionis
  dominicæ diebus,
paschalis festi gaudia celebratis,
ad ea festa, quæ lætitiis
  peraguntur æternis,
ipso opitulante, exsultantibus
animis veniatis.
R. Amen.

And may the blessing
    of almighty God,
the Father, and the Son,
    ✠ and the Holy Spirit,
come down on you and remain
    with you for ever.
R. Amen.
	Et benedictio Dei
	    omnipotentis,
	Patris, et Filii,
	    ✠ et Spiritus Sancti,
	descendat super vos
	    et maneat semper.
	R. Amen.

The final blessing formula from the Rite of Baptism of Adults or of Children may also be used, according to circumstances.

To dismiss the people the Deacon or, if there is no Deacon, the Priest himself sings or says:

Go forth, the Mass is ended, alleluia, alleluia.	Ite, missa est, alleluia, alleluia.
Or:	Vel:
Go in peace, alleluia, alleluia.	Ite in pace, alleluia, alleluia
All reply:	Omnes respondent:
Thanks be to God, alleluia, alleluia.	Deo gratias, alleluia, alleluia.

This practice is observed throughout the Octave of Easter.

The paschal candle is lit in all the more solemn liturgical celebrations of this period.

REFLECTION

✠

The story of the Creation as told in the first chapter of Genesis does not even pretend to be historical. It is a myth, which means that it teaches important basic truths in the form of a story. The story form is obvious: it is shaped by the seven days of the week, ending with the Sabbath rest day, a rest day for God after all his work. This is to show that the Sabbath-day rest, devoted to God, is part of the very stuff and pattern of the world. Obviously it is not history, for to say there were three "days" before the sun existed is a nonsense. Rather the framework is logical:

1. Light and darkness, without which no one can see anything.

2. The dome over the earth, snuggling the earth into a gap in the vast, amorphous waters.

3. Fixed objects on the land: plants and trees – no movable objects in the heavens.

4. Fixed objects in the heavens: sun, moon, stars – no fixed objects in the sea.

5. Movable objects in the sea.

6. Movable objects on the land: animals and humans.

What are the important basic truths? Everything is dependent on God. Man and woman are special (God has a little consultation, a climax, the piece of poetry, "in the image of God"). Man and woman make a single pair. They are masters of the whole earth, fill it and look after it; they are naturally vegetarian: there is no place for any killing. It is not about what happened long ago; it is about the world as we need to see it today.

The reading from Romans after the canter through the history of salvation prepares for the renewal of baptismal vows which is the centre of the Easter Vigil. It must be seen as the climax of Paul's analysis of Christ's work of redemption. Christ's act of perfect, loving obedience to his Father in the crucifixion annulled the disobedience of Adam and the whole human race. It was acknowledged by the Father in raising Christ to new life.

How does this affect me? I put myself under Christ's protection by the expression of total faith and trust in him which is Baptism, turning away from all other supports, a total act of conversion to Christ. That is, I am baptised into his death, and so enter into his death, accepting his offering of his life as my own. Neither this nor its repetition at the Easter renewal can be lightly or carelessly done. I believe that Christ's death and burial become my own death and burial. In the same way I am raised to life with Christ, and I believe that Christ's risen life is also my own risen life.

At the Mass during the Day

We know that Christ has truly risen from the dead. Yes, indeed! This is the fundamental core of our profession of faith; this is the cry of victory that unites us all today. And if Jesus is risen, and is therefore alive, who will ever be able to separate us from him? Who will ever be able to deprive us of the love of him who has conquered hatred and overcome death? The Easter proclamation spreads throughout the world with the joyful song of the Alleluia. Let us sing it with our lips, and let us sing it above all with our hearts and our lives, with a manner of life that is "unleavened", that is to say, simple, humble, and fruitful in good works. The Risen One goes before us and he accompanies us along the paths of the world. He is our hope, He is the true peace of the world.

(Pope Benedict XVI)

Entrance Antiphon Cf. Ps 138:18,5-6

I HAVE risen, and I am with you still, alleluia.
You have laid your hand upon me,
    alleluia.
Too wonderful for me,
    this knowledge, alleluia, alleluia.

Or: Lk 24:34; Cf. Rv 1:6
The Lord is truly risen, alleluia.
To him be glory and power
for all the ages of eternity, alleluia,
    alleluia.

Ant. ad introitum

R ESURREXI, et adhuc tecum sum, alleluia:
posuisti super me manum tuam,
    alleluia:
mirabilis facta est scientia tua,
    alleluia, alleluia.

Vel:
Surrexit Dominus vere, alleluia.
Ipsi gloria et imperium
per universa æternitatis sæcula,
    alleluia, alleluia.

The Gloria in excelsis (Glory to God in the highest) is said.

Collect

O God, who on this day,
    through your Only Begotten Son,
have conquered death
and unlocked for us the path
    to eternity,
grant, we pray, that we who keep
the solemnity of the
    Lord's Resurrection
may, through the renewal brought
    by your Spirit,
rise up in the light of life.

Collecta

Deus, qui hodierna die,
    per Unigenitum tuum,
æternitatis nobis aditum,
    devicta morte, reserasti,
da nobis, quæsumus,
ut, qui resurrectionis dominicæ
    sollemnia colimus,
per innovationem tui Spiritus
in lumine vitæ resurgamus.
Per Dominum nostrum Iesum
    Christum Filium tuum,

Through our Lord Jesus Christ,
    your Son,
who lives and reigns with you
    in the unity of the Holy Spirit,
one God, for ever and ever.

qui tecum vivit et regnat
    in unitate Spiritus Sancti,
Deus, per omnia sæcula sæculorum.

FIRST READING

A reading from the Acts of the Apostles   10:34,37-43

We have eaten and drunk with him after his resurrection.

Peter addressed Cornelius and his household: 'You must have heard about the recent happenings in Judaea; about Jesus of Nazareth and how he began in Galilee, after John had been preaching baptism. God had anointed him with the Holy Spirit and with power, and because God was with him, Jesus went about doing good and curing all who had fallen into the power of the devil. Now I, and those with me, can witness to everything he did throughout the countryside of Judaea and in Jerusalem itself: and also to the fact that they killed him by hanging him on a tree, yet three days afterwards God raised him to life and allowed him to be seen, not by the whole people but only by certain witnesses God had chosen beforehand. Now we are those witnesses – we have eaten and drunk with him after his resurrection from the dead – and he has ordered us to proclaim this to his people and to tell them that God has appointed him to judge everyone, alive or dead. It is to him that all the prophets bear this witness: that all who believe in Jesus will have their sins forgiven through his name.'

    The word of the Lord.

Responsorial Psalm   Ps 117:1-2,16-17,22-23. R. v. 24

R. **This day was made by the Lord;**
    we rejoice and are glad.
    Or: **Alleluia, alleluia, alleluia!**

    Give thanks to the Lord for he is good,
    for his love has no end.
    Let the sons of Israel say:
    'His love has no end.' R.

    The Lord's right hand has triumphed;
    his right hand raised me.
    I shall not die, I shall live
    and recount his deeds. R.

    The stone which the builders rejected
    has become the corner stone.
    This is the work of the Lord,
    a marvel in our eyes. R.

SECOND READING

A reading from the letter of St Paul to the Colossians   3:1-4

You must look for the things that are in heaven, where Christ is.

Since you have been brought back to true life with Christ, you must look for the things that are in heaven, where Christ is, sitting at God's right hand. Let your thoughts be on heavenly things, not on the things that are on the earth, because you have died, and now the life you have is hidden with Christ in God. But when Christ is revealed – and he is your life – you too will be revealed in all your glory with him.

The word of the Lord.

ALTERNATIVE SECOND READING

A reading from the first letter of St Paul to the Corinthians   5:6-8

Get rid of the old yeast, and make yourselves into a completely new batch of bread.

You must know how even a small amount of yeast is enough to leaven all the dough, so get rid of all the old yeast, and make yourselves into a completely new batch of bread, unleavened as you are meant to be. Christ, our Passover, has been sacrificed; let us celebrate the feast, by getting rid of all the old yeast of evil and wickedness, having only the unleavened bread of sincerity and truth.

The word of the Lord.

The sequence is said or sung on this day. On the weekdays of the Octave of Easter, its use is optional.

SEQUENCE

Christians, to the Paschal Victim
    offer sacrifice and praise.
The sheep are ransomed
    by the Lamb;
and Christ, the undefiled,
hath sinners to his Father reconciled.
	Victimæ paschali laudes
	    immolent Christiani.
	Agnus redemit oves:
	    Christus innocens Patri
	    reconciliavit peccatores.

Death with life contended:
    combat strangely ended!
Life's own Champion, slain,
    yet lives to reign.
	Mors et vita duello
	    conflixere mirando:
	    dux vitæ mortuus regnat vivus.

Tell us, Mary:
    say what thou didst see
    upon the way.
	Dic nobis, Maria,
	    quid vidisti in via?

The tomb the Living did enclose; I saw Christ's glory as he rose!	Sepulcrum Christi viventis, gloriam vidi resurgentis.
The angels there attesting; shroud with grave-clothes resting.	Angelicos testes, sudarium et vestes.
Christ, my hope, has risen: he goes before you into Galilee.	Surrexit Christus spes mea: præcedet vos in Galilæam.
That Christ is truly risen from the dead we know. Victorious king, thy mercy show!	Scimus Christum surrexisse a mortuis vere: tu nobis, victor Rex, miserere.

Gospel Acclamation   1 Co 5:7-8

R. **Alleluia, alleluia!**
Christ, our passover, has been sacrificed;
let us celebrate the feast then, in the Lord.
R. **Alleluia!**

GOSPEL

A reading from the holy Gospel according to John   20:1-9

He must rise from the dead.

It was very early on the first day of the week and still dark, when Mary of Magdala came to the tomb. She saw that the stone had been moved away from the tomb and came running to Simon Peter and the other disciple, the one Jesus loved. 'They have taken the Lord out of the tomb' she said 'and we don't know where they have put him.'

So Peter set out with the other disciple to go to the tomb. They ran together, but the other disciple, running faster than Peter, reached the tomb first; he bent down and saw the linen cloths lying on the ground, but did not go in. Simon Peter who was following now came up, went right into the tomb, saw the linen cloths on the ground, and also the cloth that had been over his head; this was not with the linen cloths but rolled up in a place by itself. Then the other disciple who had reached the tomb first also went in; he saw and he believed. Till this moment they had failed to understand the teaching of scripture, that he must rise from the dead.

The Gospel of the Lord.

As an alternative, the Gospel of the Mass of Easter Night may be read pp.235-236.
At an evening Mass, Luke 24:13-35 may be used as an alternative:

GOSPEL

A reading from the holy Gospel according to Luke   24:13-35

They recognised him at the breaking of bread.

Two of the disciples of Jesus were on their way to a village called Emmaus, seven miles from Jerusalem, and they were talking together about all that had happened. Now as they talked this over, Jesus himself came up and walked by their side; but something prevented them from recognising him. He said to them, 'What matters are you discussing as you walk along?' They stopped short, their faces downcast.

Then one of them, called Cleopas, answered him, 'You must be the only person staying in Jerusalem who does not know the things that have been happening there these last few days.' 'What things?' he asked. 'All about Jesus of Nazareth' they answered 'who proved he was a great prophet by the things he said and did in the sight of God and of the whole people; and how our chief priests and our leaders handed him over to be sentenced to death, and had him crucified. Our own hope had been that he would be the one to set Israel free. And this is not all: two whole days have gone by since it all happened; and some women from our group have astounded us: they went to the tomb in the early morning, and when they did not find the body, they came back to tell us they had seen a vision of angels who declared he was alive. Some of our friends went to the tomb and found everything exactly as the women had reported, but of him they saw nothing.'

Then he said to them, 'You foolish men! So slow to believe the full message of the prophets! Was it not ordained that the Christ should suffer and so enter into his glory?' Then, starting with Moses and going through all the prophets, he explained to them the passages throughout the scriptures that were about himself.

When they drew near to the village to which they were going, he made as if to go on; but they pressed him to stay with them. 'It is nearly evening' they said 'and the day is almost over.' So he went in to stay with them. Now while he was with them at table, he took the bread and said the blessing; then he broke it and handed it to them. And their eyes were opened and they recognised him; but he had vanished from their sight. Then they said to each other, 'Did not our hearts burn within us as he talked to us on the road and explained the scriptures to us?'

They set out that instant and returned to Jerusalem. There they found the Eleven assembled together with their companions, who said to them, 'Yes, it is true. The Lord has risen and has appeared to Simon.' Then they told their story of what had happened on the road and how they had recognised him at the breaking of bread.

The Gospel of the Lord.

The Creed is said. However, in Easter Sunday Masses which are celebrated with a congregation, the rite of the renewal of baptismal promises may take place after the homily, according to the text used at the Easter Vigil (pp.246-247). In that case the Creed is omitted.

Prayer over the Offerings

Exultant with paschal gladness,
   O Lord,
we offer the sacrifice
by which your Church
is wondrously reborn and nourished.
Through Christ our Lord.

Super oblata

Sacrificia, Domine,
   paschalibus gaudiis
exsultantes offerimus,
quibus Ecclesia tua
mirabiliter renascitur et nutritur.
Per Christum Dominum nostrum.

Preface I of Easter: The Paschal Mystery, pp.248-249.

When the Roman Canon is used, the proper forms of the **Communicantes** (In communion with those) and Hanc igitur (Therefore, Lord, we pray) are said.

Communion Antiphon 1 Co 5:7-8

Christ our Passover has been
   sacrificed, alleluia;
therefore let us keep the feast
   with the unleavened bread
of purity and truth, alleluia, alleluia.

Ant. ad communionem

Pascha nostrum immolatus
   est Christus, alleluia;
itaque epulemur
   in azymis sinceritatis
et veritatis, alleluia, alleluia.

Prayer after Communion

Look upon your Church, O God,
with unfailing love and favour,
so that, renewed by the paschal
   mysteries,
she may come to the glory
   of the resurrection.
Through Christ our Lord.

Post communionem

Perpetuo, Deus, Ecclesiam tuam
   pio favore tuere,
ut, paschalibus renovata mysteriis,
ad resurrectionis perveniat claritatem.
Per Christum Dominum nostrum.

To impart the blessing at the end of Mass, the Priest may appropriately use the formula of Solemn Blessing for the Mass of the Easter Vigil, pp.251-252.

For the dismissal of the people, the following is sung or said:

Go forth, the Mass is ended, alleluia, alleluia.	Ite, missa est, alleluia, alleluia.
Or:	Vel:
Go in peace, alleluia, alleluia.	Ite in pace, alleluia, alleluia
R. Thanks be to God, alleluia, alleluia.	R. Deo gratias, alleluia, alleluia.

REFLECTION

✠

What is this new life in Christ, which is now my life? Paul writes that we are yet to be transformed. In 2 Corinthians 3:18 he writes that through the Spirit "we are to grow brighter and brighter as we are turned into the image that we reflect"; and in Philippians 3:21, "he will transfigure these wretched bodies of ours into copies of his glorious body." These are still in the future tense. Here, however, in Colossians, the writer suggests that we have already been transformed and are waiting only to be revealed in all our glory, when Christ is revealed. What will the risen body and the risen life be like?

Some progress can be made through 1 Corinthians 15. First Paul says this is a stupid question (v. 35), but then he goes on to explain a little, in these steps:

1. There will be continuity with the present: "each sort of seed gets its own body" (v. 38).

2. There will be change: "not all flesh is the same flesh" (v. 39).

3. What is sown is perishable/contemptible/weak, but what is raised is imperishable/glorious/powerful (vv. 42-43).

4. The life principle will no longer be the human soul but the Spirit (v. 44).

These tell us little, but do tell us something. Each of the changes is a transfer into the sphere of the divine, of the God who is imperishable, glorious and powerful, and a Spirit. It is also clear in 1 Corinthians 15 that the Resurrection of Christ is the model and pattern of our own resurrection, so our body will presumably have the same properties as Christ was seen to have in the meetings after the Resurrection.

There is, of course, no story of the Resurrection itself. Only Matthew tells us that there was a great earthquake, and an angel of the Lord came to roll away the great stone. The primary evidence of the Resurrection was not the empty tomb, but the meetings with the Risen Lord, given in the traditional form by Paul (*1 Co* 15:3-5). In today's Gospel reading Peter sees the cloths, and the separation of the cloths seems to be somehow evidence that Jesus has risen, which convinces the Beloved Disciple. Perhaps the positioning of the cloths shows that somehow the risen body passed through them without disturbing them. Perhaps Peter is held in check because he has not yet annulled his triple denial of his Master by the triple confession of his love, which is to follow in John 21:15-17.

After the end of the Gospel reading the story of Mary Magdalen continues with the touching account of her encounter with the Risen Lord, whom she had mistaken for the gardener. A feature of all the meetings recorded in the Gospels is that Jesus was somehow changed, in a way which made it difficult for his friends and disciples to recognise him. But here again it is love that is important and that enables both Mary and the Beloved Disciple to recognise the Risen Lord. It is the same for all his disciples.

APPENDIX OF PRAYERS

We include some prayers that may be helpful during Holy Week. *The Stations of the Cross* are a common Lenten devotion; we give them here in the familiar text by St Alphonsus Liguori. Next are an examination of conscience and prayers for confession, to help us prepare for the Sacred Triduum. Then we give some scriptural texts arranged to help in praying the Rosary. Lastly, we give two Psalms: Psalm 21, which Jesus quoted on the Cross, and which identifies him as the Suffering Servant of the Lord, and Psalm 50, the best known of the "Penitential Psalms", professing our trust in the saving mercy of God our loving Father.

STATIONS OF THE CROSS

Meditations by St Alphonsus Liguori

Begin with:

My Lord Jesus Christ, you willingly walked this painful journey to your death on the Cross with unconditional love for each one of us, and I, how often have I ungratefully abandoned you. But now I love you with my whole soul, and because I love you I am sincerely sorry for having offended you. My Jesus, pardon me, and permit me to accompany you on this journey. You are going to die for love of me, and it is my wish also, my dearest Redeemer, to die for love of you. My Jesus, in your love I wish to live. In your love I wish to die.

The First Station

Jesus is Condemned to Death

V. (genuflecting) We adore you, O Christ, and we bless you.
R. Because by your holy Cross you have redeemed the world.

V. Adoramus te, Christe, et benedicimus tibi.
R. Quia per sanctam crucem tuam redemisti mundum.

Consider how Jesus, after having been scourged and crowned with thorns, was unjustly condemned by Pilate to die on the Cross.

My loving Jesus, it was not Pilate; no, it was my sins that condemned you to die. By the merits of this agonising journey, I implore you, help me on my journey towards eternity.

I love you, Jesus, my love, above all things; I repent with my whole heart of having offended you. Never permit me to separate myself from you again. Grant that I may love you always; and then do with me what you will.

Our Father, Hail Mary, Glory be to the Father.

V. Have mercy on us, O Lord.
R. Have mercy on us.

V. Miserere nostri, Domine.
R. Miserere nostri.

At the Cross her station keeping,
Stood the mournful
   Mother weeping,
Close to Jesus to the last.

Stabat Mater dolorosa,
Iuxta crucem lacrimosa,
Dum pendebat Filius.

The Second Station

Jesus Receives the Cross

V. We adore you, O Christ, and we bless you.	V. Adoramus te, Christe, et benedicimus tibi.
R. Because by your holy Cross you have redeemed the world.	R. Quia per sanctam crucem tuam redemisti mundum.

Consider how Jesus, in making this journey with the cross on his shoulders, thought of us, and offered for us to his Father the death he was about to undergo.

My most beloved Jesus! I embrace all the sufferings and disappointments that will come my way in this life. By the merits of the pain you suffered in carrying your cross, help me to carry mine with perfect patience and resignation.

I love you, Jesus, my love, above all things: I repent with my whole heart of having offended you. Never permit me to separate myself from you again. Grant that I may love you always; and then do with me what you will.

Our Father, Hail Mary, Glory be to the Father.

V. Have mercy on us, O Lord.	V. Miserere nostri, Domine.
R. Have mercy on us.	R. Miserere nostri.

Through her heart His sorrow sharing, All His bitter anguish bearing, Now at length the sword has passed.	Cuius animam gementem, Contristatam et dolentem, Pertransivit gladius.

The Third Station

Jesus Falls for the First Time

V. We adore you, O Christ, and we bless you.	V. Adoramus te, Christe, et benedicimus tibi.
R. Because by your holy Cross you have redeemed the world.	R. Quia per sanctam crucem tuam redemisti mundum.

Consider this first fall of Jesus under his cross. His flesh was torn by the scourges, his head was crowned with thorns; he had lost a great quantity of blood. He was so weakened that he could scarcely walk, yet he had to carry this great load on his shoulders. The soldiers struck him roughly and he fell several times.

My Jesus, it is not the weight of the cross, but of my sins, which has made you suffer so much pain. By the merits of this first fall, save me from the misfortune of falling into mortal sin.

I love you, Jesus, my love, above all things; I repent with my whole heart of having offended you. Never permit me to separate myself from you again. Grant that I may love you always; and then do with me what you will.

Our Father, Hail Mary, Glory be to the Father.

| V. Have mercy on us, O Lord. | V. Miserere nostri, Domine. |
| R. Have mercy on us. | R. Miserere nostri. |

Oh, how sad and sore distressed	O quam tristis et afflicta
Was that Mother highly blessed	Fuit illa benedicta
Of the sole-begotten One!	Mater Unigeniti!

The Fourth Station

Jesus is met by His Blessed Mother

| V. We adore you, O Christ, and we bless you. | V. Adoramus te, Christe, et benedicimus tibi. |
| R. Because by your holy Cross you have redeemed the world. | R. Quia per sanctam crucem tuam redemisti mundum. |

Consider the meeting of the Son and the Mother, which took place on this journey. Their looks became like so many arrows to wound those hearts which love each other so tenderly.

My most loving Jesus, by the sorrow you experienced in this meeting, grant me the grace of a devoted love for your holy Mother. And you, my Queen, who were overwhelmed with sorrow, obtain for me a tender and frequent remembrance of the Passion of your Son.

I love you, Jesus, my love, above all things; I repent with my whole heart of having offended you. Never permit me to separate myself from you again. Grant that I may love you always; and then do with me what you will.

Our Father, Hail Mary, Glory be to the Father.

| V. Have mercy on us, O Lord. | V. Miserere nostri, Domine. |
| R. Have mercy on us. | R. Miserere nostri. |

Christ above in torments hangs;	Quae mærebat, et dolebat,
She beneath beholds the pangs	Pia mater, dum videbat
Of her dying glorious Son.	Nati pœnas inclyti.

The Fifth Station

The Cross is laid upon Simon of Cyrene

V. We adore You, O Christ, and we bless You.

R. Because by Your holy Cross you have redeemed the world.

V. Adoramus te, Christe, et benedicimus tibi.

R. Quia per sanctam crucem tuam redemisti mundum.

Consider how exhausted Jesus had become. He was on the point of death. But, as his cruel tormentors wanted him to die the shameful death on the cross, they forced Simon of Cyrene to carry the cross behind Our Lord.

My most beloved Jesus, by your grace I will not refuse to carry the cross; I accept it, I embrace it. I accept in particular the death you have destined for me, with all the pains which may accompany it; I unite it to your death, I offer it to you. You have died for love of me; I will die for love of you. Help me by your grace.

I love you, Jesus, my love, above all things; I repent with my whole heart of having offended you. Never permit me to separate myself from you again. Grant that I may love you always; and then do with me what you will.

Our Father, Hail Mary, Glory be to the Father.

V. Have mercy on us, O Lord.

R. Have mercy on us.

V. Miserere nostri, Domine.

R. Miserere nostri.

Is there one who would not weep, Whelmed in miseries so deep, Christ's dear Mother to behold?

Quis est homo qui non fleret, Matrem Christi si videret In tanto supplicio?

The Sixth Station

Veronica Wipes the Face of Jesus

V. We adore You, O Christ, and we bless You.

R. Because by Your holy Cross you have redeemed the world.

V. Adoramus te, Christe, et benedicimus tibi.

R. Quia per sanctam crucem tuam redemisti mundum.

Consider the courage and compassion of the holy woman named Veronica. Seeing Jesus so ill-used, and bathed in sweat and blood, she wiped his face with a towel, on which he left the impression of his holy countenance.

My most beloved Jesus! Your face was beautiful before, but by the agony of your scourging, crowning with thorns and the carrying of your cross, it has lost all its beauty, and wounds and blood have disfigured it. Through your abundant grace of baptism, my soul was also once beautiful. But, alas! I have disfigured it by my sins; you alone, my Redeemer, can restore it to its former beauty. Do this by your Passion, O Jesus!

I love you, Jesus, my love, above all things; I repent with my whole heart of having offended you. Never permit me to separate myself from you again. Grant that I may love you always; and then do with me what you will.

Our Father, Hail Mary, Glory be to the Father.

V. Have mercy on us, O Lord.	V. Miserere nostri, Domine.
R. Have mercy on us.	R. Miserere nostri.
Bruised, derided, cursed, defiled,	Pro peccatis suæ gentis,
She beheld her tender Child,	Vidit Iesum in tormentis,
All with bloody scourges rent.	Et flagellis subditum.

The Seventh Station

Jesus falls for the Second Time

V. We adore you, O Christ, and we bless you.	V. Adoramus te, Christe, et benedicimus tibi.
R. Because by your holy Cross you have redeemed the world.	R. Quia per sanctam crucem tuam redemisti mundum.

Consider the second fall of Jesus under the cross. This fall renews the pain of all the wounds in his head and limbs.

My Jesus, how many times have you pardoned me, and how many times have I fallen again, and begun again to offend you. By the merits of this second fall, help me to persevere in your grace until death. Grant me the grace in all the temptations which will assail me, to turn to you in prayer for your unfailing help.

I love you, Jesus, my love, above all things; I repent with my whole heart of having offended you. Never permit me to separate myself from you again. Grant that I may love you always; and then do with me what you will.

Our Father, Hail Mary, Glory be to the Father.

V. Have mercy on us, O Lord.	V. Miserere nostri, Domine.
R. Have mercy on us.	R. Miserere nostri.
Can the human heart refrain,	Quis non posset contristari,
From partaking in her pain,	Christi Matrem contemplari,
In that Mother's pain untold?	Dolentem cum Filio?

The Eighth Station

The Women of Jerusalem Mourn for Our Lord

V. We adore you, O Christ,
and we bless you.

R. Because by your holy Cross
you have redeemed the world.

V. Adoramus te, Christe,
et benedicimus tibi.

R. Quia per sanctam crucem tuam
redemisti mundum.

Consider the courage of these women of Jerusalem. They wept with compassion when they saw Jesus in such a pitiable state, streaming with blood as he walked along. Jesus spoke to them and said, 'Daughters of Jerusalem, weep not for me, but for yourselves and for your children'.

My Jesus, laden with sorrows! I weep for the offences I have committed against you because of the pains they have deserved, and still more because of the displeasure my sinful ingratitude caused you, who have loved me so much. It is your love more than the fear of hell which causes me to weep for my sins.

I love you, Jesus, my love, above all things; I repent with my whole heart of having offended you. Never permit me to separate myself from you again. Grant that I may love you always; and then do with me what you will.

Our Father, Hail Mary, Glory be to the Father.

V. Have mercy on us, O Lord.
R. Have mercy on us.

V. Miserere nostri, Domine.
R. Miserere nostri.

Let me share with You His pain,
Who for all my sins was slain,
Who for me in torments died.

Tui nati vulnerati,
Tam dignati pro me pati,
Pœnas mecum divide.

The Ninth Station

Jesus falls for the Third Time

V. We adore you, O Christ,
and we bless you.

R. Because by your holy Cross
you have redeemed the world.

V. Adoramus te, Christe,
et benedicimus tibi.

R. Quia per sanctam crucem tuam
redemisti mundum.

Consider the third fall of Jesus Christ. His weakness was extreme, and the cruelty of his executioners excessive: they tried to hasten his steps when he could scarcely move.

My outraged Jesus, by the merits of the weakness you suffered in going to Calvary, give me strength to conquer all human respect, and my wicked passions, which have led me to despise your friendship.

I love you, Jesus, my love, above all things; I repent with my whole heart of having offended you. Never permit me to separate myself from you again. Grant that I may love you always; and then do with me what you will.

Our Father, Hail Mary, Glory be to the Father.

V. Have mercy on us, O Lord.	V. Miserere nostri, Domine.
R. Have mercy on us.	R. Miserere nostri.
O thou Mother! fount of love!	Eia, Mater, fons amoris!
Touch my spirit from above.	Me sentire vim doloris
Make my heart with yours accord.	Fac, ut tecum lugeam.

The Tenth Station

Jesus is stripped of his Garments

V. We adore you, O Christ, and we bless you.	V. Adoramus te, Christe, et benedicimus tibi.
R. Because by your holy Cross you have redeemed the world.	R. Quia per sanctam crucem tuam redemisti mundum.

Consider the violence with which Jesus was stripped by the executioners. His inner garments had stuck to his torn flesh. The soldiers dragged his clothes off so roughly that the skin came with them. Have compassion on your Saviour, thus cruelly treated.

My most innocent Jesus, by the merits of the torment you have felt, help me to strip myself of all affection to things of earth, that I may place all my love in you, who are so worthy of my love.

I love you, Jesus, my love, above all things; I repent with my whole heart of having offended you. Never permit me to separate myself from you again. Grant that I may love you always; and then do with me what you will.

Our Father, Hail Mary, Glory be to the Father.

V. Have mercy on us, O Lord.	V. Miserere nostri, Domine.
R. Have mercy on us.	R. Miserere nostri.
Make me feel as You have felt;	Fac ut ardeat cor meum
Make my soul to glow and melt,	In amando Christum Deum,
With the love of Christ my Lord.	Ut sibi complaceam.

The Eleventh Station

Jesus is Nailed to the Cross

V. We adore you, O Christ,
and we bless you.
R. Because by your holy Cross
you have redeemed the world.

V. Adoramus te, Christe,
et benedicimus tibi.
R. Quia per sanctam crucem tuam
redemisti mundum.

Consider how Jesus is roughly thrown down upon the Cross. He willingly extends his hands and offers his life to his Eternal Father as the sacrifice for our salvation. Those barbarians nail his hands and his feet to the wood and then raise the cross and allow him to die in anguish.

My Jesus, loaded with contempt, nail my heart to your feet, that it may ever remain there, to love you, and never more to leave you.

I love you, Jesus, my love, above all things; I repent with my whole heart of having offended you. Never permit me to separate myself from you again. Grant that I may love you always; and then do with me what you will.

Our Father, Hail Mary, Glory be to the Father.

V. Have mercy on us, O Lord.
R. Have mercy on us.

V. Miserere nostri, Domine.
R. Miserere nostri.

Holy Mother, pierce me through,
In my heart each wound renew,
Of my Saviour crucified.

Sancta Mater, istud agas,
Crucifixi fige plagas
Cordi meo valide.

The Twelfth Station

Jesus Dies on the Cross

V. We adore you, O Christ,
and we bless you.
R. Because by your holy Cross
you have redeemed the world.

V. Adoramus te, Christe,
et benedicimus tibi.
R. Quia per sanctam crucem tuam
redemisti mundum.

Consider how Jesus, after three hours of agony on the cross, is consumed with anguish, abandons himself to the weight of his body, bows his head and dies.

O my dying Jesus! I kiss devoutly the cross on which you died for love of me. I have merited by my sins to die a miserable death, but your death is my hope. By the merits of your death, give me grace to die embracing your feet, and burning with love for you. I commit my soul into your hands.

I love you, Jesus, my love, above all things; I repent with my whole heart of having offended you. Never permit me to separate myself from you again. Grant that I may love you always; and then do with me what you will.

Our Father, Hail Mary, Glory be to the Father.

V. Have mercy on us, O Lord.
R. Have mercy on us.

V. Miserere nostri, Domine.
R. Miserere nostri.

Let me mingle tears with You,
Mourning Him who mourned
    for me,
All the days that I may live.

Fac me vere tecum flere,
Crucifixo condolore,
Donec ego vixero.

The Thirteenth Station

Jesus is Taken down from the Cross

V. We adore you, O Christ,
    and we bless you.
R. Because by your holy Cross
    you have redeemed the world.

V. Adoramus te, Christe,
    et benedicimus tibi.
R. Quia per sanctam crucem tuam
    redemisti mundum.

Consider how, after Our Lord had died, two of his disciples, Joseph and Nicodemus, took him down from the cross, and placed him in the arms of his afflicted Mother. His mother Mary received him with unutterable tenderness, and pressed him to her bosom.

O Mother of Sorrow, for the love of this Son, accept me for your servant, and pray for me. And you, my Redeemer, since you have died for me, permit me to love you; for I wish but you, and nothing more.

I love you, Jesus, my love, above all things; I repent with my whole heart of having offended you. Never permit me to separate myself from you again. Grant that I may love you always; and then do with me what you will.

Our Father, Hail Mary, Glory be to the Father.

V. Have mercy on us, O Lord.
R. Have mercy on us.

V. Miserere nostri, Domine.
R. Miserere nostri.

For the sins of His own nation,
Saw Him hang in desolation,
Till His spirit forth He sent.

Vidit suum dulcem natum
Morientum, desolatum,
Dum emisit spiritum.

The Fourteenth Station

Jesus is Laid in the Sepulchre

V. We adore you, O Christ,
and we bless you.
R. Because by your holy Cross
you have redeemed the world.

V. Adoramus te, Christe,
et benedicimus tibi.
R. Quia per sanctam crucem tuam
redemisti mundum.

Consider how the disciples, accompanied by his holy Mother, carried the body of Jesus to bury it. They closed the tomb, and all came sorrowfully away.

My buried Jesus – I kiss the stone that entombed you. But I believe that you rose again on the third day. I beseech you, by your resurrection, to make me rise in glory with you at the last day, to be united with you always in heaven, to praise you and love you for ever.

I love you, Jesus, my love, above all things; I repent with my whole heart of having offended you. Never permit me to separate myself from you again. Grant that I may love you always; and then do with me what you will.

Our Father, Hail Mary, Glory be to the Father.

V. Have mercy on us, O Lord.
R. Have mercy on us.

V. Miserere nostri, Domine.
R. Miserere nostri.

While my body here decays,
May my soul thy goodness praise,
Safe in paradise with thee. Amen.

Quando corpus morietur,
Fac ut animæ donetur
Paradisi gloria. Amen.

In conclusion, say one Our Father, Hail Mary and Glory be to the Father, for the intentions of the Holy Father.

Prayer to Our Lady of Sorrows

O most holy Mother, Queen of sorrows, who followed your beloved Son through all the Way of the Cross, and whose heart was pierced with a fresh sword of grief at all the stations of that most sorrowful journey, obtain for us, we beseech you, O most loving Mother, a perpetual remembrance of our Blessed Saviour's cross and death, and a true and tender devotion to all the mysteries of his most holy Passion. Obtain for us the grace to hate sin, even as he hated it in the agony in the garden; to endure wrong and insult with all patience as he endured them in the judgement hall; to be meek and humble in all our trials as he was before his judges; to love our enemies even as he loved his murderers, and prayed for them upon the cross; and to glorify God and to do good to our neighbour, even as he did in every mystery of his suffering. O Queen of Martyrs, who by the sorrows of your Immaculate Heart on Calvary, merited to share the Passion of Our Most Holy Redeemer, obtain for us some portion of your compassion, that for the love of Jesus crucified, we may be crucified to the world in this life, and in the life to come may, by his infinite merits and your powerful intercession, reign with him in glory everlasting. Amen.

SACRAMENT OF RECONCILIATION

Remember that the sacrament is above all an act of God's love. It is a personal moment to be lived in a relationship of love with God. It is not routine, nor an ordeal to be gone through, but is very much part of the personal renewal which takes place in each person. You are invited, in the light of God's love, to recognise the sinfulness of your life, to have true sorrow for your sins, and a firm intention to avoid them in future.

Essential elements of a good confession

To make a good confession, we should:

1. Pray first, asking God to help us.
2. Make a sincere examination of conscience to see how we have sinned since our last confession.
3. Confess our sins simply, with humility and honesty.
4. Make our act of contrition with heartfelt sorrow and a "firm purpose of amendment", being determined that we will avoid the occasions of sin.
5. Devoutly carry out the penance prescribed and pray in thanksgiving for God's overflowing love and mercy.

Prayer before Confession

Almighty and merciful God,
you have brought me here in the name of your Son
to receive your mercy and grace in my time of need.
Open my eyes to see the evil I have done.
Touch my heart and convert me to yourself.
Where sin has separated me from you,
may your love unite me to you again:
where sin has brought weakness,
may your power heal and strengthen;
where sin has brought death,
may your Spirit raise to new life.
Give me a new heart to love you,
so that my life may reflect the image of your Son.
May the world see the glory
of Christ revealed in your Church,
and come to know that he is the one whom
you have sent, Jesus Christ, your Son, our Lord. Amen.

The Confiteor

I confess to almighty God and to you, my brothers and sisters, that I have greatly sinned, in my thoughts and in my words, in what I have done and in what I have failed to do, through my fault, through my fault, through my most grievous fault; therefore I ask blessed Mary ever-Virgin, all the Angels and Saints, and you, my brothers and sisters, to pray for me to the Lord our God.

An Act of Contrition

O my God, I am sorry and beg pardon for all my sins, and detest them above all things, because they deserve your dreadful punishments, because they have crucified my loving Saviour Jesus Christ, and, most of all, because they offend your infinite goodness; and I firmly resolve, by the help of your grace, never to offend you again, and carefully to avoid the occasions of sin.

EXAMINATION OF CONSCIENCE

Careful preparation is vital in order to make the most of this encounter with our loving heavenly Father. Find some time to be alone and quiet to reflect on your life, your relationship with God and others. An examination of conscience provides us with what we are going to say in the confessional. Without time given to such examination our confession is in danger of being incomplete. There are many ways: one is to use a gospel passage, especially one of the many healing miracles or occasions of forgiveness (eg *Lk* 15:11-32; *Jn* 4:5-42; *Mt* 18:21-35; *Lk* 18:9-14). Imagine you are the person being healed or forgiven by Jesus. Read the scripture passage, imagine you are in the scene, and listen to the words of Jesus. He speaks to you! What do you say? Alternatively, Jesus summed up and extended the Ten Commandments by his two great commandments (*Mk* 12:28-42): Love God and your neighbour.

Mortal sin is sin whose object is a grave matter and which is also committed with full knowledge and deliberate consent (*Catechism* 1857). We must confess all mortal sins. We are not obliged to confess all venial sins.

We commit venial sin when, in a less serious matter, we do not observe the standard prescribed by the moral law, or when we disobey the moral law in a grave matter, but without full knowledge or without complete consent (*Catechism* 1862). Confession of venial sins is an act of devotion. We need not be unduly anxious to confess them all, but may rather choose to focus on areas of our life that are most in need of God's grace.

The following examination of conscience can help us to measure our lives by the objective standard of Christ's teaching. We may also consider more generally how we may have failed in our lives to live fully as disciples of Christ.

Sins against God

Have I rejected my faith, refused to find out more about it?

Have I forgotten my daily prayers or said them badly?

Have I experimented with the occult or put my trust in fortune tellers or horoscopes?

Have I blasphemed against God or used bad language?

Have I shown disrespect for holy things, places or people?

Have I missed Mass on Sundays or Holydays through my own fault?

Have I let myself be distracted at Mass or distracted others?

Have I received Holy Communion in a state of mortal sin?

Have I received Holy Communion without proper reverence, care or thanksgiving?

Sins against myself and others

Have I been impatient, angry or jealous?

Have I brooded over injuries or refused to forgive?

Have I taken part in or encouraged abortion, the destruction of human embryos, euthanasia or any other means of taking human life?

Have I been verbally or physically violent to others?

Have I been racist in my thoughts, words or deeds?

Have I hurt anyone by speaking badly about them?

Have I betrayed confidences without good cause or revealed things simply to hurt others?

Have I judged others rashly?

Have I been drunk or used illegal drugs?

Have I driven dangerously or inconsiderately?

Have I spoken in an obscene way?

Have I looked at obscene pictures, films or books?

Have I been involved in any impure behaviour on my own or with someone else?

Have I been vain, proud, selfish or self-seeking?

Have I told lies to excuse myself, to hurt others or to make myself look more important?

Have I stolen anything?

Have I failed to contribute to the support of the Church in proportion to my means?

Have I been disobedient, rude or insolent to those in authority over me?

Have I been harsh, overbearing or sarcastic to those under my authority?

Have I cheated my employers or employees?

Have I misused or damaged the property of others?

Have I set my heart greedily on possessing things?

Have I given scandal or bad example?

Have I been lazy at my work, study or domestic duties?

Have I been jealous of others – of their looks, their popularity, their good work?

Have I encouraged others to do wrong in any way?

For spouses

Have I neglected to foster the warmth of my love and affection for my spouse?

Have I prolonged disagreements through resentment or failing to apologise when I have been in the wrong?

Have I mistreated my spouse verbally, emotionally or physically?

Have I used artificial means of birth control?

Have I been unfaithful to my spouse in any way?

For parents

Have I neglected to teach my children to pray?

Have I neglected the religious education of my children?

Have I failed to bring my children to Sunday Mass?

Have I argued with my spouse in front of my children?

Have I failed to exercise vigilance over what my children read, see on television or on the internet?

Have I been harsh or overbearing to my children?

Have I neglected my children's welfare in any way?

For young people

Have I been disobedient to my parents?

Have I been unhelpful at home?

Have I failed to try to understand my parents and talk with them?

Have I upset the peace of my home for selfish reasons?

Have I lost control when I have been angry?

Have I sulked or been sarcastic instead of asking for help?

Have I failed to work properly at school?

Have I treated teachers or other adults with disrespect?

Have I played unfairly at games or sports?

Have I taken part in fights?

TO CONFESSION

(You may take this prayer book with you to Confession)

Reception

The Priest welcomes the penitent warmly. The penitent and Priest begin by making the sign of the cross, while saying: ✠ **In the name of the Father, and of the Son, and of the Holy Spirit. Amen.** The Priest invites you to trust in God. You may indicate your state of life, and anything else which may help the Priest as confessor.

The Word of God

The Priest may invite you to reflect on a passage from Holy Scripture, speaking of God's mercy and call to conversion.

Reconciliation

Then you can speak in your own words or you can say: **Bless me Father for I have sinned. My last confession was ... ago** (*say roughly how long*) **and these are my sins.**

Now tell your sins simply in your own words. When you have finished, let the Priest know. You can use these words if you wish: **I am sorry for all these sins and for any that I cannot now remember.**

Listen carefully to the advice of the Priest and ask the Holy Spirit to help him to say what is best to help you to grow in the Christian life. You can ask him questions if you want. The Priest may propose an Act of Penance, which should serve not only to make up for the past but also to help begin a new life and provide an antidote to weakness. It may take the form of prayer, self-denial, and especially of service to one's neighbour and works of mercy.

Then the Priest invites you to say a prayer of sorrow (an Act of Contrition), such as:

O my God, because you are so good, I am very sorry that I have sinned against you, and by the help of your grace I will not sin again.

Wait while the Priest says the prayer of "Absolution" (where Christ forgives you all your sins). Make the sign of the cross as the Priest says: **I absolve you from your sins in the name of the Father ✠ and of the Son and of the Holy Spirit. Amen.** The Priest may say a few final words of encouragement to you as you leave.

After Confession

Take some time in the quiet of the Church to reflect on the grace of the sacrament and to thank God for his mercy and forgiveness. Here is a prayer of thanksgiving:

Father, in your love you have brought me from evil to good and from misery to happiness. Through your blessings give me the courage of perseverance. Amen.

THE ROSARY

As a Gospel prayer, centred on the mystery of the redemptive Incarnation, the Rosary is a prayer with a clearly Christological orientation. Its most characteristic element, in fact, the litany-like succession of Hail Marys, becomes in itself an unceasing praise of Christ, who is the ultimate object both of the Angel's announcement and of the greeting of the Mother of John the Baptist: 'Blessed is the fruit of your womb' (Lk 1:42).

(Pope Saint Paul VI, Apostolic Exhortation Marialis Cultus 46)

The basic form of the Rosary is well known: one **Our Father,** ten **Hail Marys** and one **Glory be** make a decade, and each decade is usually devoted to meditating on a particular mystery. These mysteries are conventionally divided into four groups of five, as given below. These groups are usually assigned to particular days of the week, although this is only a custom and is not prescriptive.

JOYFUL MYSTERIES
(MONDAYS & SATURDAYS)

The First Joyful Mystery: The Annunciation

Lk 1:26-38

[The Angel Gabriel said to Mary,] 'Rejoice, so highly favoured! The Lord is with you.'

She was deeply disturbed by these words and asked herself what this greeting could mean, but the angel said to her, 'Mary, do not be afraid; you have won God's favour. Listen! You are to conceive and bear a son, and you must name him Jesus'...Mary said to the angel, 'But how can this come about, since I am a virgin?' 'The Holy Spirit will come upon you' the angel answered 'and the power of the Most High will cover you with its shadow.'...'I am the handmaid of the Lord,' said Mary 'let what you have said be done to me.' And the angel left her.

The Second Joyful Mystery: The Visitation

Lk 1:39-47

Mary set out at that time and went as quickly as she could to a town in the hill country of Judah. She went into Zechariah's house and greeted Elizabeth. Now as soon as Elizabeth heard Mary's greeting, the child leapt in her womb and Elizabeth was filled with the Holy Spirit. She gave a loud cry and said, 'Of all women you are the most blessed, and blessed is the fruit of your womb....For the moment your greeting reached my ears, the child in my womb leapt for joy. Yes, blessed is she who believed that the promise made her by the Lord would be fulfilled.'

And Mary said:

> 'My soul proclaims the greatness of the Lord
> and my spirit exults in God my saviour.'

The Third Joyful Mystery: The Nativity

Lk 2:1-7

Now at this time Caesar Augustus issued a decree for a census of the whole world to be taken. This census – the first – took place while Quirinius was governor of Syria, and everyone went to his own town to be registered. So Joseph set out from the town of Nazareth in Galilee and travelled up to Judaea, to the town of David called Bethlehem, since he was of David's House and line, in order to be registered together with Mary, his betrothed, who was with child. While they were there the time came for her to have her child, and she gave birth to a son, her first-born. She wrapped him in swaddling clothes, and laid him in a manger because there was no room for them at the inn.

The Fourth Joyful Mystery: The Presentation

Lk 2:22-28

And when the day came for them to be purified as laid down by the Law of Moses, they took him up to Jerusalem to present him to the Lord – observing what stands written in the Law of the Lord...[Simeon] took him into his arms and blessed God; and he said:

> 'Now, Master, you can let your servant go in peace,
> just as you promised;
> because my eyes have seen your salvation...'

Simeon blessed them and said to Mary his mother, 'You see this child: he is destined for the fall and for the rising of many in Israel, destined to be a sign that is rejected – and a sword will pierce your own soul too – so that the secret thoughts of many may be laid bare'.

The Fifth Joyful Mystery: The Finding in the Temple

Lk 2:42-43,46,48-52

When he was twelve years old, they went up for the feast as usual. When they were on their way home after the feast, the boy Jesus stayed behind in Jerusalem...

Three days later, they found him in the Temple, sitting among the doctors, listening to them, and asking him questions...his mother said to him, 'My child, why have you done this to us? See how worried your father and I have been, looking for you.' 'Why were you looking for me?' he replied. 'Did you not know that I must be busy with my Father's affairs?' But they did not understand what he meant.

He then went down with them and came to Nazareth and lived under their authority. His mother stored up all these things in her heart. And Jesus increased in wisdom, in stature, and in favour with God and men.

MYSTERIES OF LIGHT
(THURSDAYS)

The First Mystery of Light: The Baptism

Mt 3:13-17

Then Jesus appeared: he came from Galilee to the Jordan to be baptised by John. John tried to dissuade him. 'It is I who need baptism from you' he said 'and yet you come to me!' But Jesus replied, 'Leave it like this for the time being; it is fitting that we should, in this way, do all that righteousness demands'. At this, John gave in to him.

As soon as Jesus was baptised he came up from the water, and suddenly the heavens opened and he saw the Spirit of God descending like a dove and coming down on him. And a voice spoke from heaven, 'This is my Son, the Beloved; my favour rests on him.'

The Second Mystery of Light: The Wedding at Cana

Jn 2:1-11

Three days later there was a wedding at Cana in Galilee. The mother of Jesus was there, and Jesus and his disciples had also been invited. When they ran out of wine...the mother of Jesus said to him, 'They have no wine.' Jesus said, 'Woman, why turn to me? My hour has not come yet.' His mother said to the servants, 'Do whatever he tells you.' There were six stone water jars standing there....Jesus said to the servants, 'Fill the jars with water,' and they filled them to the brim. 'Draw some out now' he told them 'and take it to the steward.' ...The steward tasted the water, and it had turned into wine. Having no idea where it came from...the steward called the bridegroom and said, 'People generally serve the best wine first, and keep the cheaper sort till the guests have had plenty to drink; but you have kept the best wine till now.'

The Third Mystery of Light: The Proclamation of the Kingdom

Mk 1:14-15

After John had been arrested, Jesus went into Galilee. There he proclaimed the Good News from God. 'The time has come' he said 'and the kingdom of God is close at hand. Repent, and believe the Good News.'

The Fourth Mystery of Light: The Transfiguration

Lk 9:28-36

[Jesus] took with him Peter and John and James and went up the mountain to pray. As he prayed, the aspect of his face was changed and his clothing became brilliant as lightning. Suddenly there were two men there talking to him; they were Moses and Elijah appearing in glory, and they were speaking of his passing which he was to accomplish in Jerusalem....Peter said to Jesus, 'Master, it is wonderful for us to be here; so let us make three tents, one for you, one for Moses and one for Elijah.' – He did not know what he was saying. As he spoke, a cloud came and covered them with shadow; and when they went into the cloud the disciples were afraid. And a voice came from the cloud saying, 'This is my Son, the Chosen One. Listen to him.'

The Fifth Mystery of Light: The Institution of the Eucharist

Lk 22:14-20

When the hour came he took his place at table, and the apostles with him. And he said to them, 'I have longed to eat this passover with you before I suffer; because, I tell you, I shall not eat it again until it is fulfilled in the kingdom of God.'

Then, taking a cup, he gave thanks and said, 'Take this and share it among you, because from now on, I tell you, I shall not drink wine until the kingdom of God comes.'

Then he took some bread, and when he had given thanks, broke it and gave it to them, saying, 'This is my body which will be given for you; do this as a memorial of me.' He did the same with the cup after supper, and said, 'This cup is the new covenant in my blood which will be poured out for you.'

SORROWFUL MYSTERIES
(TUESDAYS, FRIDAYS)

The First Sorrowful Mystery: The Agony in the Garden

Lk 22:39-46

[He made] his way as usual to the Mount of Olives, with the disciples following....He said to them, 'Pray not to be put to the test.'

Then he withdrew from them, about a stone's throw away, and knelt down and prayed. 'Father,' he said 'if you are willing, take this cup away from me. Nevertheless, let your will be done, not mine.' Then an angel appeared to him, coming from heaven to give him strength. In his anguish he prayed even more earnestly, and his sweat fell to the ground like great drops of blood.

...He went to the disciples and found them sleeping for sheer grief. 'Why are you asleep?' he said to them. 'Get up and pray not to be put to the test.'

The Second Sorrowful Mystery: The Scourging

Mk 15:12-15

Then Pilate spoke again. 'But in that case,' he said to them 'what am I to do with the man you call king of the Jews?' They shouted back, 'Crucify him!'

'Why?' Pilate asked them 'What harm has he done?' But they shouted all the louder, 'Crucify him!' So Pilate, anxious to placate the crowd, released Barabbas for them and, having ordered Jesus to be scourged, handed him over to be crucified.

The Third Sorrowful Mystery: The Crowning with Thorns

Mt 27:27-30

The governor's soldiers took Jesus with them into the Praetorium and collected the whole cohort round him. Then they stripped him and made him wear a scarlet cloak, and having twisted some thorns into a crown they put this on his head and placed a reed in his right hand. To make fun of him they knelt to him saying, 'Hail, king of the Jews!' And they spat on him and took the reed and struck him on the head with it.

The Fourth Sorrowful Mystery: The Carrying of the Cross

Mt 27:31-32

And when they had finished marking fun of him, they took off the cloak and dressed him in his own clothes and led him away to crucify him.

On their way out, they came across a man from Cyrene, Simon by name, and enlisted him to carry his cross.

The Fifth Sorrowful Mystery: The Crucifixion

Mt 27:33-38

When they had reached a place called Golgotha, that is, the place of the skull, they gave him wine to drink mixed with gall, which he tasted but refused to drink. When they had finished crucifying him they shared out his clothing by casting lots, and then sat down and stayed there keeping guard over him.

Above his head was placed the charge against him; it read: 'This is Jesus, the King of the Jews.' At the same time two robbers were crucified with him, one on the right and one on the left.

GLORIOUS MYSTERIES
(WEDNESDAYS, SUNDAYS)

The First Glorious Mystery: The Resurrection

Mt 28:1-8

After the sabbath, and towards dawn on the first day of the week, Mary of Magdala and the other Mary went to visit the sepulchre. And all at once there was a violent earthquake, for the angel of the Lord, descending from heaven, came and rolled away the stone and sat on it. His face was like lightning, his robe white as snow. The guards were so shaken, so frightened of him, that they were like dead men. But the angel...said to the women, 'There is no need for you to be afraid. I know you are looking for Jesus, who was crucified. He is not here, for he has risen, as he said he would. Come and see the place where he lay.'

The Second Glorious Mystery: The Ascension

Ac 1:8-9,12-14

[Jesus said to his disciples,] '...you will receive power when the Holy Spirit comes on you, and then you will be my witnesses not only in Jerusalem but throughout Judaea and Samaria, and indeed to the ends of the earth.'

As he said this he was lifted up while they looked on, and a cloud took him from their sight....

So from the Mount of Olives, as it is called, they went back to Jerusalem, a short distance away, no more than a sabbath walk; and when they reached the city they went to the upper room where they were staying; there were Peter and John, James and Andrew, Philip and Thomas, Bartholomew and

Matthew, James son of Alphaeus and Simon the Zealot, and Jude son of James. All these joined in continuous prayer, together with several women, including Mary the mother of Jesus, and with his brothers.

The Third Glorious Mystery: The Descent of the Holy Spirit

Ac 2:1-4

When Pentecost day came round, they had all met in one room, when suddenly they heard what sounded like a powerful wind from heaven, the noise of which filled the entire house in which they were sitting; and something appeared to them that seemed like tongues of fire; these separated and came to rest on the head of each of them. They were all filled with the Holy Spirit, and began to speak foreign languages as the Spirit gave them the gift of speech.

The Fourth Glorious Mystery: The Assumption

Rv 12:1-5

Now a great sign appeared in heaven: a woman, adorned with the sun, standing on the moon, and with the twelve stars on her head for a crown. She was pregnant, and in labour, crying aloud in the pangs of childbirth. Then a second sign appeared in the sky, a huge red dragon which had seven heads and ten horns, and each of the seven heads crowned with a coronet. Its tail dragged a third of the stars from the sky and dropped them to the earth, and the dragon stopped in front of the woman as she was having the child, so that he could eat it as soon as it was born from its mother. The woman brought a male child into the world, the son who was to rule all the nations with an iron sceptre, and the child was taken straight up to God and to his throne.

The Fifth Glorious Mystery: The Coronation of the Virgin Mary

Lk 1:46-53

And Mary said:

> 'My soul proclaims the greatness of the Lord
> and my spirit exults in God my saviour;
> because he has looked upon his lowly handmaid.
> Yes, from this day forward all generations will call me blessed,
> for the Almighty has done great things for me.
> Holy is his name...
> He has shown the power of his arm,
> he has routed the proud of heart.

He has pulled down princes from their thrones and exalted the lowly.
The hungry he has filled with good things,
the rich sent empty away.'

At the conclusion of the Rosary, the *Hail Holy Queen* is often said, and then the prayer following:

Hail, holy Queen, mother of mercy, hail, our life, our sweetness, and our hope. To thee do we cry, poor banished children of Eve. To thee do we send up our sighs, mourning and weeping in this vale of tears. Turn then, O most gracious advocate, thine eyes of mercy toward us, and after this exile show unto us the blessed fruit of thy womb, Jesus. O clement, O loving, O sweet Virgin Mary.

V. Pray for us, O holy Mother of God.

R. That we may be made worthy of the promises of Christ.

Let us pray.

O God, whose only-Begotten Son by his life, death and resurrection has purchased for us the rewards of eternal life, grant, we beseech you, that by meditating on these mysteries of the most holy Rosary of the Blessed Virgin Mary, we may both imitate what they contain and obtain what they promise. Through Christ our Lord. R. Amen.

PSALMS

The opening of Psalm 21 is quoted by Jesus on the Cross: see Matthew 27:46, Mark 15:34. The Psalm as a whole moves from apparent despair to trust in God's faithfulness, and is a prayer we can make our own in this week, and indeed in any other week.

The Church prays Psalm 50 every Friday in Morning Prayer; we are overborne by our sins, but God sees our repentance and grants us his Spirit, the Spirit of joy and new life.

Psalm 21
The suffering servant wins the deliverance of the nations

² My God, my God, why have you forsaken me?
  You are far from my plea and the cry of my distress.
³ O my God, I call by day and you give no reply;
  I call by night and I find no peace.

⁴ Yet you, O God, are holy,
  enthroned on the praises of Israel.
⁵ In you our fathers put their trust;
  they trusted and you set them free.
⁶ When they cried to you, they escaped.
  In you they trusted and never in vain.

⁷ But I am a worm and no man,
  the butt of men, laughing-stock of the people.
⁸ All who see me deride me.
  They curl their lips, they toss their heads.
⁹ 'He trusted in the Lord, let him save him;
  let him release him if this is his friend.'

¹⁰ Yes, it was you who took me from the womb,
  entrusted me to my mother's breast.
¹¹ To you I was committed from my birth,
  from my mother's womb you have been my God.
¹² Do not leave me alone in my distress;
  come close, there is none else to help.

¹³ Many bulls have surrounded me,
  fierce bulls of Bashan close me in.
¹⁴ Against me they open wide their jaws,
  like lions, rending and roaring.

¹⁵ Like water I am poured out,
  disjointed are all my bones.
  My heart has become like wax,
  it is melted within my breast.
¹⁶ Parched as burnt clay is my throat,
  my tongue cleaves to my jaws.

¹⁷ Many dogs have surrounded me,
  a band of the wicked beset me.
  They tear holes in my hands and my feet
^{16c} and lay me in the dust of death.

¹⁸ I can count every one of my bones.
  These people stare at me and gloat;
¹⁹ they divide my clothing among them.
  They cast lots for my robe.

²⁰ O Lord, do not leave me alone,
  my strength, make haste to help me!
²¹ Rescue my soul from the sword,
  my life from the grip of these dogs.
²² Save my life from the jaws of these lions,
  my poor soul from the horns of these oxen.

²³ I will tell of your name to my brethren
  and praise you where they are assembled.
²⁴ 'You who fear the Lord give him praise;
  all sons of Jacob, give him glory.
  Revere him, Israel's sons.

²⁵ For he has never despised
  nor scorned the poverty of the poor.
  From him he has not hidden his face,
  but he heard the poor man when he cried.'

²⁶ You are my praise in the great assembly.
  My vows I will pay before those who fear him.
²⁷ The poor shall eat and shall have their fill.
  They shall praise the Lord, those who seek him.
  May their hearts live for ever and ever!

²⁸ All the earth shall remember and return to the Lord,
  all families of the nations worship before him

29   for the kingdom is the Lord's; he is ruler of the nations.
30   They shall worship him, all the mighty of the earth;
    before him shall bow all who go down to the dust.
    And my soul shall live for him,
31   my children serve him.
    They shall tell of the Lord to generations yet to come,
32   declare his faithfulness to peoples yet unborn:
    'These things the Lord has done.'

Psalm 50
Prayer of contrition: fourth psalm of repentance

3   Have mercy on me, God, in your kindness.
    In your compassion blot out my offence.
4   O wash me more and more from my guilt
    and cleanse me from my sin.

5   My offences truly I know them;
    my sin is always before me.
6   Against you, you alone, have I sinned;
    what is evil in your sight I have done.
    That you may be justified when you give sentence
    and be without reproach when you judge,
7   O see, in guilt I was born,
    a sinner was I conceived.

8   Indeed you love truth in the heart;
    then in the secret of my heart teach me wisdom.
9   O purify me, then I shall be clean;
    O wash me, I shall be whiter than snow.

10   Make me hear rejoicing and gladness,
    that the bones you have crushed may thrill.
11   From my sins turn away your face
    and blot out all my guilt.

12   A pure heart create for me, O God,
    put a steadfast spirit within me.
13   Do not cast me away from your presence,
    nor deprive me of your holy spirit.

14   Give me again the joy of your help;
    with a spirit of fervour sustain me,

15 that I may teach transgressors your ways
    and sinners may return to you.

16 O rescue me, God, my helper,
    and my tongue shall ring out your goodness.

17 O Lord, open my lips
    and my mouth shall declare your praise.

18 For in sacrifice you take no delight,
    burnt offering from me you would refuse,

19 my sacrifice, a contrite spirit.
    A humbled, contrite heart you will not spurn.

20 In your goodness, show favour to Sion:
    rebuild the walls of Jerusalem.

21 Then you will be pleased with lawful sacrifice,
    holocausts offered on your altar.